Public and Private in Ancient Mediterranean Law and Religion

Religionsgeschichtliche Versuche und Vorarbeiten

Herausgegeben von
Jörg Rüpke und Christoph Uehlinger

Band 65

Public and Private in Ancient Mediterranean Law and Religion

Edited by
Clifford Ando and Jörg Rüpke

DE GRUYTER

ISBN 978-3-11-037102-4
e-ISBN (PDF) 978-3-11-036703-4
e-ISBN (EPUB) 978-3-11-039251-7
ISSN 0939-2580

Library of Congress Cataloging-in-Publication Data
A CIP catalog record for this book has been applied for at the Library of Congress.

Bibliographic information published by the Deutsche Nationalbibliothek
The Deutsche Nationalbibliothek lists this publication in the Deutsche Nationalbibliografie; detailed bibliographic data are available on the Internet at http://dnb.dnb.de.

Printing and binding: CPI books GmbH, Leck
♾ Printed on acid-free paper
Printed in Germany

www.degruyter.com

Acknowledgments

The conference that formed the starting point of this volume was co-financed by the University of Chicago's Center for the Study of Ancient Religions and the Kolleg-Forschergruppe "Religious Individualization in Historical Perspective," financed by the German Science Foundation (DFG). We are grateful to the Max Weber Center for hosting the conference and to Diana Püschel and Elisabeth Begemann for their aid in its organization. Our thanks likewise to Sandhya Fuchs for assistance with the copy-editing.

We offer special acknowledgment to Chris Faraone, not simply for the generous support of Chicago's Center, but also for his aid in the initial planning of this project. Conversation at the conference was notably enhanced by the participation of Claudia Bergmann, Valentino Gasparini, Richard Gordon, Kristine Iara, István Kristó-Nagy and Salvo Randazzo. Claudia Bergmann, István Kristó-Nagy and Salvo Randazzo also delivered papers on that occasion but were in the end unable to contribute to the volume. We hope that the volume reflects appropriately the courtesy and rigor of their engagement.

Table of Contents

Introduction

The distinction between public and private plays an essential role in modern understandings of nearly all aspects of social conduct. Indeed, it might even be said to be foundational in modern conceptions of the individual.[1] The terms themselves derive from Latin roots, *publicus* and *privatus*. As with all such *faux amis*, the genealogical relation between lexemes works to efface the historical specificity of the distinctions mapped by this essential polarity, as well as the very meaning of the terms themselves. For example, whereas Anglo-American liberals and most Protestants conceive of religion as an essentially private matter – albeit for different reasons, within different frameworks – Cicero's clauses on religion in *On the Laws* assign to all individuals both public and private religious lives, the one entailed by citizenship, the other normatively familial (Cicero *De Legibus* 2.19).

The aim of this volume, as of the conference in which it originates, is to explore the public-private distinction in two grand normative domains of life in the ancient Mediterranean, law and religion. From its inception, the project has taken two principles as axiomatic: first, for all the weight with which the distinction is freighted, its definition and salience within particular ideological contexts are highly contingent. Second, notions of public and private (insofar as these have reasonable correlates in the cultures under study) themselves interact with highly charged but equally contingent concepts: the household, the family, and the people as political collectivity among them. For these reasons, we planned a conference and volume that were avowedly comparative and historicist.[2] In this way, the project aspires to shed light not simply on why, when and where boundaries are drawn, but also, *ex comparatione*, on where they are not.

By way of setting the stage, we might set in dialogue with each other and with our own project some notable works of scholarship in related domains. In some contexts – American search and seizure law, for example – the household or, more properly, the walls of one's dwelling, are taken as a boundary between the public and private.[3] In Athenian political thought, the household is not simply a site privileged and protected in law; it is also accorded an ontology prior to that of the political. In Aristotle's *Politics*, for example, the *oikos* pre-

1 A point stressed by Eidinow in her chapter.

2 This aspiration to comparatism differentiates this project from several very fine recent works on aspects of the public-private distinction in antiquity, notably de Polignac and Schmitt Pantel 1998, Macé 2012, and Dardenay and Rosso 2013.

3 Davies 1999 offers an idiosyncratic history.

cedes the *polis* and, indeed, political communities can be regarded as formed from an agglomeration of households. And yet, as Susan Lape has shown, the intertwined notions of family and *oikos* have a history, and an intensely political one at that: it was Solon who established the intergenerational and conjugal household as the normative basis for social reproduction.[4] The contingency and cultural specificity of the Roman household, by contrast, is emphasized not simply by Roman lawyers speaking to the peculiarity of *patria potestas*,[5] but also by the myth of Rome's origin in Romulus' asylum: in that history, Rome is founded through a gathering of individual males, and its households are necessarily established both later and by exogamy.

In the Greco-Roman, liberal and republican traditions, at least, what one establishes as prior to the political is necessarily naturalized, and is thereby often removed from the reach of statal power. Within this heuristic, Athens and Rome are two different worlds.

Of course, the notional autonomy of the household – its existence beyond statal control – is largely an ideological artifact. We are therefore compelled to ask, in the interest of whose power, and whose subjugation, were these narratives crafted, modified and retold. Of course, Athenian and Roman households were similar in being patriarchal, but the reach of ideologies of household and family structure do not end there. Rather, social and religious authority in the household is regularly established in explicit homology to the structures of authority in the public sphere.[6] In this way, the notional autonomy of the household has historically often operated to naturalize patriarchy in public magistracy, and vice versa: so in Athenian tragedy, the health and purity of king's household is often treated as synecdochic for the health and purity of the community as a whole, while at Rome, the authority of the household is often figured as dependent upon the status of the elite male in the public sphere. That said, whatever the explicit direction of analogy in argument, the prevalance of patriarchy in the two domains is de facto mutually constitutive or, one might say, they are mutually dependent and (logically, at least) equally fragile. This quarrel over the ontology of the household and its relation to the political is mirrored at the dawn of Anglophone political theory, in the sharp disagreement between Hobbes and Locke about the parties to the social contract and, indeed, the equality of women to men.[7] Not for nothing, therefore, have principal aims of the feminist

4 Lape 2002/3; see also Lape 2003.

5 On which point see the chapter by Evans Grubbs, p. XXX.

6 Ando 2009: 180.

7 Hobbes of course posited individuals as the contracting parties and argued for the radical equality in nature, at least, of all persons.

traditional overall, and the Anglo-American feminist critique of liberalism in particular, been to analyze the "politics" and "economy" of the family and to call to account normative distinctions between public and private.[8]

The concept of the public deserves similar scrutiny and historicization, but, outside Roman law, this has been slow to happen in classical studies.[9] On this topic the essential provocation should have been the historical argument of Jürgen Habermas in *Strukturwandel der Öffentlichkeit* (1962), to the effect that antiquity had no notion of "the public sphere" as a non-private, non-familial but also non-statal space: this was a development of early modern England and, to a point, the Netherlands.[10] Was it in fact true that antiquity lacked the ability to conceptualize non-familial collectivities and non-household spaces except through the paradigm of the public?[11] If so, what implications would this hold for associational life, including but not limited to cult? As a related matter, the priority of the public in Roman ontologies of the political has the effect of establishing "the private" in dependency upon it: the private becomes merely that from which the public has withdrawn its claim.[12] Our ability to recognize the very different structure of ancient thought in this matter is hampered by the simultaneous persistence in contemporary thought of quite distinct notions of both public and private, which are often discussed using identical language. Alongside a notion of the public as communal and explicitly non-statal exists a notion of the public as citizenly and universal; corresponding to these are a range of understandings of public goods, from an aggregate arising from possessive individualism or interest-group pluralism to republican, communitarian, progressive or social democratic goods; and finally, we should acknowledge historical, cross-cultural and merely political variation in how one understands the agency of the public.[13]

---

8 Abbey 2011 provides a contemporary overview; see also Gavison 1992 and Brettschneider 2007.

9 A limited but valuable exception is Kuhn 2012; for some historical, theoretical and normative reflections on this topic see Ando 2012.

10 Habermas 1989 [1962]; Withington 2007 offers a useful summary of the reception of Habermas's work among historians.

11 For some brief remarks on the use by Roman jurists of analogical arguments drawing on public law to explain the structures of "private" associations see Ando 2015, chapter 2.

12 The starting point for any future inquiry into Roman understandings of the public must be Thomas 2002a and 2002b.

13 Horwitz 1982 provides a survey from a legal perspective; Gilens and Page 2014 provides an excellent survey of theories of democratic politics and, implicitly, their underlying notions of public goods. On the communal as public (or, another faux ami, "civic") see the classic works Putnam 2000 and Skocpol 2003.

Finally, to return to a theme announced above, distinctions between public and private regularly have quite distinct geographic, topographic and material aspects. Here, a principal achievement in recent decades has followed upon the crucial insight of Andrew Wallace-Hadrill, to the effect that for all their status as enclosed spaces – and their potential thereby actually to exclude non-members – Roman aristocratic houses offered a number of spaces that served public functions, just as, one might say, an aristocrat's *otium*, his leisure time, was always in fact open to public scrutiny as a measure of his suitability for public affairs.[14] But two further historical problems lie latent and underexplored in this literature, both arising from the normative status of the city in virtually all theorizing of politics and the public and private in the western tradition. It is often assumed, indeed, essential to theory, that public spaces are monumentalized spaces, and private spaces are urban dwellings. Tom Habinek has raised the question whether the emergence of sexuality as an analytically distinct component of theories of identity rested crucially on the forms of social interaction and demographic background of the ancient megalopolis.[15] His work challenges us to think, with Eidinow, about how ancient notions of the person, individual or *privatus* stand in relation to the modern individual or, indeed, the subject. Furthermore, was the public/private distinction drawn differently in the grand metropolitan centers, where individuals existed in more atomized relation to one another, than they were in mid-size municipalities, or villages, for that matter? Do changes occur in relation to mere population growth or are they better indexed to some increase in heterogeneity? Finally, we must not forget that there were normative traditions in the ancient world in which urbanism was explicitly dispreferred in relation to pastoralism (as one possibility): the book of Genesis is an important locus for such thought. Such traditions challenge the very fundamentals whereby the publicness of spaces can be conceptualized.

The papers in this volume engage these and related themes in a sequence of detailed and interrelated historicizations of the public/private distinction in Greek, Roman, Christian, Jewish and Islamic antiquity.

Edward Harris addresses the complex case of homicide and concepts of pollution associated with it, which might appear to have partially discontinuous histories in criminal and religious law. The chapter is able to show that ideas about pollution are not mere survivals from earlier period, but vigorous and functional. Legally, it remained the primary duty of the family to deal with homicide without

---

14 Wallace-Hadrill 1988 and 1994, which serve as points of departure for the chapters of both Begemann and Evans Grubbs in this volume.
15 Habinek 1997.

interference by the community. The ascription of pollution served a double purpose. It puts pressure on the family to swiftly deal with the crime. At the same time it acknowledges the wider effects of such crimes on the community as a whole. Public and private are thus perspectives that could apply at one and the same time to single events and situations.

"Public/private" is a distinction frequently employed in describing Athenian law in order to differentiate the status conferred in several respects to the household as a private sphere, including instances of judicial power, for instance over slaves, and situations of legal self-help against intruders. By concentrating on law enforcement, however, Adriaan Lanni is able to identify mechanisms employed both by courts and within judicial contexts whereby seemingly private conduct was exposed to public scrutiny and, indeed, to sanction. It is the whole life conduct of a person beyond and unrelated to the actual case at hand that was thematized and used in argument in litigation. In this way, norms of deviance were formulated and informal control and vituperation were encouraged. The mechanisms of communication and the range of such information and their influence were, however, difficult to assess.

Esther Eidinow considers a notion of the private very much in dialogue with one important to the chapter by Ahmed El-Shamsy. Commencing from some reflections on the inability of models of polis-religion to allow for a strong public-private distinction, even at the level of analysis, Eidinow suggests a turn at once to theories of mind and, as a related matter, to what might appear a theological conundrum, namely, whether the Greeks believed the gods could know thoughts and intentional states that remained unvoiced. The twinned consideration of notions of human interiority and divine knowledge opens up many new approaches to the texts under consideration.

In her chapter on the conflict of Marcus Tullius Cicero after his return from exile in 55 BCE, with Publius Clodius Pulcher, who had in meantime consecrated a temple of Liberty in Cicero's house, Elisabeth Begemann analyses a well-documented case from the late Roman republic. Public and private, *publicus* and *privatus*, are concepts at the very heart of the political, religious, and legal case. Given the fact that the very character of a house of a Roman *nobilis* and politician defies classification as either "public" or "private," by virtue of its use for receptions of colleagues and clients, for formal meetings of priesthoods as for the accessible display of wealth, all arguments based on the distinction have to be very carefully framed, as the chapter shows in its detailed analysis of Cicero's speeches, his insinuations and omissions. In the end, it is contingent circumstances, the whereabouts of the statue, and the personality of Clodius, rather than general rules, that had to carry the case.

William van Andringa offers a case study from a slightly later epoch, a temple foundation at Pompeii in 3 CE. The podium of the temple of Fortuna Augusta was built on private property, but the necessary stair leading up to the sanctuary covered not only public space, but even changed the urban layout by narrowing a street. This difference in the legal status of the property concerned is marked by the use of visibly different building materials. Van Andringa situates this move of Marcus Tullius (not related to Cicero) within the strategies of contemporary members of the elite and their attempts at building relationships to the local community as well as the central figure of the emperor. The epigraphic formula *solo et pecunia sua*, the author claims, is thus intended to denote these political as well as property facts.

Judith Evans Grubbs takes up a problem that might seem to exist strictly within the domain of law and, indeed, within private social relations, to wit, the legal status of illegitimate children. But Evans Grubbs shows, through detailed chronological consideraton of the evidence, first, that illegitimate children were of many types: slave-born natural beings, *naturales*; freeborn children from non-legal couplings, *spurii*; and, as a special case, children from incestuous marriages. By contrast with the other cases, incest was a matter of religious concern and therefore fell within the domain of public law. Although juristic and documentary evidence from the classical and immediately post-Antonine period shows some flexibility toward a form of relation common among certain non-Roman peoples, Diocletian's legislation marks a severe change toward censuring such unions as both un-Roman and offensive to the gods.

Harry Maier turns to early Christian texts and the importance of a discourse on the household and domestic life in them. After a fashion kindred to the theological discourses studied by Eidinow and El-Shamsy, Maier reveals a discourse in which private conduct is the object of an evaluative gaze. In his case, however, the scrutiny is not divine, nor the discourse theological: private social relations, occurring within household spaces, become a proxy of religious worthiness and the interior spaces of houses become the object of a very public gaze. His essay has an affinity to the excellent and more material work of Kim Bowes on a later period and they might usefully be read together.[16]

The chapters by Rubina Raja and Natalie Dohrmann examine topics in many respects the inverse of Maier's. Whereas Maier's Christians nominally respect a distinction between public and private only to upend it, in seeking to expose the notionally private and domestic to public scrutiny, Raja and Dohrmann investigate notionally public spaces and discourses that are by varied means re-

16 Bowes 2008.

stricted in use, access or audience. Raja studies *tesserae* discovered (largely) in temple complexes of Roman Palmyra. The consensus holds these to have been used as tickets for banquets held at the temples. Raja contends that many of the banquets may have departed from the avowed status of the temples in two respects: first, the events appear to have been private, or at least restricted in attendance to invitees; and second, they may well have been held in honor of gods, or of priests of gods, other than the divinity to whom the temple space was dedicated.

Dohrmann examines the paradox of a normative discourse, that of the rabbis, that on her intrepretation sought simultaneously to claim a public authority but instantiated itself as ephemeral, as oral. The claim to public authority arises from the very form of the discourse the rabbis adopted, that of law. At the same time, they toiled to circumscribe the claims they made on its behalf. Inter alia, it was not the law of a statally constituted community and did not position itself as such in the terms standard to the day, which demanded material and manifest publication and an explicit claim to jurisdiction, over a population and a space. Dohrmann views the turn to oral law and its forms as complexly mimetic of Roman law or, at least, as deserving study on analogy with Roman law: as she puts it, the turn to oral law must be understood as an effort to make rabbinic discourse both authoritative and invisible in the landscape of the (imperial) rabbinic city.

Catherine Hezser, too, situates a problem in rabbinic law in analogical relation to arguments within Roman law, though she is concerned with a specific doctrinal issue. In the Palestinian Talmud, an earlier category of uncertain status, *carmelit*, emerges to temporary prominence. In short, earlier tannaitic sources describe as *carmelit* spaces of definitional ambiguity, materially and therefore ritually situated uneasily between private and public. In the Talmud, by contrast, *carmelit* emerges as a positive category, not so much liminal and uncertain as bridging. Hezser likens the carmelit to various forms of property in Roman law identified as property of no one (*res nullius*). In both traditions, she urges, thinkers reacted to the limitations and constraints of a rigid public/private distinction, with the crafting of some tertium quid that allowed certain practicalities to go forward.

Ahmed El-Shamsy addresses the Islamic distinction of public and private in the light of the notion of an all-seeing God. The strict separation of two spheres of action correlated to two different audiences or better: fellow human observers, that is, society on the one hand, and only God, on the other. The difference is conceptualized in terms of visibility, of cover and display. Earlier notions of sin and shame were re-elaborated in this framework. The unhindered – and unhinderable – view of God informed the development of an individual self and ethic. In the long run it might have helped to shape a conduct and ethic suitable to the rise of urbanism within the growing Islamic Empire.

Works cited

Abbey, R. 2011. *The Return of Feminist Liberalism.* Montreal and Kingston.

Ando, C. 2009. "Evidence and orthopraxy." *Journal of Roman Studies* 99 (2009): 171–181.

Ando, C. 2012. "Empire, state and communicative action," in C. Kuhn, ed., *Politische Kommunikation und öffentliche Meinung in der antiken Welt:* 219–229. Stuttgart.

Ando, C. 2015. *Roman Social Imaginaries. Language and thought in contexts of empire.* Toronto.

Aubert, J.-J., ed. 2003. *Tâches publiques et enterprise privée dans le monde romain.* Geneva.

Bowes, K. 2008. *Private worship, public values, and religious change in late antiquity.* Cambridge.

Brettschneider, C. 2007. "The Politics of the Personal: A Liberal Approach." *American Political Science Review* 101.1: 19–31.

Dardenay, A. and E. Rosso, eds. 2013. *Dialogues entre sphère publique et sphère privée dans l'espace de la cité romaine: vecteurs, acteurs, significations.* Bordeaux.

Davies, T.Y. 1999. "Recovering the original Fourth Amendment." *Michigan Law Review* 98: 547–750.

de Polignac, F. and P. Schmitt Pantel, eds. 1998. *Public et privé en Grèce ancienne. Lieux, conductes, pratiques.* Ktèma 23.

Gavison, R. 1992. "Feminish and the Public/Private Distinction." *Stanford Law Review* 45.1: 1–45.

Gilens, M. and B.I. Page. 2014. "Testing theories of American politics: elites, interest groups, and average citizens." *Perspectives on Politics* 12: 564–581.

Habermas, J. (1989) [1962]. *The structural transformation of the public sphere. An inquiry into a category of bourgeois society,* translated by Thomas Burger with the assistance of Frederick Lawrence, Cambridge, 1989 = *Strukturwandel der Öffentlichkeit,* Darmstadt, 1962.

Habinek, T. 1997. "The invention of sexuality in the world-city of Rome," in T. Habinek and A. Schiesaro, eds., *The Roman Cultural Revolution:* 23–43. Cambridge.

Horwitz, M. J. 1982. "The History of the Public/Private Distinction." *University of Pennylsvania Law Review* 130.6: 1423–1428.

Kuhn, C. ed. 2012. *Politische Kommunikation und öffentliche Meinung in der antiken Welt.* Stuttgart.

Lape, S. 2002/3. "Solon and the Institution of the 'Democratic' Family Form." *Classical Journal* 98: 117–139.

Lape, S. 2003. "Racializing Democracy: The Politics of Sexual Reproduction in Classical Athens." *Parallax* 9: 52–63.

Macé, A., ed. 2012. *Choses privées et chose publique en Grèce ancienne. Genèse et structure d'un système de classification.* Grenoble.

Putnam, R.D. 2000. *Bowling alone: the collapse and revival of American community.* New York.

Skocpol, T. 2003. *Diminished Democracy: From membership to management in American civic life.* Norman.

Thomas, Y. 2002a. “La construction de l’unité civique. Choses publiques, choses communes, choses n’appartenant à personne et représentation.” *Mélanges de l’École française de Rome, series Moyen Âge* 114, 7–39.

Thomas, Y. 2002b. “La valeur des choses. Le droit romain hors la religion.” *Annales: Histoire, Sciences Sociales*, November-December 2002, 1431–1462.

Wallace-Hadrill, Andrew (1988). “The Social Structure of the Roman House”, *PBSR* 56: 43–97.

Wallace-Hadrill, A. (1994). *Houses and Society in Pompeii and Herculaneum.* Princeton University Press.

Withington, P. (2007). “Public discourse, corporate citizenship, and state formation in early modern England.” *American Historical Review* 112: 1016–1038.

Edward M. Harris

1. The Family, the Community and Murder: The Role of Pollution in Athenian Homicide Law

Abstract: Scholars have recently argued that pollution for homicide was a religious belief that originated in the Homeric period and was fading away by the late fifth century BCE. This chapter presents evidence to show that beliefs about pollution continued to shape the legal procedures for homicide into the fourth century BCE. Plato's rules about pollution for homicide in his *Laws* therefore reflect contemporary beliefs and were not the product of religious "conservatism." These beliefs had both an instrumental and an expressive function and were closely connected with the development of the state. On the one hand, they placed pressure on the victim's family and the community to bring the killer to justice. On the other, pollution for homicide was a way of expressing society's disapproval for a crime that threatened the state's monopoly of legitimate force.

Introduction

Normally when one brought a private charge (*dike idia*) in Athenian law such as theft, damage, or for the recovery of a dowry, one summoned the defendant to appear before a magistrate on a certain day.[1] When the two parties met, the plaintiff submitted his charge in writing.[2] The case was then assigned to a public arbitrator. If either of the parties was not satisfied with the arbitrator's decision, he could appeal the decision to one of the courts.[3] There were no special rituals to be performed. Homicide was also a private charge in Athenian law: only the relatives of the victim could bring the charge.[4] Unlike other private charges, however, there were certain religious practices that had to be performed as part of a prosecution for homicide. First, when one initiated the charge, one had to swear

1 Harrison 1971, 85–94. References to works in Ancient Greek use the abbreviations found in the *Oxford Classical Dictionary.*

2 On the plaint see now Harris 2013a.

3 On arbitration see Harrison 1971, 66–69. This procedure was introduced after 403 BCE. Before 404 BCE private cases appear to have gone directly to court.

4 For a brief analysis of the sources see Kidd 1990. For a more extensive treatment see Tulin 1996, with the criticism of Harris 2006, 261 f.

an oath (Antiphon 5.11–12). The oath was very solemn; the accuser swore that the charge was true and called down destruction on himself, his relatives and his household if it were not. Second, after the *basileus*, the archon who had jurisdiction in cases of homicide, received the charge, he made a proclamation that the defendant had to keep away "from lustral water, libations, bowls of wine, holy places, and the marketplace" (Dem. 20.158; Antiphon 6.35–36; cf. Arist. *Ath. Pol.* 57.4; Soph. *OT* 236–42). Third, the case did not go to an arbitrator or a court immediately, but was reviewed at three preliminary hearings called *prodikasiai*, heard over three months (Antiphon 6.42). Fourth, the case was not heard before one of the regular courts manned by panels drawn from the 6,000 judges who served every year, but by special courts. The Areopagus heard cases of deliberate homicide (*ek pronoias*), the Palladion tried cases of involuntary homicide (*akousios*) and attempted homicide (*bouleusis*), and the Delphinion tried cases of "just" homicide or homicide "according to the laws" (Arist. *Ath. Pol.* 57.3–4. Cf. Dem. 23.22–61).[5] There were two other curious courts: one was located at Phreatto and was held for special cases involving charges brought against those in exile for involuntary homicide. The defendant stood in a boat offshore and delivered his reply to the charges without setting foot in Attica. There was another court at the Prytaneion held for homicide caused by animals and inanimate objects. Fifth, trials for homicide were not held inside buildings but were tried in the open air (Antiphon 5.11). Sixth, the successful accuser had to swear another oath after the trial that his charges were true (Aeschin. 2.87–88). A sacrificial animal was cut into pieces, and the accuser swore his oath standing in the middle.[6] Seventh, the normal penalty in a private suit was a payment of damages to the victim or their family. The person convicted of deliberate homicide was either put to death or sent into permanent exile with confiscation of his property by the state (Dem. 21.43). The person convicted of involuntary homicide was sent into exile until the relatives of the victim pardoned him (Dem. 37.59). Finally, there was a statute of limitations in private cases, which barred any suits brought five years after the offense (Dem. 36.25–7; 38.17).[7] By contrast, there was no statute of limitations in homicide cases (Lys. 13.83). Even though homicide was a private charge, there were

5 For the translation of *ek pronoias* ("deliberate" or "intentional") see Harris 2013b, 182–189.
6 When one swore an oath in Ancient Greece, it was customary to cut an animal in pieces (*tomia*) and stand in the middle of them. On this ritual see Arist. *Ath. Pol.* 55.5; Antiphon 5.88; Plato *Laws* 753d. For a Hebrew parallel see Jeremiah 34.18–19. Stengel 1910, 78–85 argued that the *tomia* were the testicles of the animal, but see Casabona 1966, 211–215.
7 See Charles 1938.

therefore eight major differences between procedure in homicide cases and that for other private charges.

Why did the Athenians create these rules for homicide law and not for other kinds of private charges? In three of the features that set the homicide courts apart from the regular courts, it is clear that concerns about pollution played an important role. The proclamation by the *basileus* was aimed at preventing the defendant from spreading his pollution by contact with public rituals and holy places. As Antiphon (5.82–83) observes, the presence of a polluted person at a sacrifice would cause the offering to fail.[8] The unusual features of the court at Phreatto were obviously designed to keep the defendant's pollution from touching Attica (Dem. 23.78 [not touching land]; Pollux 8.120 [placing neither gangway nor anchor onto land]). And the requirement that trials for homicide take place in the open air was imposed, as Antiphon (5.11) says, so that the judges would not enter the same place as someone whose hands were unclean, that is, polluted.

Over the last fifty years there has been a tendency among scholars to play down the importance of pollution in homicide law or to explain it away. In his study of homicide law published over fifty years ago, D. M. MacDowell played down the importance of pollution.[9] The most influential treatment of the topic has been that of Robert Parker in his *Miasma* published thirty years ago.[10] Parker claimed that views about pollution for homicide originated in the Homeric period (despite the absence of any evidence in the *Iliad* and *Odyssey*) and were the product of a society without formal legal institutions. After the growth of the law and the courts in Classical Athens, these beliefs tended to die out and had virtually vanished by the fourth century BCE. The book about homicide law of E. Carawan relies heavily on Parker's views.[11] In an article of 2006 Sealey has argued that pollution for homicide is only found in tragedy and belongs to the world of myth. It had no impact on Athenian law and legal procedure.[12] Arnaoutoglou takes a similar view.[13]

This chapter falls into two parts. The first part examines the evidence for beliefs about pollution for homicide in the Classical period and shows how these beliefs continued to shape legal procedures for homicide into the fourth century

---

8 For failed sacrifices see Naiden 2013, 131–182.

9 MacDowell 1963, 140–50, esp. 150: "it is unwise to take for granted that a belief in pollution was fundamental to Athenian homicide law." Cf. Gagarin 1981, 164–167.

10 Parker 1983, 104–143. Eck 2012 (*non vidi*) appears to follow Parker.

11 Carawan 1998, 17–20.

12 Sealey 2006.

13 Arnaoutoglou 2000.

BCE (*pace* Parker). The second part analyzes the role that beliefs about pollution for homicide played and their instrumental and expressive functions. On the one hand, the belief in pollution compelled the relatives of the victim to prosecute the murderer and the community to see that he was punished. On the other, beliefs about homicide expressed important views about the use of deadly violence in community. Far from being a survival from an earlier stage of social evolution, beliefs about pollution articulated the state's attempt to monopolize the use of legitimate force.

1. Pollution for homicide as a survival from an earlier period

Parker devotes a chapter of forty pages in his *Miasma* to pollution for homicide, but his main points can be easily summarized. Parker believes that "the appropriate context for beliefs of this kind about murder-pollution is surely a society that lacks more formal legal institutions."[14] Parker therefore traces the origin of beliefs in pollution for homicide to the period of the Homeric poems. After the growth of the *polis* with its formal legal and political institutions, there was no longer any need for such beliefs because their function had been taken over by the officials and the courts of the *polis*. "If the proper place for a belief in murder pollution is in a society without courts, we would expect it to wither away or change in meaning once courts were established."[15] Even though there was a system of courts in Athens from the time of Draco and Solon in the late seventh and early sixth centuries, Parker claims that the fear of pollution did not abate until the early fourth century. "After Aeschylus and Antiphon, however, the dangers of pollution seem to recede."[16] In support of his view, Parker points to Lysias' speech *Against Eratosthenes*, in which a man named Euphiletus defends himself a charge of homicide, and the speech he delivered against another Eratosthenes, who he claimed was responsible for the death of his brother Polemarchus. "The first speech of Lysias, a defence in a case of justified killing, is quite free from the language of pollution, and it appears only fleetingly even in the prosecution of Eratosthenes."[17] As a result, Parker claims that prosecutions for homicide in the fourth century did not mention the danger of pollution. "But

14 Parker 1983, 125.
15 Parker 1983, 126.
16 Ibid.
17 Parker 1983, 128.

it is reasonable to suppose that, in a fourth-century prosecution, murder would have been presented as a threat to society on a secular far more than on a religious level. This secularization probably has complex causes, but it is tempting to suggest as one of them that murder-pollution had outlived its utility."[18] Parker then attempts to explain away the rules about pollution in the section about homicide in Plato's *Laws* written in the middle of the fourth century. "The prominence of pollution in the *Laws* is characteristic of that work's profound religious conservatism."[19] Parker is also forced to explain away the numerous references to pollution in Antiphon's *Tetralogies*.[20]

There are several objections to Parker's analysis. First, it is not correct to state that there were no courts or administration of justice in the Homeric world. One thinks immediately of the trial scene on the shield of Achilles in the *Iliad* (18.497–5-8). The *basileis* of the Homeric and Hesiodic poems certainly exercise judicial functions by enforcing justice and *themistes*, which are clearly legal norms, and resolve disputes (*Il.* 9.297–298).[21] Even though the Assembly fails to support Telemachus' charges against the suitors in the second book of the *Odyssey*, it is clear that the Assembly could also exercise judicial functions. It is also striking that murderers are never said to be polluted or to require ritual purification in the Homeric poems.[22] For instance, when the people of Ithaca gather after the death of the suitors in the *Odyssey* (24.412–471) to discuss what to do with Odysseus, not a single person says that they must punish Odysseus because he is polluted or because his pollution threatens the safety of the community. When Theoclymenus flees Argos after killing a man, he tells Telemachus that he fears the revenge of the victim's relatives but says nothing about pollution driving him out (*Od.* 15.271). After Odysseus kills the suitors, he orders his slave women to "clean the house" but this cannot be considered a religious purification because it involves no sacrifice to the gods (*Od.* 23.438–440, 451–453).[23] By contrast, when the Achaeans purify their army in the *Iliad*, they remove

---

18 Ibid.

19 Ibid.

20 Parker 1983, 130: "It seems that the author of the *Tetralogies* has taken the doctrine of pollution to a theoretical extreme some way beyond the level of unease that in practice it created." But the attitude toward pollution in the *Tetralogies* appears to be no different from that found in Antiphon 5.

21 See Pelloso 2012 and more briefly Burchfiel 1994.

22 Schol. T *Il.* 11.690; schol. T *Il.* 24.480.

23 Heubeck in Heubeck, Fernández, and Russo 1992, 296 claims that "the cleaning of the hall is not merely hygienic, but also a ritual cleansing of pollution." The language of pollution is however absent in the passage, and ritual purification required a sacrifice to win back the god's favor, which does not occur in this passage. The verb *kathairo* in this passage means "cleanse" all traces of pollution (*lumata*) and then perform a sacrifice to Apollo (*Il.* 1.312–317).[24] Because the society of the Homeric poems did not consider the murderer polluted, there was no need for purification after homicide, which is also absent from the *Iliad* and *Odyssey* (see Appendix 1).[25]

Second, if the creation of courts removed the need for pollution as a means of repressing violence, why did it take so long for beliefs about homicide to die out? Even if we believe that there was no formal system of justice in the Homeric period, why didn't fears of pollution vanish in the decades after the legislation of Draco (roughly 630 BCE) and Solon (594 BCE)? Yet Parker admits that views about the dangers of pollution are still found in Aeschylus and Antiphon, almost two hundred years later.

Third, the reason why Euphiletus does not mention pollution for homicide in his speech defending his killing of Eratosthenes is because he claims that the murder of Eratosthenes was just and according to the laws (Lys. 1.26–36),[26] and this type of homicide incurred no pollution (Lycurg. *Leocrates* 125; Dem. 9.44; Dem. 20.158).[27] There was therefore no reason for him to mention pollution. One cannot therefore use this speech as evidence for the argument that the Athenians no longer were concerned about homicide in the early fourth century BCE.

Fourth, one cannot toss out the evidence of Plato's *Laws* because of "that work's profound religious conservatism". In the *Laws* and other works Plato accepts the traditional rituals of Greek religion but does not attempt to resuscitate religious practices that had fallen into desuetude or were no longer widely practiced. As McPherran has shown, Plato followed Socrates by "appropriating, reshaping, and extending – but not entirely rejecting – the religious conventions

in the non-ritual sense (cf. *Od.* 6.17, 93; 20.152). Parker 1983, 114 claims that Odysseus "purifies" his house but also observes that Odysseus does not purify himself, which would have been necessary in purification for homicide.

24 Cf. Kirk 1985, 84–5: "to rid their bodies of pollution."

25 The attempt of Parker 1983, 130–143 to explain away the absence of purification for homicide in the Homeric poems is not convincing. On the other hand, Parker 1983, 136 does note that some scholars have noted that "those heroes whose monstrous pollution fill the Attic stage are viewed by Homer and other early poets with a certain complaisance" but tries to explain this away by claiming "Killing a parent is, it seems, just one of the ordinary ups and downs of a hero's career." But if it is one of the "ordinary ups and downs of a hero's career," this does still not explain why the tragic poets treat these murders in a different way from Homer. Cf. Adkins 1960, 87: "In Homer ... the murderer is not polluted in what will be shown to be the fifth-century sense."

26 On this passage see Harris 2006, 283–295.

27 See also Hewitt 1910.

of his own time in the service of establishing the new enterprise of philosophy."[28] Like his teacher Socrates, Plato respected the traditional religious practices of his day. In the *Apology* (20d-23c) Socrates undertakes his philosophical questioning in obedience to the god Apollo and accepts the truth of the god's oracle at Delphi. In some cases, Plato accepts traditional stories about the gods. For instance, in the *Timaeus* (40d-e) Plato accepts stories about deities in the past who were said to be children of the gods and sees no need to doubt them. But in the *Republic* he criticizes at length the way the gods are portrayed by the poets (*Resp.* 377d-e). He rejects as false stories about the struggle between Uranus and Cronus (*Resp.* 377e-378a), about gods at war with each other (*Resp.* 378b-c. Cf. *Euthphr.* 6b), Hera being chained by Hephaestus (*Resp.* 378d), and Zeus giving mortals good and bad (*Resp.* 379b-d). He wishes to delete passages from the *Iliad* and *Odyssey* depicting the afterlife as unpleasant (*Resp.* 386c-387b), the gods laughing (*Resp.* 388e-389a), and Zeus being distracted from his plans by desire for Hera (*Resp.* 390b-c). In the *Laws* Plato denies the traditional tales about Hermes' thefts (*Leg.* 941b) and claims that the Cretan wrongly invented the story of Zeus' passion for Ganymede to justify their own illicit desires (*Leg.* 636c). The old story that Hera drove Dionysus mad dishonors both gods (*Leg.* 672b-c). In the proposals for the new state of Magnesia, Plato maintains the traditional division between Olympian and Chthonic deities (*Leg.* 717ab) but innovates by placing all worship for the latter in one special month dedicated to Pluto (*Leg.* 828c).[29]

In the ideal state sketched in the *Republic* Plato preserves a role for sacrifices (*Resp.* 419a), hymns to the gods (*Resp.* 607a) and temples, prayers, festivals, and (*Resp.* 427b-c). But if Plato retains the outward form of traditional rituals for Magnesia, he subtly alters their function. To win the gods' favor, the worshipper must not just offer them gifts but must try to imitate their nature (*Laws* 716c-717c). The role of festivals and hymns is to "provide virtue-training pleasures, pleasures that can be associated as stimuli with self-control and internal harmony that

---

28 McPherran 2006, 244. Cf. Morrow 1960, 399 who finds that in the *Laws* Plato "transforms the spirit, while adhering to the form, of the worship he finds among his countrymen." Cf. Morrow 1960, 401: "It is not a new religion that Plato proposes for his state, but the old religion, purified of its unwitting errors, and illuminated by a more penetrating conception of the meaning of religious worship ... Plato pours new wine into old bottles ..." and Reverdin 1945, 247: the religion of Plato's city "c'est, à bien des égards, la religion grecque repensée, épurée, spiritualisée."
29 Sacrifices to Chthonic deities occurred throughout the calendar of Classical Athens. For instance, the Mysteries, which involved worship of the Chthonian deities Persephone and Demeter, took place in Anthesterion (Plut. *Demetrius* 26.1 with Mikalson 1975, 120) and in Boedromion (Mikalson 1975, 55–60, 65). According to Apollodorus (*FGrHist* 244 F 109), quoted in Athenaeus 7.325a, there were *deipna* given to Hecate on the thirtieth of every month.

is productive of virtuous behavior."[30] Cult thus goes beyond to become a means of "imitating god." Moreover, Plato's conception of the afterlife as contemplation of the Forms (*Phd.* 79c-84c; *Resp.* 490a-b; *Phdr.* 247d-e) owes nothing to contemporary religious notions.[31] Plato's views about the role of the Demiurge who created the Cosmos as "a work of craft, modelled after that which is changeless and is grasped by a rational account, that is, by Wisdom" (*Ti.* 29a6-b1) departs considerably from traditional cosmogonies (e.g. Hesiod *Theogony*).[32] And in the *Laws* (909d-910b) Plato takes the radical step of banning private cults, which were permitted in Athens and other city-states.[33] It would be more accurate to state that Plato accepts the main rituals of his time and in some cases reforms them. The almost obsessively detailed rules about pollution and purification in the regulations about murder in the *Laws* (see Appendix 2) are therefore better viewed as a reflection of contemporary beliefs, which Plato accepted and reformed by adding new categories of homicide.[34] Plato's views about pollution for homicide are certainly not a throwback to the beliefs of an earlier period.

Fifth, if the Athenians did not take the dangers of pollution seriously at the end of the fifth century and early in the fourth century, why didn't they remove the regulations about pollution when they revised the laws of Draco and Solon during the revision of the law code between 410 and 399 BCE?[35] According to a speaker in Lysias' speech *Against Nicomachus* there were many changes in laws about religious activities (Lys. 30.17, 19–21). Why did the Athenians then allow the rules about pollution to remain in law code after 400 BCE if they no longer considered pollution a serious threat?

Sixth, *pace* Parker it is not true that litigants in court during the fourth century do not mention the dangers of pollution for homicide and other offenses. The Athenians believed that pollution was contagious: if one associated with a person who was polluted, one risked becoming infected by his pollution and thereby incurring the anger of the gods. If one truly believed that someone had committed murder, one attempted to shun his company to avoid catching his pollution. On the other hand, if one did not think that a person was guilty

30 McPherran 2000, 104 with *Laws* 653c-d, 654c-d, 659d-e, 665a-c, 887d.

31 McPherran 2006, 247.

32 On Plato's myths see most recently Morgan 2000, 132–292.

33 On Plato's ban on private cults see Morrow 1960, 491–94. For the numerous private cults in contemporary Athens see Arnaoutoglou 2003.

34 Cf. Reverdin 1945: "Plus qu'un novateur, l'auteur des lois nous est apparu comme un réformateur.' For Plato's innovations in homicide law see Harris 2013b, 189, 207 f.

35 For the revision of the laws in the late fifth century see now Canevaro and Harris 2012, 110–116.

of murder, one would freely associate with him and allow him to hold public office. In the middle of the fourth century when Meidias charged that Demosthenes murdered Nicodemus, Demosthenes argued that Meidias clearly did not believe in the truth of his accusation because he had allowed Demosthenes to conduct sacrifices and to preside over rituals for the entire city (Dem. 21.114). This argument would only have been convincing if the court considered pollution a serious threat. Later, in 343, Aeschines (2.148) repeated Meidias' allegation and accused Demosthenes of entering the agora when he was unclear – *ou katharos* – that is to say, polluted.[36] Why use this language if the court had no concerns about pollution? One also finds the language of pollution for homicide and ritual purity for innocence in several other speeches from the fourth century BCE (Dem. 9.44; 20.158; 23.72; 37.59; Lycurgus *Leocr.* 125). Finally, one finds the language of ritual purity for just homicide in the law of Eucrates dated to 336 BCE about killing tyrants (*SEG* 12.87). If pollution was not a concern in this period, why did the law state that the person who killed a tyrant was free from pollution? In fact, we see concerns about pollution for homicide as late as the second century BCE: the Achaeans objected to the Roman request to take back the exiles who were responsible for the death of their fellow citizens because "their hands were unclean" (οὐ καθαρῶν χεῖρας) (Pausanias 7.9.7).

I think there is a basic fallacy lying at the root of Parker's conception of the development of Greek Law in the Archaic and Classical periods. This is the assumption that there was an evolution in Greek society from a primitive stage in which power derived from religious authority and other "irrational" and "emotional" beliefs to the more advanced stage of the *polis*, which was rational, and political authority was not based on religion.[37] In the words of Louis Gernet, there was a development from *prédroit* to *droit*.[38] According to this view, pollution was an emotional reaction that expresses primitive horror at bloodshed. In fact, Adkins believed that views about pollution were not based on moral concepts but were an expression of revulsion at the act of killing: "It must be held that certain acts *per se* engender 'pollution', and the emotions originally engendered by despair and disaster will be transferred to the act of killing in its own right. There will thus be a horror of the killer, but not a moral horror which will conform to moral categories ..."[39]

---

36 The accusation of impiety mentioned at Dem. 22.2 also presumes a belief in pollution for homicide.

37 For good criticisms of such evolutionary assumptions see Evans-Pritchard 1965, 5, 29, 31, 37–8, 52, 108.

38 For this view see Gernet 1948–49 = Gernet 1968, 175–260.

39 Adkins 1960, 98.

There are two objections to this view. Even though there was much political development between the Homeric period and the Classical period, the realms of religion, law and politics still remained inextricably connected in Athens during the fifth and fourth centuries BCE. Religious business remained a regular item on the agenda of the Assembly (Arist. *Ath. Pol.* 43.5). The laws and decrees passed by the Assembly dealt with both sacred and secular matters. The Council was responsible for managing festivals and other religious practices as well as their secular duties.[40] Public officials might perform sacrifices and supervise religious festivals as part of their duties. The Eponymous Archon arranged the procession at the Thargelia and the one for Asclepius, Zeus the Savior and the Dionysia (Arist. *Ath. Pol.* 56.4–5). The Basileus looked at the Mysteries and the Lenaea festival and settled disputes about priestly privileges (Arist. *Ath. Pol.* 57.1–2). The Polemarch made sacrifices to Artemis the Huntress and Enyalius (Arist. *Ath. Pol.* 58.1). And it was not unusual for speakers in the Assembly to produce oracles and use them to support arguments about public policy.[41]

The second objection is that the rules about pollution were based on moral and legal distinctions. The rules about pollution for homicide served to articulate Athenian views about guilt and moral responsibility. There existed not one type of pollution but several, each one calibrated to indicate a different level of culpability. The most serious was ineradicable pollution, which could only be removed by the removal of the killer from the community either by death or permanent exile and confiscation of property. This was the type of pollution incurred by the person who committed deliberate homicide. Because this was the most serious kind of homicide, it was the one that deserved the most serious penalties and the highest level of pollution (Soph. *OT* 95–101; Dem. 21.43–46). The next level of pollution was that which could be removed by purification. This kind of pollution attached to the person who committed homicide against his will (Dem. 23.72; 37.59). Because this offense was not as serious as deliberate homicide, it merited a lesser penalty, only exile without confiscation of property. The killer also had the chance to return to Attica if he could gain pardon from the victim's relatives. This possibility was also expressed in ritual terms: just as the killer might be pardoned and his punishment ended, his pollution could also be removed by purification. The ritual of purification could also be used as a way of expressing regret. When a master killed his own slave, he could not be prosecuted in Athenian law because the slave was his property, and he had the right to do

40 See Rhodes 1981, 127–131.

41 Thuc. 8.1.1; Arist. *Hipp. passim.* On the interpenetration of religion, law and politics in Classical Athens see Harris 2006, 50–57.

whatever he wished with his slaves (Antiphon 6.4). There would also be no one to prosecute him because the slave had no kin recognized by law, and cases for homicide had to brought by the victim's kin. But the master still might feel a sense of regret for killing a human being and might therefore feel polluted by his action. He might therefore undergo purification to remove this sense of guilt. There is no evidence that the law required this ritual; it was optional and served to express his sense of regret. Finally there was the zero degree of pollution, that is, ritual purity, conveyed by the word *katharos*. When the homicide was done in accordance with the law or justly, the killer was not considered guilty and could not be convicted in court (Lycurg. *Leocr.* 125; Dem. 9.44; Dem. 20.158). Just as he was free of guilt, he was also free of pollution. The different types of pollution were therefore not a separate group of categories, set apart from the legal categories, but served to express different levels of legal and moral responsibility. Because pollution made the same kinds of distinctions that the law did, it was in this sense a "rational" practice rooted in moral beliefs, not a primal, emotional reaction to the horror of bloodshed.[42] The rules about pollution are therefore inextricably bound to contemporary legal notions about the gradation of penalties, not some primitive and irrational survival from an earlier stage of social development.[43]

Even though the specific rules about homicide are clearly the product of the city-state and associated with its laws and legal procedures, the basic notion behind the concept of pollution is rooted in two concepts that go back to the period of the Homeric and Hesiodic poems. One of these beliefs is the view that the evil deeds of one person can bring destruction on those associated with him. According to Hesiod (Op. 240–46):

> Often an entire city is destroyed because of an evil man,
> who sins and devises evils deeds. The son of Cronus
> brings suffering from heaven, plague and famine,
> and the people waste away. Or he destroys their
> vast army or their walls, or far-seeing Zeus
> punishes their ships at sea.

---

42 *Pace* Osborne 2011, "the behaviour regulated by notions of pollution complemented the behaviour regulated by law." As the evidence shows, pollution applied to the same behaviour as the law.

43 Cf. Evans-Pritchard 1965, 111: "it is not sound scientific method to seek for origins, especially when they cannot be found. Science deals with relations, not with origins and essences. In so far as it can be said that the facts of primitive religion can be sociologically explained at all, it must be in relation to other facts, but those with which it forms a system of ideas and practices and other social phenomena associated with it."

This view is also found in the *Iliad:* when Agamemnon dishonors Chryses by refusing his gifts and rejecting his request for his daughter's return, the priest prays to Apollo for vengeance (*Iliad* 1.8–42). The god punishes Agamemnon by bringing a plague on his troops, who opposed his refusal to return Chryseis but nevertheless suffer by their association with the king (*Iliad* 1.43–52). In the *Odyssey* Aeolus tells Odysseus to leave his kingdom because he believes that the gods hate him and that his presence might cause his own destruction (*Odyssey* 10.72–75). One cannot argue that this was a primitive belief that died out with the advent of the *polis.* Aeschines quotes the passage from Hesiod's *Works and Days* not once but twice, in his *On the False Embassy* (2.158) and in *Against Ctesiphon* (3.135). He calls his opponent Demosthenes "accursed" (*prostropaion*), a ritual term, and claims that he should not be allowed to enter the Assembly, which the Athenians purify before meetings. The continuity of belief is clear. The other view is that moral transgressions can cause disruptions in the natural world in the form of plagues, storms, earthquakes and crop failures (Hesiod Op. 225–237; *Iliad* 16.384–393). Conversely, moral virtue in a community and its leaders brings fertility and good weather (*Odyssey* 19.109–114). Concerns about pollution for homicide are certainly based on these beliefs. Fears of pollution therefore did not "arise" in one period and then die out. They were rooted in beliefs that can be found in the Homeric poems and continued right down into the Classical period.

2. Pollution for Homicide: Instrumental and expressive aspects

But why did the city-state of Athens believe that homicide caused pollution while other private offenses did not? What accounts for the difference between the attitude toward homicide in Homeric society and that found in Classical Athens? Here one must place Athenian homicide law within the context of Athenian law in general to understand the role of the rituals associated with these procedures. Athenian law divided legal procedures into two basic categories: public actions and private actions. Public actions were brought against crimes that harmed or threatened the community or against offenses against individuals that were so serious that they merited public attention. These actions could be brought by anyone who wished (*ho boulomenos*). Examples of the former are treason, embezzlement of public funds, and cowardice (a military offense); examples of the latter are outrage or aggravated assault (*hybris*), harm done to an heiress, and wounding with intent. The punishments for conviction in public actions ranged from death or exile with confiscation of property to fines to be paid to the Treasury (imprisonment was possible but normally used only for those who had not yet paid fines). In general, the accuser did not receive payment from the defendant (Dem. 21.28). Private actions were brought against offenses done to individuals such as theft, damage to property, failure to return a dowry, embezzling the funds of a ward by a guardian, failure to vacate property belonging to another person. Only the victims or their representatives could bring these suits. If the plaintiff won his suit, he received financial compensation from the defendant.

Homicide was anomalous in this scheme for several reasons. It was classified as a private suit for the obvious reason that the harm was done to an individual. But it departed from the standard private suit in several ways. First, the victim of the offense could not bring the action himself because he was no longer alive. Second, there could be no compensation paid to the victim. In deliberate homicide the principle of reciprocity could only be maintained if the killer were to be put to death. Alternatively he might be driven into exile with confiscation of property by the state (Dem. 21.43). In involuntary homicide the convicted man remained in exile until he received pardon from the relatives of the victim (Dem. 37.58). These punishments (death and exile) were normally reserved for public actions.

The reason why the Athenians believed that homicide caused pollution was a way of recognizing that homicide was a special type of private action and setting it apart from other private actions to express communal views about the gravity of the offense. As Demosthenes (20.157) says, preventing homicide is the most serious aim of the legal system. For other serious crimes, there were public actions, which served to express the community's views about the gravity of the offense. In the case of homicide, the community used rituals to convey the seriousness of the crime. In fact, Antiphon states this explicitly in his speech *On the Chorister* (6.6).

For these reasons the laws, the oaths, the sacrifices, the proclamations, and all the other rituals which are performed for cases of homicide are very different from those for other private cases because it is of supreme importance that a correct decision be reached about matters which involve much danger.

One finds a similar view in the *Third Tetralogy* attributed to Antiphon (4.1.1–2).

> It has been established by law that those who judge cases of homicide correctly pay the greatest attention to ensuring that accusations and testimony are made according to justice by not acquitting the guilty and not putting the ritually pure on trial. For when god wished to create the human race and brought our earliest ancestors into existence, he gave them

> the land and the sea to feed them so that they would not die before the end of old age through lack of necessities. Since god considers our life so valuable, the person who kills illegally commits impiety toward the gods and destroys the laws of men. The dead man who has been deprived of god's gifts rightly leaves behind him the wrath of avenging spirits as god's punishment. Those who decide a case or give testimony unjustly therefore join in the perpetrator's impiety and bring into their private houses another man's pollution.

Why was homicide considered such an important matter? Here we need to place the issue in the wider context of Athenian attitudes about violence and the community.[44] By the fifth century, Athens had developed the three main features of state institutions. First, it had clearly marked geographical borders.[45] Second, it had a concept of citizenship and made a strict distinction between those who held political rights in decision-making and in holding office and those who did not. In short, there was a distinction between *politai* on the one hand and *metoikoi* and *xenoi* on the other. Third, and most important for our topic, there was a distinction between public officials and private citizens. These public officials represented the interests of the community and possessed what Max Weber called "a monopoly of legitimate physical violence within defined borders" ("innerhalb eines bestimmten Gebietes... das Monopol legitimer physischer Gewaltsamkeit für sich (mit Erfolg) beansprucht"). There were some cases in which private citizens in Athens had the right to use deadly force (just as they do in modern states), but these were exceptions to the general rule that citizens should not use violence to enforce their rights against others.[46]

This was one of the major differences between the Greek city-state of the Classical period and the Homeric community. In the Homeric poems there were three main responses to homicide: first, the family of the victim could accept compensation from the killer (*Il.* 9.632–636). Second, the killer could flee abroad (e.g. *Od.* 15.271–282). In this case the family of the victim appears to have considered this adequate retribution because one never finds any evidence for vicarious punishment in the Homeric poems. Third, a relative of the victim could kill the murderer as Orestes does with Aegisthus.[47] The rule in Athens was very different: one was not allowed to kill a murderer or to accept payment in compensation for deliberate homicide. Demosthenes (23.69) states the principle very clearly in his *Against Aristocrates:* "If the accuser is judged to have made an honest accusation and he convicts the guilty man on a charge of murder, not

44 On Athens as a state and the monopoly of legitimate force see Harris 2013b, 21–59.

45 For the borders of Greek *poleis* see Daverio Rocchi 1988 and Rousset 1994.

46 For the exceptions see Harris 2013b, 50–59.

47 For references see Appendix 1, no. 1.

even then does he gain power over the convicted man. No, the laws and the officials assigned to this task have the power to punish him. The accuser can witness the penalty inflicted by law, nothing more." If a murderer was convicted in court, sentenced to exile, and respected the terms of his exile, no one was allowed to kill him. If someone did, he could be prosecuted for homicide (Dem. 23.35–43). All those accused of homicide were entitled to a trial before a court, and the state's officials alone had the right to inflict punishment.[48] The use of deadly force by a private individual was therefore the greatest threat to the state's monopoly of legitimate force. The Athenians also banned the practice of accepting compensation for the murder of a relative.[49] Homicide was now considered such an important offense that it had to be punished by either death or permanent exile; a murderer could no longer buy off his victim's relatives. Even though the relatives of the victim were to bring the case against the offender, it was the state that determined what his punishment would be.

The special rituals contained in homicide procedure were a way of expressing the community's disapproval of violence used by private individuals and of setting it apart from other private offenses that did not represent the same type of threat to the state. Such rituals did not have a place in the Homeric world because there was no state that attempted to monopolize the use of legitimate force. Homicide was an offense similar to many others, and disputes arising from murder could be resolved by an agreement between private individuals like any other offense such as theft or damage.

The close link between the procedures for homicide and the rise of state institutions is clear in their common approach to public and sacred space. In the Homeric poems Greek communities inhabit geographical areas, but these territories are not carefully defined by fixed borders marked by *horoi* (boundary-markers) or mutually agreed physical features of the landscape (rivers, mountain ranges).[50] In similar fashion, the *agora* in the *Iliad* and the *Odyssey* is only a meeting place at a central location but is not formally set apart by boundary-markers (e.g., *Il.* 1.490; 2.93; 7.382; 19.45, 88, 173, 249; *Od.* 2.10, 37, 150; 20.146, 362; 24.420). By contrast, the community of Athens had formally designated borders on land (e.g., Thuc. 2.12.1–3).[51] These play an important role in the regulations for homicide: if the murderer who is convicted and sentenced to exile remains outside of these boundaries, he cannot be killed (Dem. 23.37–42. Cf. *IG*

---

48 One finds a reflection of the new attitude in Euripides' *Orestes* 496–517.

49 Dem. 58.28–9 and Harpocration *s.v.* ὑποφόνια with MacDowell 1963, 8f.

50 The word οὖρος in the sense of "boundary-marker" occurs only once in the Homeric poems and refers to a boundary of private property – see *Iliad* 21.405.

51 See the works cited in note 44.

i³ 104, lines 26–29). By the sixth century the Athenians had set up *horoi* around the *agora* in the city center, marking it out as a sacred space.[52] They had also appointed special officials *(agoranomoi)* to police this area and to enforce regulations about its use.[53] This public sacred space was also important in the procedure for homicide: after a charge of murder was made, the *basileus* who received the charge made a declaration banning the defendant from the *agora* and other public places (Aeschin. 2.148; Antiphon 5.10; Dem. 20.158; Antiphon 6.35–36; Arist. *Ath. Pol.* 57.4; cf. Dem. 23.80; 24.60).[54]

According to Mary Douglas, beliefs about pollution "can have another socially useful function – that of marshalling moral disapproval when it lags (...). This accords with the general principle that when the sense of outrage is adequately equipped with practical sanctions in the social order, pollution is not likely to arise. Where, humanly speaking, the outrage is likely to go unpunished, pollution beliefs tend to be called in to supplement the lack of other sanctions."[55]

This may be true in regard to some offenses in some societies, but does not apply to pollution for homicide in Athenian society. In Classical Athens there existed adequate procedures for prosecuting homicide. In addition to the private action for murder, an accuser could also use a special procedure against *kakourgoi* to prosecute a killer.[56] Even though one or more relatives of a victim might not have wished to bring a charge, most victims would have had enough relatives to ensure that someone was willing to bring the victim's killer to court.[57] If there was a disagreement among the relatives of the victim about whether to accuse the killer or not, the decision of the person who wished to prosecute would prevail. According to Demosthenes (21.116), someone could also call upon the Council to investigate a homicide and make an arrest. Finally, one should recall that it would have been a matter of honor for the victim's family to seek revenge, and

52 See Lalonde in Lalonde, Langdon and Walbank 1991, 10–11 with H25–28.

53 For the *agoranomoi* at Athens see most recently Oliver 2012.

54 For the distinction between *agora* as a sacred space and *agora* in the secular sense of market-place see de Ste. Croix 1972, 267–284, 397 f.

55 Douglas 1966, 131 f. A similar view of pollution is taken by Osborne 2011, 180: "notions of pollution in the classical Greek world serve to reach parts, types of behaviour, which formal law cannot reach, and where the society is not sufficiently small and close knit for shame, which is entirely without threat of sanction, to be relied on." Osborne does not explain why formal law "cannot reach" acts of homicide. As this essay shows, there were several procedures created to prosecute homicide, which were used by families on many occasions.

56 This procedure appears to have been used in the prosecution of Agoratus for the murder of Dionysodorus (Lys. 13.87, with Harris 2006, 396 f.) and in the prosecution of the murderer of Herodes (Antiphon 5.8–19, 85–96 with Gagarin 1989, 17–29).

57 See *IG* i³ 104, lines 13–19 with Gagarin 1981, 48–54.

this would have exerted social pressure on the family to bring the killer to justice.[58] Beliefs about pollution for homicide worked like curses added to laws and decrees of the Greek city-states: for offenses that the community considered very serious, the law attempted to harness all available forces, both secular and religious, to punish offenders. Religious rituals did not act in this case as a substitute for legal procedures but worked with political officials to enforce compliance to human and divine standards.[59]

To use the terms of Mary Douglas, the rituals associated with the legal procedures for homicide had both an instrumental and an expressive function.[60] On the one hand, they served to place pressure on the relatives of the victim to see that the murderer received the appropriate punishment. These rituals also encouraged the judges at homicide trials to take their responsibility seriously: failure to punish the guilty man or the conviction of an innocent man might bring about crop failure, disease, storms or earthquakes. On the other hand, the unusual features of homicide procedure expressed the community's views about the use of deadly force. Homicide was such a serious crime that accusers had to swear a special oath when bringing the charge and after a successful conviction, the *basileus* had to conduct not one, but three preliminary hearings and banish by proclamation the defendant from holy places and public rituals. The state had to assign special courts to try these cases. It was the most serious crime not only because it was the greatest harm that one could do to an individual, but was also the greatest threat to the community because the killer in effect attempted to usurp the state's monopoly of legitimate force. There is therefore no need to view beliefs about pollution for homicide as a survival from an earlier stage of social development. The best way to explain the rituals associated with homicide procedure is to place them in the context of the legal, political and religious institutions of Classical Athens.

The laws and legal procedures for homicide in Classical Athens were an attempt to reconcile the private interests of the family with public interests of the community. On the one hand, the laws left the prosecution of homicide primarily in the hands of relatives of the victim. The community did not wish to weaken family ties or to discourage citizens from defending the honor of their relatives. The family was one of the building blocks of the community, and the community as a whole would be weakened if the ties linking its constituent units were weak-

---

58 For social pressure exerted to avenge a relative by marriage see [Dem.] 59.12.

59 Cf. Douglas 1966, 3: "The whole universe is harnessed (i. e. through pollution) to men's attempts to force one another into good citizenship."

60 For the distinction between expressive and instrumental aspects of ritual see Douglas 1966, 3.

ened. The family was not viewed as a threat to the *polis*; the family was considered a microcosm of the *polis* (Soph. *Ant.* 661–2; Aeschin. 1.30; 3.78; Xen. *Mem.* 3.14.2; 6.14). A good member of the family would become a good citizen. The law retained a place for the private interests of the family in homicide law, and the beliefs about pollution served to encourage (if not compel) family members to do their duty and avenge their relatives.

On the other hand, the laws recognized the state's monopoly of legitimate force by removing from relatives the power to execute murderers. Beliefs about pollution for homicide expressed the view of the community that individuals did not have the right to use deadly force (except in exceptional circumstances). The special rituals associated with the legal procedures for homicide also placed pressure on all citizens to punish those who committed homicide and served to mark out this private action as one that concerned everyone in the community.

Appendix 1
Homicide and the Consequences of Homicide in the *Iliad* and the *Odyssey*

This list is based on Gagarin (1981) 6–10 with some modifications.

1. *Il.* 2.661–670: Tlepolemus killed his father's maternal uncle and, threatened by others, went into exile in Rhodes; Zeus made him wealthy. No mention of pollution or purification.
2. *Il.* 13.694–697 (cf. 15.333–360): Medon killed the brother of his stepmother and is living in exile. No mention of pollution or purification.
3. *Il.* 15.431–439: Lycophron killed a man and came to live with Ajax, where he was greatly honored. No mention of pollution or purification.
4. *Il.* 16.572–575: Epigeus killed his cousin and joined Achilles' forces. No mention of pollution or purification.
5. *Il.* 18.497–508: On Achilles' shield a trial is being held concerning compensation for a man who was killed. For discussion see Pelloso (2012). No mention of pollution or purification.
6. *Il.* 23.85–90: As a boy, Patroclus killed another boy in anger over a dice game but against his will; he goes into exile and joins Achilles. No mention of pollution or purification.
7. *Il.* 24.480–483: The amazement felt by Achilles when seeing the suppliant Priam is compared to that felt by those who see an exiled killer seeking the protection of a wealthy man. No mention of pollution or purification.

8. *Od.* 1.29–30, 35–43, 298–300; 3.193–919, 234f., 248–252, 255–257, 303–310; 4.91f., 519–537, 546f.; 11.387–389, 409–434; 24.20–22, 96–97, 199–202: Aegisthus killed Agamemnon and was killed in turn by Agamemnon's son Orestes. No mention of pollution or purification.
9. *Od.* 11.422–430: Clytemnestra killed Cassandra and helped to kill Agamemnon; she was later killed and buried by Orestes. No mention of pollution or purification.
10. *Od.* 3.309f.: Orestes killed Aegisthus and was praised. No mention of pollution or purification.
11. *Od.* 4.536f.: The followers of Agamemnon and Aegisthus all killed each other. No mention of pollution or purification.
12. *Od.* 11.273–280: Oedipus killed his own father in ignorance, but his father's identity was later revealed. He continued to rule in Thebes but was tormented by his mother's Erinyes. Oedipus does not go into exile to avoid pollution, and there is no mention of purification.
13. *Od.* 13.259–275: In one of his false stories, Odysseus says that he was deprived of booty and then killed a man in ambush at night, then left the country. No mention of pollution or purification.
14. *Od.* 14.380f.: A killer from Aetolia flees and is received by Eumaeus on Ithaca. No mention of pollution or purification.
15. *Od.* 15.271–282 (cf. 15.224): Theoclymenus kills a fellow tribesman in Argos and flees to Pylos. Telemachus takes him under his protection but does not purify him.
16. *Od.* 21.24–30: Heracles kills his guest Iphitus for his horses; he suffers no punishment and undergoes no purification.
17. *Od.* 22.1–33: Odysseus kills Antinous. The suitors think that he has done it against his will and intend to kill him. No mention of pollution.
18. *Od.* 22: Odysseus and Telemachus kill the suitors. The reconciliation takes place without any mention of purification.
19. *Od.* 22.465–472: Telemachus kills twelve slave-girls by hanging and feeds their bodies to the dogs.[61] For their status and treatment see Harris 2012, 14.

There are several attempted murders or plots to murder.

1. *Od.* 4.669–74; 16.374–405: The suitors attempt to kill Telemachus. The people of Ithaca would be angry if they knew and drive them out, but there is no indication that the suitors fear pollution.

---

61 Gagarin calls these women "maid-servants," which is misleading, and does not mention what Telemachus does to their corpses.

2. *Il.* 6.167–190: Proetus hesitates to kill Bellerophon and sends him to this father-in-law, who tries unsuccessfully to have him killed.
3. *Il.* 9.458–461: Phoenix wanted to kill his father but did not out of fear for the bad reputation acquired by parricides.
4. *Il.* 24.583–586: Achilles tries to avoid killing Priam in anger and thereby anger Zeus. He is not said to fear pollution.
5. *Od.* 14.402–406: Eumaeus, if he were to kill his guest, would have a bad reputation and would pray to Zeus. There is no mention of a need for purification.

For the possibility of the killer obtaining pardon by paying blood-money see also *Il.* 9.632–636. This practice was outlawed in Classical Athens.

The word *miaros* occurs only once in Homer (*Il.* 24.420) and means "dirty" without any connotation of ritual impurity. The word *miasma* and *katharmos* are completely absent. The word *katharos* is never used in the sense of ritually pure as opposed to "clean."

Appendix 2
Regulations about Homicide in Plato's *Laws*

<u>Violent and Involuntary Homicide</u> (865a–b)
<u>Purification</u> required as Delphi directs. No punishment.
<u>Doctors</u> (865b)
- If the patient dies against the doctor's will, the doctor is <u>pure</u>.

<u>Homicide by Killer's Hand</u> but <u>Involuntary</u> (865b–866d)
- Slaves – The killer must pay the owner the value of the slave. If he does not, the owner may bring an action for double the value (determined by judges). A greater degree of <u>purification</u> than in previous cases (because the offense is more serious).
- Free Citizens – The same kind of <u>purification</u> as for slaves and the penalty of exile for one year.
- Free Foreigner – Same as for a free citizen but with the additional penalty of exile from the victim's country.
- If the killer violates the terms of exile, the relatives of the victim can prosecute and the penalty is doubled. If the relatives do not prosecute, they incur pollution and can be prosecuted by anyone. The penalty is exile for five years.

- Foreigner Kills a Foreigner – Anyone may prosecute. Metics are punished with exile for a year (purification required); foreigners are exiled in perpetuity (purification required). If the foreigner returns, the Nomophylakes are to execute him and hand his property to the next of kin. If he is shipwrecked off the coast, he must remain in the sea and look for a ship to take him. If he is brought back by force, the first official who sees him must free him and send him over the border unharmed.

Homicide Committed in Anger (θυμῷι) (866d–868a)
- Free man kills free man in anger and without intent, he goes into exile for two years.
- Free man kills free man in anger and with deliberate intent, he goes into exile for three years (more serious crime, greater penalty).
- When the exile ends, the Nomophylakes sent twelve to the border who decide whether to grant pardon and to allow them to return.
- For a second offense, the penalty is permanent exile.

Homicide Committed in Anger, Unusual Cases: Slaves, Spouses, Parents, Children (868a–869c)
- If the victim slain in anger is a slave, the master will purify himself. If he kills another man's slave in anger, he pays double damages.
- If any of these offenders violates the law and enters the market, games or meetings (implicit concern about pollution), anyone can prosecute the kin of the victim who permit this and the killer himself. Monetary penalty.
- If a slave kills a master in rage, the relatives must kill the slave in any way they wish and are ritually pure.
- If a slave kills anyone else, the owner must turn him over to the victim's family for execution.
- If a father or a mother kills a child in anger by blows or other violence, the killer must be purified and go into exile for three years. After return from exile, the killer must divorce his spouse, and they can never have children or share the same home or same rites.
- If a husband kills his wife in anger or wife a husband, they must be purified and go into exile for three years. After return, the killer must not join in worship with his children or share the same table. Those who disobey can be prosecuted for impiety.
- If a child kills a parent in anger, the killer is pure if the victim pardons him before dying and if he undergoes purification. If there is no pardon, the penalty is death.

Civil Strife (869c–e)

- If a brother kills a brother after being struck during civil strife, he is pure. The same holds true for citizens who kill citizens or foreigners who kill foreigners. If a citizen kills a foreigner after being struck, he is pure, and the same if a slave kills a slave. If a slave kills a free man after being struck, he is subject to the same laws as one who kills a father.
- If any victim pardons his killer before dying, the killer will be purified and go into exile for one year.

Homicide Done Willingly and With Planning (869e)

- The person who kills deliberately and unjustly anyone of the tribe must stay away from shrines, market, harbors and any other gathering place.
- Anyone who does not prosecute the killer when he should or does not warn him about his status is also polluted. The person who prosecutes will perform certain rituals.
- Penalty for deliberate homicide is death and will not be buried in the land of the victim.
- If the killer flees and does not return, he is condemned to permanent exile. If he returns, the relatives of the victim will slay him or give him to the official who judged the case for execution.
- The prosecutor must demand sureties, and the defendant will produce three sureties (approved by the court) who will guarantee his appearance. If he does not produce them, he will be put in prison.
- If a man does not kill with his own hand, but plots death, he will be prosecuted in the same way except that he can be buried at home.
- The same rules apply to cases between foreigners, those between citizens and foreigners, and between slaves and slaves.
- If a slave kills a free man, the public executioner will flog the slave in front of the victim's tomb. If the slave is still alive after the flogging, he will be put to death.
- If someone kills a slave from fear of being denounced, he will be subject to same procedures as for a free person.

Murder of Kin (872c–873b)

- For killing mother or father, there is no purification until killing expiates killing. The same warning for exclusion before the trial. The man who is convicted is put to death by the assistants of the judges and the officials. All the officials will cast a stone on the head of the corpse and thus purify (ἀφοσιούτω) the entire state and then cast the body out unburied.

Suicide (873c–d)
– The person who kills himself because of laziness and cowardice will be buried in an isolated place on the borders of the twelve districts that are barren and nameless without a tombstone or name to indicate the location of the tomb.

Works cited

Adkins, A. W. H (1960). *Merit and Responsibility: A Study in Greek Values.* Oxford.
Arnaoutoglou, I. (2000). "Pollution in the Athenian Homicide Law," *Revue internationale des droits de l'antiquité*[3] 40: 109–137.
Arnaoutoglou, I. (2003). *Thusias heneka kai sunousias: private religious associations in Hellenistic Athens.* Athens.
Benson, H. (2006). *A Companion to Plato.* Malden and Oxford.
Burchfiel, K. (1994). "The myth of 'pre-law' in early Greece," in Thür (1994): 79–104.
Canevaro, M. and Harris, E. M. (2012). "The Documents in Andocides' *On the Mysteries*," *CQ* 62: 98–129.
Cantarella, E., ed. (2007). *Symposion 2005: Vorträge zur griechischen und hellenistischen Rechtsgeschichte.* Vienna.
Capdetrey, L. and Hasenohr, C., eds. (2012). *Agoranomes et édiles: Institutions des marchés antiques.* Bordeaux.
Carawan, E. (1998). *Rhetoric and the Law of Draco.* Oxford.
Casabona, J. (1966). *Recherches sur le vocabulaire des sacrifices en grec, des origines à la fin de l'époque classique.* Aix-en-Provence.
Charles, J. F. (1938). *Statutes of Limitations at Athens.* Chicago.
Daverio Rocchi, G. (1988). *Frontiera e confini nella Grecia antica.* Rome.
Douglas, M. (1966). *Purity and Danger: An Analysis of the Concepts of Pollution and Taboo.* London.
Eck, B. (2012). *La mort rouge: Homicide, guerre et souillure en Grèce ancienne.* Paris.
Evans-Pritchard, E. E. (1965). *Theories of Primitive Religion.* Oxford.
Faraguna, M., ed. (2013). *Legal Documents in Ancient Societies* IV. Trieste.
Gagarin, M. (1981). *Drako and Early Athenian Homicide Law.* New Haven.
Gagarin, M. (1989). *The Murder of Herodes: A Study of Antiphon 5.* Frankfurt am Main.
Gernet, L. (1948–49). "Droit et prédroit en Grèce ancienne," *L'année sociologique* 3: 21–119.
Gernet, L. (1968). *L'anthropologie de la Grèce antique.* Paris.
Hansen, M. H. (1998). *Polis and City-State. An Ancient Concept and its Modern Equivalent.* (*Acts of the Copenhagen Polis Centre* vol. 5). Copenhagen.
Harris, E. M. (1989). "Demosthenes' Speech against Meidias," *Harvard Studies in Classical Philology* 92: 117–36.
Harris, E. M. (2000). "Open Texture in Athenian Law," *Dike* 3: 27–79.
Harris, E. M. (2004a). "More Thoughts on Open Texture in Athenian Law," in Leão, Rosetti and Fialho (2004): 241–263.
Harris, E. M. (2004b). "Le rôle de l'*epieikeia* dans les tribunaux athéniens," *Revue historique de droit français et étranger* 82: 1–13.

Harris, E. M. (2006). *Democracy and the Rule of Law in Classical Athens. Essays on Law, Society and Politics.* Cambridge.
Harris, E. M. (2007). "Who Enforced the Law in Classical Athens?" in Cantarella (2007): 159–176.
Harris, E. M. (2010). "Is Oedipus Guilty?" in Harris, Leão, and Rhodes (2010): 122–46.
Harris, E. M. (2012). "Homer, Hesiod, and the 'Origins' of Greek Slavery," *REA* 114: 1–22.
Harris, E. M. (2013a). "The Plaint in Athenian Law and Legal Procedure," in Faraguna (2013): 156–175.
Harris, E. M. (2013b). *The Rule of Law in Action in Democratic Athens.* Oxford.
Harris, E. M., Leão, D. and Rhodes, P. J., eds. (2010). *Law and Drama in Ancient Greece.* London.
Harrison, A. R. W. (1971). *The Law of Athens: Procedure.* Oxford.
Heubeck, A., Fernández, M., and Russo, J. (1992). *A Commentary on Homer's* Odyssey. Vol. 3. Oxford.
Hewitt, J. W. (1910). "The Necessity of Ritual Purification after Justifiable Homicide," *TAPA* 41: 99–113.
Kirk, G. (1985). *The Iliad: A Commentary.* Vol. 1: Books 1–4. Cambridge.
Kraut, R. ed. (1992). *The Cambridge Companion to Plato.* Cambrigde.
Lalonde, G. V., Langdon, M. and Walbank, M. B. (1991). *Agora XIX: Horoi, Poletai Records, Leases of Public Land.* Princeton.
Leão, D, D. Rosetti and M. Fialho, eds. (2004). *Nomos – estudos sobre direito antigo.* Coimbra.
MacDowell, D. M. (1963). *Athenian Homicide Law in the Age of the Orators.* Manchester.
MacDowell, D. M. (1990). *Demosthenes: Against Meidias.* Oxford.
McPherran, M. L. (1996). *The Religion of Socrates.* University Park, PA.
McPherran, M. L. (2000). "Does piety pay? Socrates and Plato on Prayer and Sacrifice," in Smith and Woodruff (2000): 89–114.
McPherran, M. L. (2006). "Platonic Religion," in Benson (2006): 244–259.
Mikalson, J. D. (1975). *The Sacred and Civil Calendar of the Athenian Year.* Princeton.
Morgan, K. A. (2000). *Myth and Philosophy from the Presocratics to Plato.* Cambridge.
Morgan, M. L. (1990). *Platonic Piety.* New Haven.
Morgan, M. L. (1992). "Plato and Greek Religion," in Kraut (1992): 227–247.
Morrow, G. (1960). *Plato's Cretan City: A Historical Interpretation of the Laws.* Princeton.
Naiden, F. S. (2013). *Smoke Signals for the Gods: Ancient Greek Sacrifice from the Archaic through Roman Periods.* New York and Oxford.
Nenci, G. and G. Thür, eds. (1990). *Symposion 1988. Vorträge zur griechischen und hellenistischen Rechtsgeschichte.* Cologne.
Oliver, G. (2012). "*Agoranomoi* at Athens," in Capdetrey and Hasenohr (2012): 81–100.
Osborne, R. (2011). *The History Written on the Classical Greek Body.* Cambridge.
Parker, R. (1983). *Miasma. Pollution and Purification in Early Greek Religion.* Oxford.
Pelloso, C. (2012). *Themis e dike in Omero: ai primordi del diritto dei Greci.* Alessandria.
Reverdin, O. (1945). *La religion de la cité platonicienne.* Paris.
Rhodes, P. J. (1981). *A Commentary on the Aristotelian Athenaion Politeia.* Oxford.
Rickert, G. (1989). *HEKON and AKON in Early Greek Thought.* Atlanta, GA.
Rousset, D. (1994). "Les frontières des cités grecques. Premières réflexions à partir du recueil des documents épigraphiques," *Cahiers du Centre Gustave Glotz* 5: 97–126.

Rubinstein, L. (2007). "ARAI in Greek Laws in the Classical and Hellenistic Periods: Deterrence or Concession to Tradition?" in Cantarella (2007): 269–86.

Sealey, R. (2006). "Aristotle, *Athenaion Politeia* 57.4: Trial of Animals and Inanimate Objects for Homicide," *Classical Quarterly* 56.2: 475–85.

Smith, N. D. and Woodruff, P. B., eds. (2000). *Reason and Religion in Socratic Philosophy.* Oxford.

Solmsen, F. (1942). *Plato's Theology.* Ithaca.

de Ste. Croix, G. E. M. (1972). *The Origins of the Peloponnesian War.* London.

Stengel, P. (1910). *Opferbräuche der Griechen.* Berlin.

Thür, G., ed. (1994). *Symposion 1993: Vorträge zur griechischen und hellenistischen Rechtsgeschichte.* Cologne.

Tulin, A. (1996). *Dike Phonou: The Right of Prosecution and Attic Homicide Procedure.* Stuttgart.

Adriaan Lanni

2. Public and Private in Classical Athenian Legal Enforcement[1]

Abstract: This essay explores the extent to which the distinction between a public and private sphere is a meaningful one in Athenian law enforcement. Athenian law did treat the household as a private sphere in some respects: the head of the household enjoyed near-exclusive power to discipline its members and retained the legal right to use self-help to protect the *oikos* long after public legal institutions had become dominant in other areas of life. On the other hand, the notion of a sphere of private conduct free from practical state interference was a myth. While Athenian statutes did not directly regulate private matters, in practice Athenian courts enforced norms of private conduct through character evidence raised by the litigants. Finally, the operation of informal means of social control (such as social sanctions and gossip) and the formal court system were so interdependent that the traditional dichotomy between "private" and "public" or "formal" and "informal" mechanisms of enforcing norms does not apply to the Athenian legal system.

1. Introduction

According to the traditional view, classical Athenians did not enjoy negative liberty in the sense of freedom from government interference into private matters.[2] More recently, several scholars have suggested that in classical Athens there was effectively a "private sphere" of conduct free from state interference because Athenian law regulated only conduct that affected the state's interests (as the Athenians broadly defined it).[3] This essay seeks to complicate this picture, focusing in particular on the extent to which the distinction between public and private is meaningful in Athenian law enforcement. After a brief introduction to the

1 Throughout, Athenian speeches are cited by the abbreviation for the speechwriter (Aesch. for Aeschines; Andoc. for Andocides; Ant. for Antiphon; Dem. for Demosthenes; Din. for Dinarchus; Hyp. for Hyperides; Is. for Isaeus; Lyc. for Lycurgus; Lys. for Lysias) followed by the speech and section number. The Loeb Classical Library includes all these authors; modern English translations and notes can be found in the University of Texas Press' *Oratory of Classical Greece* series edited by Michael Gagarin.

2 The locus classicus is Berlin 1969: xl–xli.

3 Hansen 2010; Cohen 1991; Wallace 1997.

Athenian legal system, I argue that the household did operate as a private sphere in some respects: the head of the household enjoyed near-exclusive power to discipline its members and retained the legal right to use self-help to protect the *oikos* long after public legal institutions had become dominant in other areas of life. While Athenian statutes did not directly regulate private matters, in practice Athenian courts enforced norms of private conduct through character evidence raised by the litigants. Finally, the operation of informal means of social control (such as social sanctions and gossip) and the formal court system were so interdependent that the traditional dichotomy between "private" and "public" or "formal" and "informal" mechanisms of enforcing norms does not apply to the Athenian legal system.[4]

2. The Athenian Legal System

It may be helpful to begin with some background on the Athenian legal system. The vast majority of cases, including cases involving religious offenses like impiety or theft of sacred property, were tried in the popular courts, manned by citizen juries. There were, however, specialized homicide courts manned by ex-magistrates that dealt with cases of homicide, wounding, and some religious offenses such as destroying sacred olive trees.

Athenian courts were largely, but not entirely, the province of adult male citizens. Foreigners and resident aliens were permitted to litigate in certain circumstances, most notably in commercial suits.[5] With a few exceptions, slaves could serve neither as plaintiffs nor defendants.[6] When a slave was involved in a dispute, the case was brought by or against the slave's owner. Similarly, women were forced to depend on their male legal guardians to act on their behalf in court, as in almost every forum in Athenian society.[7]

In what the Athenians called "private cases" (*dikai*), the victim (or his family in the case of homicide) brought suit. In "public cases" (*graphai*), any adult male citizen was permitted to initiate an action, though in our surviving *graphai* the prosecutor tends to be the primary party in interest or at least a personal enemy of the defendant with something to gain by his conviction. Although no ancient source explains the distinction between *graphai* and *dikai*, *graphai*

4 Forsdyke 2012:144–13 also challenges the distinction between formal and informal means of law enforcement in Athens, though with a very different emphasis.

5 MacDowell 1978: 221–224; Todd 1993: 196.

6 Todd 1993: 187.

7 Todd 1993: 208.

seem to have been cases regarded as affecting the community at large.[8] This division is not quite the same as the modern criminal-civil distinction; homicide, for example, was a *dike* because it was considered a crime against the family rather than the state. The provision of generalized standing in public cases brought with it the potential for abuse. To prevent vexatious litigation, the Athenians imposed penalties on volunteer prosecutors who dropped their case or failed to gain one-fifth of the jurors' votes at trial.[9]

With few exceptions, litigants were required to deliver their own speeches to the jury.[10] Each Athenian litigant was allotted a fixed amount of time to present his case. Some private cases were completed in less than an hour, and no trial lasted longer than a day. Although a magistrate chosen by lot presided over each popular court, he did not interrupt the speaker for any reason or permit anyone else to raise legal objections, and did not even instruct the jury as to the relevant laws.

Cases in the popular courts were heard by juries[11] chosen by lot from adult male citizens and generally ranged from 201 to 501 in size.[12] There was no process like our *voir dire*, meant to exclude from the jury those with some knowledge of the litigants or the case. On the contrary, Athenian litigants at times encouraged jurors to base their decision on preexisting knowledge.[13] A simple majority vote of the jury, taken without deliberation, determined the outcome of the trial. No reasons for the verdict were given, and there was no provision for appeal.[14]

Athenian jurors did not feel constrained to strictly apply the statute under which the case was brought.[15] The treatment of law in our surviving speeches is consistent with Aristotle's characterization of laws as a form of evidence, similar to contracts and witness testimony, rather than a decisive guide to a ver-

---

8 Todd 1993: 102–109.

9 Todd 1993: 93.

10 A litigant could donate some of his time to another speaker (Rubinstein 2000).

11 I have been using the term "jurors" as a translation for the Greek *dikastai* to refer to the audience of these forensic speeches, but some scholars prefer the translation "judges". Neither English word is entirely satisfactory, since these men performed functions similar to those both of a modern judge and a modern jury. I refer to *dikastai* as jurors to avoid the connotations of professionalism that the word judges conjures up in the modern mind.

12 Hansen 1991: 187.

13 Aesch.1.93.

14 A dissatisfied litigant might, however, indirectly attack the judgment by means of a suit for false witness or might bring a new case, ostensibly involving a different incident and/or using a different procedure. Some of our surviving speeches point explicitly to a protracted series of connected legal confrontations (Osborne 1985: 52).

15 For fuller discussion, see Lanni 2006: 41–74.

dict.[16] The Athenian laws were inscribed on stone *stelai* in various public areas of Athens. Litigants were responsible for finding and quoting any laws they thought helped their case, though there was no obligation to explain the relevant laws. There appears to have been no rule setting forth the range and types of information and argument appropriate for popular court speeches.[17] Speakers were limited only by the time limit and their own sense of which arguments were likely to persuade the jury.

While the punishment for some offenses was set by statute, in many cases the jury was required to choose between the penalties suggested by each party in a second speech.[18] Unlike modern jurors, Athenian jurors were generally made aware at the guilt phase of the statutory penalty or the penalty the prosecutor intended to propose if he won the case. For this reason, the guilt decision often incorporated considerations typically limited to sentencing in modern courts, including questions of the defendant's character and past convictions.[19]

Imprisonment was rarely, if ever used as a punishment;[20] the most common types of penalties in public suits were monetary fines, loss of citizen status (*atimia*), exile, and execution.[21] With some exceptions, the fine in a public suit was paid to the city.[22] In most private cases damages were paid to the prosecutor, though the penalties for some *dikai* included public fines in addition to compensation.[23]

3. A private sphere? Private discipline, self-help, and the *oikos*

The *oikos*, or household, is the natural place to begin looking for evidence of a distinction between public and private in Athenian law. In some respects, Athe-

16 Aristotle, *Rhetoric*, 1.15.

17 The "Constitution of the Athenians" attributed to Aristotle (67.1) refers to an oath to speak to the point taken by litigants in private cases, but this oath is never mentioned in our surviving popular court speeches and if in fact it existed, it appears to have had no effect (Lanni 2006: 113 with n.4).

18 Todd 1993: 133–135.

19 Lanni 26: 53–59.

20 Hunter 1997.

21 On penalties generally, see Allen 2000: 217–43; Todd 1993: 139–44.

22 In some special procedures, such as *phasis* and *apographe*, the prosecutor was entitled to a portion of the fine collected (MacDowell 1978: 257).

23 MacDowell 1978: 257.

nian law treated the *oikos* as a private realm: the head of the household enjoyed exclusive and near-complete disciplinary control over its members, and private protection of the *oikos* was one of the few examples of legally-sanctioned self-help in the classical period. Discipline within the household involved the imposition of punishment determined and administered privately, without official involvement. Private discipline played a critical role in regulating the behavior of slaves, women, and minors, who were largely excluded from the various mechanisms through which the formal legal system enforced order. Although Athenian laws and norms increasingly encouraged resort to law rather than self-help, we will see that the right to protect the *oikos* by killing night burglars and sexual offenders was never rescinded. It seems that the notion of the *oikos* as a separate sphere subject to private protection and governance endured long after public legal institutions became the dominant mechanism for resolving serious disputes.

3.1. Private discipline within the *oikos*

The discipline of privately-owned slaves operated entirely apart from the formal legal system.[24] Masters had complete discretion to determine when and how to punish their slaves, except that a master was prohibited from killing his slave unless he had been condemned by the state.[25] At least one source suggests that women as well as men could punish slaves in the household.[26] The most common private punishments in our sources were whipping and other physical abuse; the most common infractions leading to slave punishment were stealing, lying, and laziness of various sorts.[27] It seems that with few exceptions only masters were legally permitted to discipline their slaves;[28] the proper recourse for an

24 There are a handful of examples of slave offenses enforced by magistrates, though these were generally used against public slaves, slaves who operated businesses in the market, and slaves who committed capital offenses. For discussion, see Hunter 1994: 155–157.

25 Ant. 5.48; 6.4.

26 Xenophon, *Oikonomikos* 9.14.

27 E.g. Dem. 45.33; Lys. 1.18; Aristophanes, *Wasps* 440–450; 1292–6; *Frogs* 542–5; *Wealth* 190–192; 1139–1140; *Knights* 101–102; Menander *Samia* 306–7; *Heros* 1–5; for discussion see Hunter 1994: 162–173; Herman 2006: 299–300.

28 [Xenophon] *Constitution of the Athenians* 1.10 states that it was not permitted to hit a slave in Athens. Despite the general prohibition on hitting a slave who was not your own, it is clear that disciplining another's slave was considered much less serious than harming a free person and may have occurred in practice. One speaker recounts how his opponent deliberately sent a free boy onto his property to steal flowers in the hope that he would mistake the boy for a slave and

individual outside the *oikos* who was wronged by a slave was to bring suit to seek damages from the owner.[29] Presumably the master would in turn inflict punishment or, in the case of slaves operating independent businesses, use funds from the business to cover for any damages awarded in a suit. The master's prerogative to privately discipline his slaves extended to recapturing runaway slaves by force.[30]

Women's compliance with public norms was similarly achieved primarily through private means. A woman could be directly sued only for capital offenses;[31] the head of the household (typically her husband or father) was responsible for privately disciplining a woman who failed to comply with norms. Women, of course, had much more informal power within the household than slaves,[32] and it is impossible to know how and how often *kyrioi* imposed discipline for infractions that that were not so severe as to threaten the integrity and legitimacy of the family. While our sources are largely silent on the acceptability of husbands physically punishing their wives,[33] it is clear that beating was a common and accepted form of private discipline for minor children within the household.[34] In sum, with the exception of very serious infractions, members of the *oikos* were governed and disciplined privately without interference from the polis.

---

hit him, inviting a suit for *hubris* (Dem. 53.16). The implication is that hitting a trespassing slave would not constitute *hubris*, or at least would not be considered serious enough to merit a lawsuit. Todd (1993: 189) suggests that these two passages, taken together, imply that a free man was permitted to hit another's slave when there was clear justification; MacDowell (1978: 81) views discipline of another's slave caught stealing produce as an exception to the general rule.

29 MacDowell 1978: 81. The suit could be brought in the slave's name if the slave was acting without his owner's permission (Dem. 55.31), but the owner was still responsible for defending the suit in court and for any damages awarded.

30 E.g., Dem. 53.6; 59.9.

31 E.g. Ant.1 (homicide); Dem. 57.8 (impiety); for discussion, see Todd 1993: 208.

32 On the gap between women's formal incapacities and social practice, see, e.g. Hunter 1994: 9–42.

33 Fisher (1999: 77) and Ruiz (1994: 174) speculate that wife-beating was likely a regular practice, despite the understandable absence of explicit discussion of it in our sources. There are a few hints of physical abuse of wives: Alcibiades was said to have physically dragged his wife Hipparete back to his home after she attempted to leave (Plutarch, *Alcibiades* 8.4; Lys. 14.42; Andoc. 4.10); and one fragment from Aristophanes includes women discussing their husbands' committing violence towards them (Aristophanes. Frag. 10E).

34 Fisher 1999: 77.

3.2. Self-help to protect the *oikos*

Self-help—that is, private punishment meted out by the victim without official involvement in the determination of guilt or penalty—was explicitly permitted by law in three limited circumstances: catching a sexual offender caught in the act[35] or a thief at night,[36] or defending oneself or one's property from forcible attack or seizure.[37]Although these situations were not limited to events occurring within the house, they appear to have been designed in large part to protect the household from serious intrusions. Over time, norms shifted toward using official legal institutions to address these (and other) offenses, but the law continued to carve out a space for self-help in defense of the *oikos*.

The first major category of sanctioned self-help involved the permissible use of deadly force to protect against thieves and attackers in certain limited circumstances.[38] The speaker in Demosthenes 23 reports that Draco's justifiable homicide statute permitted the use of deadly force to defend life or property against violent attack.[39] Another Athenian statute listed deadly self-help as one legitimate response to encountering a thief at night:

> For a theft in day-time of more than fifty drachmas a man might be arrested summarily and put into custody of the Eleven [the magistrates who summarily executed admitted "wrongdoers" (*kakourgoi*)]. If he stole anything, however small, by night, the person aggrieved might lawfully pursue and kill or wound him, or else put him into the hands of the Eleven, at his own option.[40]

Although the laws justifying deadly force in cases of forceful theft and nocturnal theft could apply to situations outside the household, it seems likely that the archetypal case contemplated by these statutes was house burglary.[41] Nocturnal theft by stealth, without force, presumably applied most commonly to house burglars. The Draconian statute permitting homicide in response to any forcible

---

35 Dem. 23.53–54.

36 Dem. 24.113.

37 Dem. 23.53–54, 60.

38 For discussion of the sources, see, e.g. Christ 1991: 522–525; Ruiz 1994: 35–36.

39 Dem. 23.60. Antiphon's *Third Tetralogy* (4.b1) also suggests that deadly force was permitted in self-defense when attacked by another without provocation.

40 Dem. 24.113 (trans. Murray 1939). This passage also provides that daytime thefts of greater than fifty drachmas were liable to the summary *apagoge* procedure. Cohen 1991: 118 argues that this law permitting killing only the nocturnal thief and not the daytime thief is a newer law that partially conflicts with the older justifiable homicide law that permitted killing any thief using force. He further argues that the Athenians never resolved the conflict.

41 Christ 1991: 522 and Cohen 1991: 112f. who also see these statutes as aimed at housebreakers.

theft would permit individuals to defend their household from violent theft in remote situations where it might be more difficult to call on help from passersby to repel a daytime thief than in public spaces such as the market.

It is possible that self-help was not the most common response even in the limited situations where deadly force against thieves was explicitly permitted by law. As Cohen has pointed out,[42] it seems likely that the law permitting the killing of nocturnal thieves was enacted after the Draconian justifiable homicide law that permitted killing in response to any violent theft. The provision for self-help in the more recent nocturnal theft law appears to have been narrower than the older justifiable homicide law: it permitted self-help only in the case of nocturnal thefts, and provided that daytime theft of a significant sum should be handled through the official *apagoge* procedure, whereby the victim hauled the wrongdoer before a board of magistrates for possible summary execution.[43] Moreover, even in the case of nocturnal thieves the law provides for violent self-help as only one option alongside the official summary procedure.[44] The newer summary arrest procedure was also available for a range of crimes which might in some cases qualify as forcible theft, including kidnappers, clothes-stealers, house burglars, and pickpockets.[45] While the older violent theft law remained in force throughout the classical period, the newer law may reflect a shift in norms and social practice away from exercising one's legal right to self-help against thieves in favor of the use of the official summary procedure.

The second category of legally-sanctioned self-help involved the treatment of sexual offenders—principally adulterers and fornicators—caught in the act. While many of the details of the laws addressing adultery and fornication are uncertain,[46] this much seems clear: although Athenian law expressly permitted the killing of an adulterer taken in the act, in practice Athenians tended to favor non-deadly forms of self-help such as humiliation and demands for compensation.

Our sources refer to several potential forms of self-help against sexual offenders. The "Draconian" justifiable homicide statute discussed above also included a provision for killing adulterers and fornicators caught in the act: "If

---

42 Cohen 1991: 118.

43 Dem. 24.113. Wrongdoers who confessed, and perhaps also those who were manifestly guilty, were summarily executed; all others were tried before a court.

44 Dem. 24.113.

45 *Ath. Pol.* 52.1; Aesch. 1.91; Ant. 5.9; Dem. 35.47; 54.1; Isoc. 15.90; Lys. 10.10; Xenophon, *Memorabilia* 1.2.62.

46 I do not summarize all the scholarly controversies here. For in-depth discussion of the debates over the Athenian treatment of adultery, see, e.g., Scafuro 1997: 194–216; D. Cohen 1991: 98–132.

a man kills another ... in intercourse with his wife, or mother, or sister, or daughter, or concubine kept for procreation of legitimate children, he shall not go into exile for these reasons."[47] As has often been pointed out, Euphiletus' apparent defensiveness when pleading that killing his wife's lover was not only permissible but indeed compelled by the city's laws[48] suggests that by the fourth century killing the adulterer was not the typical or accepted response in such a situation.[49]

Physical humiliation and compensation appear to have been more common. It is possible, but not certain, that a statute permitted the sexual offender caught in the act to be subjected to physical abuse and humiliation short of death.[50] Regardless of whether the law explicitly provided for physical abuse of sexual offenders caught in the act, our sources suggest that as a matter of social practice the Athenians condoned abuse and humiliation of the adulterer by means such as physical blows, "radishing" (inserting a radish into the anus), and depilation of pubic hair using hot ash.[51] Confining the sexual offender and demanding compensation is also attested;[52] though this practice does not appear to have been directly permitted by statute.[53] The law did, however, acknowledge and indirectly condone confinement of sexual offenders by providing a remedy in cases where a man alleges that he has been falsely taken as a sexual offender.[54] Under this law, if the complainant prevails, he and his sureties are released from their promise to pay compensation; if, however, the complainant is adjudged guilty

---

47 Dem. 23.53 (trans. Scafuro).

48 Lys. 1.34.

49 For the view that killing the adulterer was unusual, see, e.g, Cohen 1991: 98–132; Scafuro 1997: 214 f.

50 The statement in Lys. 1.49 that the laws permit anyone taking a *moichos* to "treat him in any way he likes" does not explicitly prohibit killing the adulterer, but is sometimes read, in conjunction with the law limiting abuse of a convicted sexual offender (Dem. 59.66–7) as a paraphrase of a law that referred to humiliation and abuse short of death. For discussion, see, e. g. D. Cohen 1991: 115–119; Scafuro 1997: 198 f.

51 Is. 8.44; Xenophon, *Memorabilia* 2.2.5; Lys. 1.25; Aristophanes, *Clouds* 1083; Aristophanes, *Wealth* 168. Cohen (1985: 385–387) expresses doubts about comic evidence of radishing and depilation, but Carey (1993: 53–55) and Kapparis (1995: 66 f.) argue that it was a common practice.

52 Lys. 1.25; Dem. 59.41–42, 64–66.

53 In fact, as Scafuro (1997:199 n.26) points out, the speaker's statements in Lysias 1.28 suggest that the laws did not provide for compensation in response to taking an adulterer in the act.

54 Dem. 59.66.

of adultery or fornication, the man who arrested him is permitted to abuse the offender in court in whatever way he wishes provided he does not use a knife.[55]

While many of the details surrounding remedies for sexual offenses remain controversial, it is clear that the use of self-help was considered an acceptable response to discovering an adulterer or fornicator in the act. The rationale behind permitting the use of self-help in sexual offenses is similarly uncontroversial: it preserved the *kyrios*'s prerogative to protect the house (*oikos*) from intrusion. Adulterers posed a threat to the household by raising doubts about the children's legitimacy and inheritance rights, by disrupting family relations,[56] and by penetrating the house and therefore violating the head of the household's honor.[57] Thus Athenian law explicitly permitted self-help where the integrity of the *oikos* was endangered by a thief, attacker, or sexual offender.

4. The fiction of the limited state

Athenian democratic ideology included the notion that the state did not interfere with private conduct that did not impinge on the state's interests.[58] The locus classicus of this ideal is Thucydides' account of Pericles' funeral oration:

> And, just as our political life is free and open, so is our day-to-day life in our relations with each other We do not get into a state with our next-door neighbor if he enjoys himself in his own way, nor do we give him the kind of black looks which, though they do no real harm, still do hurt people's feelings We are free and tolerant in our private lives; but in public affairs we keep to the law.[59]

Scholars have interpreted such statements, along with Athenian legal practice, as evidence of a "private sphere" of conduct free from legal regulation.[60] These scholars have pointed out that in Athens there was no morals legislation as such; legislation was limited to activity that harmed a specific victim or affect-

---

55 Dem. 59.66. Physical abuse in court is not a form of private self-help in our sense, but rather a court-ordered punishment.

56 Hence the (much debated) statement in Lysias 1.32 that adultery was considered more severe than rape in Athenian law.

57 On protection of the *oikos* as the primary rationale behind the self-help remedies for adultery, see, e.g. Scafuro 1997: 197 f.; Carey 1995: 416; D. Cohen 1991: 112–114. On the rationale for including concubines (*pallakai*), see Scafuro 1997: 197 f.; Carey 1995: 416.

58 Cohen 1991: 229 provides examples, including Dem. 22.51; Lys. 25.33; Arisitotle, *Politics* 1320a30.

59 Thuc. 2.37 (trans.Warner 1972).

60 Hansen 2010; Cohen 1991; Wallace 1997.

ed the state's interest.[61] Thus there was no provision to prosecute an adulterer in the courts because Athenian law "did not aim at regulating adultery as a form of sexual misconduct."[62] Rather, the law sought to regulate adultery "as a source of public violence and disorder" by addressing only a limited situation: what options were available to a man who caught an adulterer in the act.[63] Similarly, the law generally permitted homosexuality and prostitution. In fact, prostitution was subject to state taxes and the state condoned the practice by treating contracts for sexual services just like any other enforceable contract.[64] But several laws protected young boys from homosexual advances by older men.[65] And a citizen who had been a prostitute was not permitted to speak in the Assembly, apparently on the theory that such a man was morally unworthy of democratic leadership.[66] For the Athenians, limited state interference in private conduct (as they defined it, more narrowly than a modern would) was one of the primary characteristics of a democracy.[67]

While conduct that did not affect the public interest was not directly regulated by statute, in practice the courts enforced norms of private conduct. The broad approach to relevance in Athenian courts meant discussion of the parties' character and private conduct was common in court speeches and likely influenced court decisions.[68] Litigants regularly criticize their opponents' treatment of family members and rail against their private vices, while of course touting their own virtue. When particular types of arguments such as these are used many times over by different speechwriters in a wide array of cases, we can surmise that these arguments were thought to be persuasive. In this way, the public courts indirectly regulated activity within families and households and other "private" conduct.

The surviving court speeches include many discussions of litigants' behavior toward relatives. Discussion of these norms appear in legal disputes of all sorts,

61 Cohen 1991; Wallace 1997.

62 Cohen 1991: 124.

63 Ibid.

64 Aesch. 1.119, 160 – 161; Lys. 3.22 – 26; Aesch. 1.160 – 161.

65 If a relative or guardian hired out a boy as a prostitute, both the relative/guardian and the customer could be prosecuted under a *graphê* (Aesch. 1.13 – 14). A separate law provided that acting as a pimp for a free boy was punishable by death (Aesch. 1.14). For a discussion of this topic, see Cohen 1991: 176.

66 Aesch. 1.19 – 20, 28 – 32; Cohen 1991: 175 – 186; Fisher 2001: 36 – 52.

67 Thuc. 2.39; Dem. 25.25. Aristotle, *Politics* 1310a30; Plato, *Republic* 557b, 560 – 1, 565b, Plato, *Laws* 700a; Cohen 1991: 124.

68 For a more in-depth discussion, see Lanni 2009.

from charges of political corruption[69] to inheritance disputes.[70] Litigants commonly describe how they dutifully took care of their female relatives[71] and charge that their adversary mistreated his parents or other close kin.[72] The prosecutor charging the defendant with being a state debtor in *Against Aristogeiton* provides a long list of the defendants' violations of these norms: he charges that Aristogeiton failed to bail his father out of prison, refused to pay for his subsequent burial, physically abused his mother, and even sold his own sister into slavery.[73] We have seen that the legal regulation of sexual activity appears to have been limited to behavior that was perceived to threaten public order, yet litigants regularly informally charge their opponents with sexual deviance of all sorts.[74] Litigants also criticize their opponents for everything from extravagance,[75] poor money management,[76] and drunkenness[77] to walking quickly and talking loudly,[78] and cite their own moderation and private virtue.[79] Aeschines' personal attacks on Timarchus when prosecuting him under a law forbidding former male prostitutes from speaking in the Assembly is particularly memorable: he charges that Timarchus squandered his family estate and "was a slave to the most shameful pleasures, fish-eating, extravagant dining, girl-pipers and escort-girls, dicing, and the other activities none of which ought to get the better of any man who is well-born and free."[80] The relevance of "private" conduct in court extended to members of litigants' household. Litigants occasionally charge the female members of their opponent's *oikos* with violations of extra-statutory norms in an effort to influence the verdict.[81]

---

69 e.g., Din. 2.8, 11, 14.
70 e.g., Is. 5.39–40.
71 e.g., Lys. 16.10; Is. 10.25.
72 e.g., Dem. 24.107, 201; 25.54f.; Din.2.8; Lys. 10.1–3; Lys. 14.28; 32.9, 11–18; Is. 5.39f.; 8.41; Aesch. 1.102–4; 3.77f..
73 Dem. 25.53–55.
74 E.g., Aesch. 2.151; 3.238; And. 1.100, 124–127; Lys. 13.66; 14.25–26; Is. 6.18–21; 8.44; Dem. 36.45.
75 Dem. 21.133f., 158; 36.45; 38.27; Aesch. 1.95–100; Din. 1.36.
76 Lys. 14.27; Aesch. 1.97–105; Din. 1.36; Is. 5.43.
77 Lys. 3.5–9; 24.25–29; 30.2; Dem. 38.27.
78 Dem. 37.52.
79 Lys. 5.2; Andoc. 1.144–145; Isoc. 16.22–24; Is. 10.25.
80 Aesch. 1.42. (trans. Fisher 2001). On fish-eating as paradigmatic gluttonous behavior, see Fisher 2001: 174f.
81 Dem. 25.26 (past crime committed by mother); Is. 6.49–50 (religious morality); Dem. 40.50 (extravagance). Discussion of women is much more common in attempts to raise doubts about an oppnent's citizenship status (e.g. Aesch. 2.78; for discussion see Hunter 1994: 111–115).

Failure to adhere to these informal "private" norms could be used to publicly embarrass a litigant before hundreds of jurors and potentially influence the jury against his case. In this sense the courts did, in effect, regulate "private" conduct and served an important disciplinary function with respect to these norms.

5. The interdependence of public and private forms of enforcement

In the absence of stringent rules of evidence, Athenian court speakers addressed not only the parties' private conduct, but also whether the parties had adhered to legal norms unrelated to the charge at hand, including prior convictions and past crimes and bad acts that had not been prosecuted.[82] Discussions of past crimes were not limited to charges similar to the present case; any prior violation of the law by a litigant could be used against him. For example, when Alcibiades the Younger, the son of the famous general, was charged with deserting the ranks, his prosecutor provides a long list of his past crimes, including adultery and attempted murder.[83] In essence, when you walked into an Athenian courtroom, your entire life was on trial. As a result, litigants had incentives to uncover and then publicize in court any prior bad acts by their opponent, even if they were victimless crimes or committed against someone other than the litigant, and even if they were completely unrelated to the present case.

The Athenian approach of enforcing norms unrelated to the case in court compensated for deficiencies in the operation of both informal social control and formal legal enforcement. Athenian trials facilitated informal enforcement of norms by publicizing norm violations and by serving as shaming ceremonies. The Athenian approach also compensated for problems in law enforcement stemming from a private prosecution system. In this way, private (or informal) means of social control such as social sanctions and gossip were inextricably intertwined and with the public mechanisms of court institutions.

The courts complemented, rather than supplanted, informal sanctions. Broadcasting accusations of unprosecuted wrongdoing at a public trial assisted the informal enforcement of legal norms in two ways. First, the trial can be seen as a form of public shame sanction, as litigants were attacked before hundreds of jurors and spectators. Second, the courts publicized norm violations, making

---

82 See Lanni 2009.
83 Lys. 14.30 f.

informal enforcement more likely. As Athens was not a face-to-face society, information about norm violations would not always become known to potential business partners or the small group of neighbors and fellow demesmen who were in a position to enforce social sanctions. The courts may have assisted informal norm enforcement by improving information flow. The courts gave litigants incentives to ferret out their opponents' norm violations, and court speeches publicized these violations, making it more likely that other citizens in small village communities would impose informal social sanctions.[84] Litigants clearly feared the effect that allegations of wrongdoing might have on their reputation. Aeschines states, for example, that even if he wins his suit he will consider his life not worth living if anyone is convinced by his opponent's suggestion, unrelated to the charges in the case, that he had committed *hubris* against a woman.[85]

The use of publicity to facilitate informal enforcement also helped compensate for difficulties of enforcement stemming from a system that relied on private prosecution and enforcement. Because litigants had incentives to bring up their opponents' unrelated past bad acts, Athenians could not blithely commit victimless crimes or injure those who might be powerless to sue them; these offenses could come back to haunt them if they ever found themselves in court for any reason in the future. Demosthenes is quite explicit about how consideration of unrelated crimes can compensate for problems of under-enforcement. He lists the many people his opponent, Meidias, has wronged in the past, noting that most of them did not bring suit because they lacked the money, or the speaking ability, or were intimidated by Meidias.[86] He then urges the jury to punish Meidias for these unprosecuted crimes: "for if a man is so powerful that he can commit acts of this sort and deprive each one of you of exacting justice from him, now that he is securely in our power, he should be punished in common by all of us as an enemy of the state."[87] In this way, informal and formal mechanisms of social control were closely intertwined.

In summary, the general picture that emerges from our sources is more complicated than either a clear public–private distinction or the absence of a meaningful dichotomy. In some respects the household did operate as a private sphere. While the Athenians had an ideology of freedom in private affairs and Athenian law did not directly regulate matters that did not affect the community,

84 Hunter 1994: 117.
85 Aesch. 2.5.
86 Dem. 24.141.
87 Dem. 24.142.

in practice public legal institutions played an important disciplinary role with respect to "private" conduct.

Works cited

Allen, D.S. (2000). *The World of Prometheus: The Politics of Punishing in Democratic Athens.* Princeton.
Berlin, I. (1969). *Four Essays on Liberty.* Oxford.
Carey, C. (1995). "Rape and adultery in Athenian law," *Classical Quarterly* 45: 407–417.
Carey, C. (1993). "Return of the radish or just when you thought it was safe to go back into the kitchen," *Liverpool Classical Monthly* 18: 53–55.
Christ, M.R. (1998). "Legal self-help on private property in classical Athens," *American Journal of Philology* 119: 521–545.
Cohen, D. (1991). *Law, Sexuality, and Society: The Enforcement of Morals in Classical Athens.* Cambridge.
Cohen, D. (1985). "A note on Aristophanes and the punishment of adultery in Athenian law," Zeitschrift der Savigny Stiftung 102: 385–387.
Cohen, D. (1983). *Theft in Athenian Law.* Munich.
Fisher, N.R.E. (2001). *Aeschines: Against Timarchos.* Oxford.
Fisher, N.R.E. (1999). "Workshop of villains: Was there much organised crime in classical Athens?" in K. Hopwood, ed., *Organised Crime in Antiquity:* 53–96. Swansea.
Forsdyke, S. (2012). *Slaves Tell Tales And Other Episodes in the Politics and Popular Culture of Ancient Greece.* Princeton.
Hansen, M.H. (2010) "Athenian democratic *eleutheria* and modern liberal democrats' conception of freedom," in M.H. Hansen, ed., *Démocratie athénienne-démocratie modern: Tradition et influences.* Entretiens sur l'Antiquite Classique 56: 307–339. Vandoeuvres.
Hansen, M.H. (1991). *The Athenian Democracy in the Age of Demosthenes.* Oxford.
Herman, G. (2006). *Morality and Behaviour in Democratic Athens.* Cambridge.
Hunter, V. (1997). "The Prison of Athens: A comparative perspective," *Phoenix* 51: 296–326.
Hunter, V. (1994). *Policing Athens: Social Control in the Attic Lawsuits.* Princeton.
Kapparis, K. (1996). "Humiliating the adulterer: the law and the practice in classical Athens," *Revue Internationale des Droits de l'Antiquité* 43: 63–77.
Lanni, A. (2009). "Social norms in the ancient Athenian courts," *Journal of Legal Analysis* 1: 691–736.
Lanni, A. (2006). *Law and Justice in the Courts of Classical Athens.* Cambridge.
MacDowell, D.M. (1978). *The Law in Classical Athens.* London.
Murray, A.T. (1939) (Trans.) *Demosthenes with an English translation.* Cambridge.
Osborne, R. (1985). "Law in action in classical Athens," *Journal of Hellenic Studies* 105: 40–58.
Rubinstein, L. (2000). *Litigation and Cooperation: Supporting Speakers in the Courts of Classical Athens.* Stuttgart.
Ruiz , F. (1994). *The Use and Control of Violene in Classical Athens.* PhD. Dissertation, Johns Hopkins University.

Scafuro, A. (1997). *The Forensic Stage: Settling Disputes in Graeco-Roman New Comedy.* Cambridge.
Todd, S.C. (1993). *The Shape of Athenian Law.* Oxford.
Wallace, R.W. (2007). "The legal regulation of private conduct at Athens: Two controversies on freedom" *Etica & Politica/Ethics & Politics* 9: 155–171.
Warner, R. (trans.) (1972). *Thucydides: History of the Peloponnesian War.* New York.

Esther Eidinow

3. φανερὰν ποιήσει τὴν αὐτοῦ διάνοιαν τοῖς θεοῖς: Some Ancient Greek Theories of (Divine and Mortal) Mind

Abstract: 'Does private reflection occur in private spaces?' This question, posed in the conference description, provides the spur for this paper, which sets out to explore some perceptions, ancient and modern, of the limits of the 'public', and the nature of what is 'private', with reference to the individual, and in particular the individual's mind, in the context of ancient Greek religion.

As the conference description observes, scholarship on ancient Greek religion has examined and questioned the relevance of the public-private distinction. Nevertheless, it continues to be employed, although with a range of meanings. In general, it is used to describe the religious activity of social groups: the ways in which 'private' may relate to the individual (individual experience/the individual mind) are generally not regarded as accessible. This approach is shaped, at least in part, by the '*polis* religion' model that emphasises the 'public' aspect of religious praxis, and by conceptions of the nature of the individual within that model, which draw on particular conceptions of self and of the mind.

This paper suggests that consideration of alternative models—of ancient Greek religion, the nature of the individual, and theories of mind—raise questions about the ancient conceptions of the individual experience and mind—and lead to a reconsideration of the nature of 'private reflection in private spaces'.

1. Introduction

This paper was inspired by the question posed in the conference description: 'Does private reflection occur in private spaces?' Starting with modern views, the ultimate private realm is generally accepted to be that of our own minds: the prevalent contemporary Western model of the person emphasises the individual's separate existence and their autonomy; their mental state is something to which only that person has privileged access.[1] This depiction of the mind un-

1 See Solomon 2006, 414. Although this model of the mind has been shaped by work by and on

derpins, indeed, is essential for our understanding of the individual as capable of objective, independent decision-making, a conception that forms the basis for multiple dimensions of Western life, ranging, for example, from the realm of law to that of scientific research.[2] Nevertheless, relatively recently, more complex conceptions of the cognitive processes of the individual have developed, which recast the relationship between individual, society and environment. These include, for example, embodied cognition (in which the mind is rooted in bodily structures), situated cognition approaches (which emphasise the contextual instantiation of cognition), and distributed cognition (which describes the mind in terms of collective cognitive processes); all of these approaches explore the idea that the cognitive activities of the mind are not bounded by the individual.[3] Questions about our model of the mind and mental processes are also prompted by anthropological exploration of theories of mind: these demonstrate both the cultural specificity of theories of mind (across a number of dimensions) and also indicate how particular contexts or experiences may prompt a change in theories of mind held by individuals or groups.[4]

These different approaches to the individual, the mind and mental processes, may introduce nuances, if not challenges, to the models that currently underpin historical research. When we turn to scholarship on ancient Greek religion, we find the relevance of the public/private distinction has been examined, questioned, and employed with a range of meanings; in general, it is used with reference to the activities of groups rather than individuals. Indeed, within the schema of '*polis* religion', although the individual is described as 'the basic, cultic unit', it is stressed that 'the modalities of individual acts of worship are the same as those of group worship', and '[t]his suggests a religious mentality in which the individual's act of worship is not different in nature from that of the group's'.[5] This seems to result in a paradox: acknowledgment of a private ex-

the philosophy of Descartes, the extent to which that philosopher understood the mind and body to be separate is a matter of debate: see, for example, Rorty 1992 on Descartes' approach to 'thinking with the body' and Cottingham 2008 on the 'myth of "Cartesian privacy"'.

2 Subotsky 2010, 143. Robert Wilson (2004) observes that there is little consistency between different scientific disciplines, which conceive of individuals differently—leading to specific explanations of particular behaviours.

3 A large and increasing literature; examples include, on embodied cognition, Varela, Thompson and Rosch 1991, Damasio 1994; on situated cognition, Kirshner and Whitson 1997, Robbins and Aydede 2009; on distributed cognition, Hutchins 1995; and the extended mind, Clark and Chalmers 1998.

4 Luhrmann 2011, and on relational approaches Strathern 1988, LiPuma 1998.

5 Sourvinou-Inwood 2000b, 44.

perience that can only be described in public terms: in this context, it is difficult to know what to make of the idea of 'private reflection in a private space'.

This paper sets out to explore perceptions, ancient and modern, of the limits of the 'public', and the nature of what is 'private', with reference to the individual, in the context of ancient Greek religion. To do this, it introduces some possibilities for a reconsideration of the notions of public and private, drawing on work that highlights alternative models of ancient Greek religion, of the individual, and of theories of mind.

2. Public and Private in Scholarship on Ancient Greek Religion

i) Public and Private Activities

The elusive nature of the public/private distinction in scholarship on ancient Greek religion is well known. In addition to public vs. private, other axes that have been used in an attempt to map this space, and categorise the ritual activities of an ancient community, include 'official' or 'civic' vs. 'popular', or 'informal' or 'elective'; sometimes, the terms refer to specific social groups, such as 'family' or 'friends'. The most obvious challenge that this presents is a lack of clear agreement about how to use this vocabulary.[6] It seems to be commonly agreed that 'public' may be used to indicate cult that was funded and administered by the *polis*; however, as has frequently been observed, the ways in which the state intervened in religious activity, and interacted with different sub-groups or familial organisations (not to mention panhellenic and federal religious structures) varied.[7]

After the debate about the 'public' nature of support, comes the question of the nature of control. Andrea Purvis, for example, in her study of individual ritual practice focuses on ritual activity where 'individuals' choices and means of establishing or modifying cults are clearly their own.'[8] She designates the cults she discusses as 'individual ritual practice' on the grounds that they are '"private," "elective," and "non-official," in that they lack regulation and funding

6 As Aleshire 1994, 11, who cites Feaver 1957, 145, n. 75.
7 As Parker (1996, 5) observes 'the general distinction between "public" and "private" cannot be maintained'. See Purvis 2003, 1–2, who also cites: Davies 1988, 379, Sourvinou-Inwood, 2000a and 2000b, Aleshire, 1994; Parker 1996, 5–7.
8 Purvis 2003, 2.

by the *polis*, sub-political units, or familial associations.'[9] For Purvis, regulation means administrative organisation. In contrast, Robert Parker has argued that among cults designated as public should be included those that are 'products... of publicly sanctioned convention'—and this widens the remit considerably.[10] Under this definition, regulation includes not just legislation, but unwritten, sometimes even unspoken standards. Civic sanction and convention are obviously closely related, especially in the amorphous arena of *asebeia* accusations—and, it appears that for Parker, even the potential for prosecution is itself a form of regulation. As he puts it, the idea that there was no activity exempt from being 'arraigned as "impious"' indicated that there was 'no authentically private religious domain in Attica'.[11] We must assume that under this (implicit) criterion, to achieve privacy is to achieve total social autonomy; otherwise, the public sphere encompassed everything. However, this approach is not without its problems: as Aleshire observed, 'the fact that the state *could* regulate an aspect of cult behaviour does not, in the absence of confirming evidence, mean that it *did* so in each individual case', and, one might add, it does not mean that it was expected to do so.[12] In his more recent writing, Parker also modulates his approach in this direction, admitting, for example, that there were limits to the control that the *polis* might exercise.[13] In practice, a level of autonomy, closer to the kind his earlier discussions required, may have been achieved, or at least actively maintained for a while by some religious practitioners. Nevertheless, he still regards this as *polis* control, a description that keeps the dichotomy clearly in play, even while appearing to deny that one part of it—privacy—could ever have been realised.

These discussions take for granted the idea of the public, and focus on the limits of the private. But perhaps the nature of 'the public' should also be examined: almost every trial began with an individual's choice to prosecute, and the process of regulation comprised individuals competing for the right to impose a penalty sanctioned by a civic procedure. It is not surprising to find that 'public' prosecutions, rooted in the will and desires of an individual, could be motivated by 'private' concerns.[14] Specifically to this enquiry, in the case of *asebeia* accusations, it has been observed from antiquity that trials for impiety often seem to

---

9 *Ibid.*
10 Parker 1996, 7.
11 Parker 1996, 7.
12 Aleshire 1994, 12.
13 Parker 2011, 59–61.
14 Eidinow 2010 and 2014.

overlap with relationships of personal enmity.[15] It may be difficult to identify, on the grounds of the potential for regulation, an 'authentically private' religious domain; but it is similarly hard to describe the process of its regulation as 'authentically public'.

The integrated nature of ancient Greek religious practice and belief means that it does not respond well to rigid etic definitions. The observance of the official religion of the state, in civic festivals or sacrifices, did not preclude or conflict with the religious activity of the family, or of groups of friends, or of a mixture of the two.[16] But is the cult activity with family or friends to be regarded as public or private activity? Is a domestic cult private until friends are brought to worship at it, or should it still be described as private even when friends arrive, because it was founded through individual initiative—or has it never been 'private' because social pressures expect that it should be founded, and nobody so far has been prosecuted for impiety? As we try to subsume everything within one classification of 'public', the 'private' slips quietly back into view; as with a kaleidoscope, with the flick of a definition, the one becomes the other—private is public and the public is part of the private realm.

ii) Models and Categories

It is, perhaps, adherence to a particular aspect of the model of *polis* religion that has ensured that the dichotomy of public and private activities is set so firmly at the heart of scholarship on Greek religion—and why there appears to be so little room for what is private. In Christiane Sourvinou-Inwood's two seminal papers, the notion of the private is, explicitly, subsumed within the *polis:* 'A point that needs to be stressed is that all cult acts, including those which some modern commentators are inclined to think of as 'private', are (religiously) dependent on the *polis*.'[17] She goes on to discuss the public nature of religion in the *oikos*. We have seen, above, how the individual is similarly positioned vis-à-vis the group: 'individual acts of worship are the same as those of group worship'.[18] Moreover, as I have noted elsewhere, there is little consideration of even the presence of certain religious activities: Sourvinou-Inwood notes that some man-

15 Plut. *Per.* 32 on prosecutions for impiety brought by enemies of Perikles against his circle; see discussion by Todd 1993, 308–10 on impiety charges and political enmity, discussed further below.
16 As Parker 2005, 44–45.
17 Sourvinou-Inwood 2000b, 51.
18 Sourvinou-Inwood 2000b, 44.

ifestations of 'non-institutionalised sectarian discourse of the Orphic type... may have been perceived as lying outside the authority of *polis* discourse' but the observation, which comes only at the end of her second essay, is never developed.[19]

To explore this aspect, and in an attempt to maintain some consistency in this discussion of *polis* religion, I return to the work of Robert Parker, whose approach is perhaps closest to that of Sourvinou-Inwood and is based on a profound understanding of its dimensions. In this area, he describes the relevant activities as those that 'took place on the edge of our field of vision'; he includes initiations for Sabazios, the Corybantes, Orphic cults; Dionysiac *thiasoi*, ad hoc *thiasoi*, privately conducted rites for Pan/Aphrodite/Hekate, semi-permanent cult associations of diverse types (for heroes, Asklepios, Mother)—and much else besides.[20] This description incorporates these activities within the *polis* model, but marks their difference by placing emphasis on their relative size compared to other more visible ritual activities, and by noting that they took place within different 'channels'.[21] The choice of this term seems to signal only an external dissimilarity—a change of social context or action—from what may be perceived as usual. But this is to beg the question, far from resolved, of the possible internal (mental, emotional or physical) aspects of these activities: that is, what was the nature of the experience of those worshippers who chose to pursue these activities?

iii) Private and Public Experience

At least since the work of Jane Harrison, it has been maintained by scholars that it is in the arena of 'private' religious activity that religion gained serious meaning for individuals, perhaps because elective cults seem to offer more personal relationships with certain kinds of gods, who oversaw healing, divination or mysteries.[22] But although he asks if such religious activities 'stir depths of feeling untouched' by more public behaviour, Parker's final analysis is that elective cults offered 'à la carte access to a familiar range of religious experiences, rather than something fundamentally different'. This approach reveals why use of the

---

19 *Ibid.*, 55; see discussion Eidinow 2011a.

20 Parker 2005, 373.

21 Parker 2005, 374: 'what proportion... of the total volume of Athenian religious traffic went through these channels' (although earlier he describes this as (373) 'much ritual activity.') He notes that Aristophanes and Theophrastus, two of our chief sources for elective cults, describe festivals of the city and its subgroups far more frequently than they allude to private societies.

22 E.g., Zaidman and Schmidt Pantel 1992, 14–15.

word 'channels' (above) may be apposite, but it still leaves a number of questions unanswered. One puzzling aspect is the way it ignores the very context it describes, one in which these worshippers were choosing to participate in a potentially dangerous ritual activity.[23] But a more basic difficulty is that the parameters it sets as a comparison—the 'familiar range of religious experiences'—are never defined.

Rather than offering illumination, this reference to the familiar experiences of our historical subjects takes us back to some of the questions already raised about the role of the individual—and the nature of what is deemed private in ancient Greek religion. The '*polis* religion' model offers us a very 'public' notion of religious privacy. The individual that we find is an opaque unit: like the figure at the heart of a Russian doll, he or she is simply the smallest of a series of demarcated public realms that comprise the formal social structures of the *polis*. Even though there is increasing work being done on individual activity at cult sites the discussion about Greek religion has tended not to move below the level of formally identified social groups. The traditional model of embedded Greek religion, for example, focuses on the mutual constitution of social groups and religious activity; what happens below the level of the social group—what kinds of individual cognitive processes we are taking for granted, how the individual participates in the process of 'embedding'—is left unexplored.[24] Within such a religious schema the question of how we may understand the meaning of 'private reflection in private spaces' in a religious context is left unanswered and unanswerable. But although criticisms of aspects of the *polis* religion model have regularly been raised, it is not clear how scholars might reshape their approach.[25]

---

23 E.g., the observation (374) that priestesses of such cults could be prosecuted and the kinds of gods they worshipped so regarded that they might be (if only in Aristophanic fantasy) expelled from the city. (And yet presumably they exist within the *polis* and are therefore *polis* religion; we are prompted to ask at what point they cease to be *polis* religion) Laying aside the question of depth, it is hard to see how choosing to join, and then participating in, a religious activity that brings with it the potential threat of prosecution might not involve an extra-ordinary experience.
24 Cf. see Purvis 2003 and Eidinow 2014.
25 Criticisms of *polis* religion have regularly been made: for a selection, see Aleshire 1994, Cole 1995, Burkert 1995, Woolf 1997, Jameson 1997, Bendlin 2000, Hansen and Nielsen 2004, Bremmer 2010, Kindt 2012.

3. Networks: Models for Thinking about Greek Religion

The language of public and private, the elision of the individual within the group, offers a series of problems rooted in the inflexibility of the *polis* religion model. Building on the basic facets of this structure, an approach is needed that allows us to engage with the fluidity of both the ritual interactions and the emerging identities of those participating in these interactions. Effectively, the *polis* religion model has treated the *polis* as the sole network within which an individual was placed in classical Greece. But this picture may be transformed if we reconceptualise the individual's religious position in ancient Greece in terms of a plurality of networks of relations of different, interacting types.[26]

i) Embodied

First of all, we may imagine overlapping physical and social networks, reflecting the different ways in which individuals and groups were involved in religious practice. This initial configuration helps, for example, to rethink our understanding of 'embedded religion', so that it no longer simply emphasises the relationship between one particular social structure, the *polis*, and religious practice. Instead, a network theory of embeddedness describes the multiple, different relationships that comprise the different dimensions of a single person—so that to be embedded is to be 'embodied' within social networks.[27]

Such a model allows us to encompass the connections and relationships created by those activities that we 'glimpse out of the corner of our eye', without needing to quantify them in contrast to more visible activities; it also allows us to include, for example, itinerant oracle sellers, who moved from *polis* to *polis*, explaining their relationship to the *polis*, rather than simply excluding them from a *polis* religion model. The individual emerges each time in a new

26 Eidinow 2011a offers an initial attempt at creating such a model, based on the work of Harrison White (2008). Others who have raised the idea of a network as a model for Greek religion: Aleshire 1994, 10, argues that 'a full map of Athenian cult connections, if that were possible, would resemble a network or a web more closely than a pyramid.' Sourvinou-Inwood makes reference to networks in passing in her essays on *polis* religion, see (2000a, 17): 'Greek religion, then, consists of a network of religious systems interacting with each other and with the Panhellenic religious dimension' (and 'nexus': 2000a, 27 and 30).
27 See Eidinow 2014, on a reconsideration of 'embeddedness' in a network setting.

role, depending on the configuration of relationships. It is this configuration that determines the nature of each interaction. As soon as the range of networks in which an individual participates is considered, it becomes apparent that rigid distinctions such as 'public/private' are inappropriate, since they fail to describe a variety of circumstances in which individuals are involved.

ii) Embedded

In addition, a network model offers a way of beginning to discuss the processes involved in the creation and sharing of religious culture, including the role of individuals. Physical and social networks help to create cognitive embeddedness: they comprise individuals and groups participating in shared activity, who create and share meaning, shaping key concepts.[28] Conceptual networks overlap with, emerge from, and, in turn, help to form physical and social networks: the relationships between physical/social networks and conceptual networks are dynamic, reflecting the ongoing employment of concepts across different settings, by and within different groups, and or individuals, for different purposes. This approach, in terms of a plurality of networks, can illuminate the interface between shared, external culture and internal cognition, and the process by which cultural meanings converge.

As an example, conceptual networking can be illuminated by tracing the use, and nuances of use, of the concept of *asebeia* in surviving Athenian law-court speeches.[29] In that evidence, we see how speakers drew on shared ideas of *asebeia*, consolidating and developing its meanings. In specific contexts the concept was manipulated and developed, shaped through various rhetorical approaches, as speakers linked it with risks that threatened dikasts, citizens, the city itself, even the gods in different ways.[30] Examining the rhetoric of the courtroom, the crafting of narratives and negotiation of meanings, can illuminate some of the ways in which Athenian citizens participated in the co-creation of the concept of *asebeia*, and, in turn, the ways in which networks of concepts were involved in the formation of social networks.

This approach can further clarify how and why ancient Greek religion may be described as 'embedded'. Whereas previous models of embedded religion evoked this very powerful idea (in a variety of different ways) as dependent on

---

28 Eidinow 2011a emphasises the role of narrative in the formation of meaning; and the multiple identities of individuals in creating those narratives.

29 See further Eidinow 2014.

30 See Demosthenes 21 and 59, Lysias 6, Andokides 1.

social groups within the *polis*, in contrast, a networked version of embedded religion focuses on relational ties between individuals and between individuals and groups. Consideration of the conceptual as well as physical/social networks draws our attention to the dynamic cognitive processes, both group and individual, involved in the creation of the concepts and practices of ancient Greek religion. Thus, a networked model of ancient Greek religion suggests that it was by means of individual relationships, consisting of stories, narratives and other forms of discursive communication, that ancient Greek religious culture was both experienced and manipulated, transmitted and shaped by those involved.

This suggests that it may be possible to explore some aspects of the ancient Greek understanding of 'private reflection in private spaces' by paying closer attention to patterns of incidental discourse concerning experiences of the supernatural. What follows will briefly consider some of the evidence for one kind of experience in particular: the idea that the gods can, somehow, enter one's mind; this is related to questions of divine omniscience. This not only offers some insights into how individuals expected to experience the divine; it also raises questions about the roles of and relations between gods and mortals in a network model of Greek religion.

4. Models of the Mind

i) Oversight and Deduction

This brings me then to the quotation in the title of this paper, which is from the peroration of Lykourgos *Against Leokrates*, where the speaker is threatening the jury with the oversight of the gods. This is, according to Henk Versnel, in a note in his awe-inspiring *Coping with the Gods*, one of the very few references to the idea that the gods are all-knowing. He goes on, 'The interesting fact, however, is not so much that they occur, but that their occurrence is so rare... In other words: gods may be able to see everything, but do so only when their own interest is involved.'[31] Versnel's discussion is primarily focused on the question of omnipotence, which he concludes cannot be summarised with a 'monolithic or general statement', and he treats omniscience rather in passing as included in this larger theme.[32] This apparent autonomy of divine representation is a matter of expres-

31 Lyk. Leok. 146–147. Versnel 2011, 399, n. 59.

32 Versnel 2011, 400: 'These testimonia give rise to the suspicion that any monolithic or general statement concerning omnipotence or lack of omnipotence (including omniscience) in Greek religion is bound to be overturned by the next piece of evidence'.

sion—but the emphasis on discourse remains important. Although he criticizes those who put such inconsistent views down to rhetoric, nevertheless, his own argument appears to embrace this idea, and elsewhere he notes how these powers appear or disappear according to literary context, and argues that we should not hold the Greeks to be consistent in their approach to the gods.[33] He summarises that 'any god may be taken to see everything that one wishes whenever it suits the adorant'.[34] But closer attention to the evidence—and the question of divine omniscience and divine 'seeing'—complicates these conclusions.

Lykourgos' speech provides a particularly apposite example for this paper because of the way in which the speaker explores what has been described as a public/private distinction: Lykourgos lays emphasis on the 'public nature of his suit' and plays rhetorically with the themes of public and private.[35] Where other prosecutors may recount the personal aspects of their relationship with the defendant, or other details of his personal life, Lykourgos provides a series of quotations from Euripides, Homer, Tyrtaeus, two monuments, Spartan law and other unknown writers: the sentiments focus on the responsibilities of the individual to the city and fatherland.[36] The connections between personal passion and public prosecution in the Athenian lawcourts are well known, but, as Allen has pointed out, Lykourgos' speech stands out for his refusal to link the two. (In social network terms, we might recast the public/private distinction in terms of the types and extent of network ties to which Lykourgos is appealing: τὰς ἰδίας ἔχθρας denotes a limited set of 'strong' ties, while τὰ κοινά, translated above as 'public', could perhaps be translated as 'shared' or 'in common', to indicate the greater number of 'weak ties' that the speaker is urging.[37])

Lykourgos argues that the private is in danger of becoming public (that is, in network terms, it is spreading across a wider set of ties for whom it has little or no relevance), when it is public matters that should be felt as deeply as those that are usually private (i.e., that usually circulate across a smaller set of network ties). This is demonstrated by the stress he lays on the important educational impact of punishment imposed for the 'right' reasons.[38] In line with that argument, we find the gods introduced as arbiters into this forensic network: first, the decree 'περὶ εὐσεβείας' is read aloud, then the dikasts are threatened with the responsibility of their own role: εὖ δ' ἴστε, ὦ ἄνδρες, ὅτι νῦν κρύβδην ψηφιζόμε-

33 Versnel 2011: 438.
34 Versnel 2011, 437.
35 Discussed by Allen 2000, esp. 6–7.
36 Lyk. *Leok.* 5–6.
37 Compare Granovetter's (1973) insights into 'the strength of weak ties'.
38 See Lyk. *Leok.* 10; discussed by Allen 2000, 20–23.

νος ἕκαστος ὑμῶν φανερὰν ποιήσει τὴν αὑτοῦ διάνοιαν τοῖς θεοῖς' ("Know well, gentlemen, that even as you vote in secret, each of you makes his thought visible to the gods"). Thus, the speaker aligns a decree of the city—the broader network, as it were—with the oversight of the gods, and uses this to threaten the dikasts.

A similar context can be observed for the other three examples of this kind of threat found in the forensic corpus. First, in Lysias' *Against Andokides:* the speaker asks the dikasts a series of rhetorical questions, which powerfully, albeit indirectly, highlight their responsibility to condemn Andokides by referring to the gods' view of their secret actions.[39] Again, the argument is so presented that it draws attention to the social context in which the dikaste decision is to be made; it emphasizes the socio-political network to which they belong—and it sets the god within this web of oversight. Two further examples offer a similar context: In *Against Neaira*, Apollodoros notes how the vote of the dikasts cannot escape the gods (λήσειν τοὺς θεούς), who are also connected to the case as victims—alongside the Athenians.[40] In *About the False Embassy* Demosthenes observes that even a vote taken in secret cannot escape the gods (λήσει τοὺς θεούς). Again, the gods are established as part of the civic network that is both part of and oversees the outcome of the legal system.[41]

There are no further examples from the forensic corpus—and it is worth bearing in mind that these expressions, or rather the lack of them, raise a question for Versnel's notion that they simply occur as they are useful to the speaker. If this were the case, then we would expect to see them more frequently, and more emphatically employed. Nevertheless, the sentiment behind them is perhaps not so rare. It can be argued that the threats they make comprise a more detailed version of a warning quite frequently made in *graphai*, where the speaker appeals to the need to protect the city and its inhabitants, and underlines the risk of the dikasts committing *asebeia*.[42] The reference to the gods here provides an extension of a quite mundane, indeed, importantly mundane, idea, which speakers frequently use to stress the interconnections of individual, citizens, city and god.

39 Lysias 6 dated to 400/399 BCE in Todd 2000, 61. Lys. 6.53. See Dover 1974: 257–58, who argues that these indicate that 'gods read our thoughts' (p. 257).

40 MacDowell 2010, 487; and on Dem. 59 (343–339BCE), *ibid.*182.

41 [Dem.] 59.126 and Dem. 19.239. Dover adds misdeeds that are contemplated but not acted upon which receive punishment—Hdt. 1.159.4 and 6.86.γ.2—but as he points out, these are spoken aloud to an oracle, so although they involve a judgment of concealed intent, the mind-reading aspect is not evident.

42 For example, in Antiphon's speeches, and in Lysias 6 and Andokides 1, and Demosthenes 21 (see Eidinow 2014).

The connections of language between these four quotations suggest that there is some intertextuality—and, perhaps, a common idea being drawn upon. There are also various similarities of context: first, these examples arise in situations where the speaker wants to emphasise the dangers looming over the city, and imply that the gods, in their role as protective deities, are on his side. In addition, there is a chronological aspect: both Lysias and Lykourgos were bringing their prosecutions long after the crime in question. The need to take the long view in matters of justice, indeed, in matters of justice that safeguard the city, is given extra emphasis by introducing these divine guardians/overseers alongside their mortal counterparts. To support this idea, we can turn briefly outside the forensic corpus to Herodotus 8.106.3, which offers a further example of the idea of escaping the gods (θεοὺς λήσειν). Here it is used by Hermotimos as he reveals who he is and what he plans to do, as he takes his terrible revenge on Panionios for castrating him and selling him into slavery. The theme of that speech is justice, and the context is one in which, it can be argued, the extreme cruelty of the act about to take place perhaps requires an extreme justification. In turn, both these observations may also bear on the case against Neaira—as well as concerning activities that had taken place some time before, it could be argued that the prosecution of a woman was sufficiently unusual that it required some additional explicit divine support.

Looking at these examples in this light may help clarify the goals of the speaker's rhetoric, but the precise implications of these threats remains puzzling. We may gloss this as omniscience, but the way in which that knowledge is gathered demands more attention: this is not a mysterious process of mind-reading. Lykourgos' description, κρύβδην ψηφιζόμενος ἕκαστος ὑμῶν φανερὰν ποιήσει τὴν αὑτοῦ διάνοιαν τοῖς θεοῖς ("even as you vote in secret, each of you makes his thought visible to the gods"), appears to describe a process in which a god observes an individual perform an action in secret, which in turn makes clear his *dianoia* to the god: it is a process of deduction that is being described. The same can be noted of the examples from the speeches of Lysias and Demosthenes. In each case, the implication is that it is an action—a showing of favour, a vote being cast, albeit one done in secret—that makes the mental state of the mortal individual clear to the gods. This process of gods learning from and about particular mortals—one of action, inference, clarity—turns on its head the onerous process of sign/ambiguity/interpretation which is the experience of mortals seeking information from gods.

But this raises the question of what is meant by *krubden*, 'in secret'. Other examples may help: they also use the term to describe actions that are *in some ways* hidden. Thus, in *Od.* 11.455, Agamemnon gives Odysseus instructions to moor his ship in secret, when he sails home; and in *Od.* 16.153, the term is used to describe a maid sent out on an errand. These are actions that are meant to be concealed from some, but are known about by others (including, of course, the audience of the poem); they are conducted in plain sight for those standing in the right place at the right time—although their full significance may not be clear. Returning to the courtroom, in terms of voting, *krubden* is used to describe a process that is in contrast to an overt procedure, that is a show of hands; but, as Lysias says (12.91), in the end, even that act of voting does not remain secret: 'Nor should you suppose that your voting is in secret for you will make your judgement manifest to the city.' The implication is not so much that the gods can see what cannot be seen by any other mortal—but that they are able to see and make sense of actions concealed from some mortals.[43]

This is far from a comprehensive analysis—my intention is not to stray too far from the lawcourts—but it does suggest an intriguing limit to the remarkable nature of divine omnisicience: although the material discussed above offers evidence for knowledge of mortal mental states or ideas, these are not startling examples of divine 'superpowers'. Although these episodes certainly describe divine knowledge as better than that of mortals, the process of divine deduction mirrors familiar mortal activities, and the gods themselves are treated as an extension of the existing mortal context—the monitoring and oversight of individuals by members of the *polis* community.[44]

ii) Manipulation and Deliberation

The discussion so far suggests the human mind was not regarded as accessible. And yet, other evidence reveals that the ancient Greek self was considered to be permeable: it is a widespread trope that personified abstract concepts could

43 In the *Memorabilia* (1.1.19), Xenophon reports that 'Socrates thought that they [the gods] know all things, our words and deeds and secret purposes; that they are present everywhere, and grant signs to men of all that concerns man' (trans. Marchant), but Socrates is rare in this regard: he states that other men think that the gods know some things but do not know other things. Even here, the list of things the gods see are actions/activities—words and deeds —while the phrase τὰ σιγῇ βουλευόμενα (translated 'secret purposes') may mean something plotted in secret (that is, kept quiet from some, but obviously not others) rather than plans conceived of and contemplated with absolutely no external indication. Neatly reflecting this process of divine deduction, in Xenophon's *Symposium* (4.47) the statement that all men believe in the gods is presented as an inference based on mortal activities.

44 For those interested in a cognitive approach to the characterisation of ancient Greek gods, this may conform to a minimally counter-intuitive attribute (see Boyer 1992).

enter and direct the individual.[45] Even in the forensic speeches, where the question of responsibility is a primary factor, we find both prosecution and defence alleging that supernatural powers have intervened in an individual's mental processes. The theme is used to explain those actions that a speaker wants to underline as being extraordinary or inexplicable. For example, in Lysias 6, Andokides' choice to return home to Athens, and the alternative penalties that he has proposed, are remarkable, the speaker claims, and so must have been put there by a god.[46] Once this trope is established, Lysias uses it to shape other arguments, for example, the idea that Andokides' choice to go to trial is similarly inexplicable and so prompted by a supernatural force.[47] From Andokides' speech in response we learn of a further argument in which this trope appears—in prodding a mortal towards a particular action, the gods are ensuring that he will receive punishment.[48] The idea that supernatural powers are engineering one's fate also occurs in Lykourgos' *Against Leokrates* (92), where the moral character of that individual is made explicit, and the point is driven home with a traditional (and pointedly unattributed) quotation that the audience is encouraged to regard as an oracular utterance.[49]

In terms of our attempt to understand the nature of the mental realm as a 'private space', these descriptions remind us that this was a culture in which the risk of divine invasion could threaten anyone, and elements of the human mind were considered manipulable by unseen supernatural forces. *Gnome* can be 'destroyed'; *dianoia* can be 'led in a wrong direction'; while the divine provision of forgetfulness can influence the choices a mortal makes. These descriptions remind us of the range of ways in which the gods were portrayed as shaping mortal mental states in ancient Greek tragedy.[50] It appears that the dramatic depiction of an individual's mentality—their mental processes and motivations—was also considered relevant to a legal setting. Indeed, speakers on both sides introduce this explanation almost incidentally, suggesting that it was a familiar argument in the Athenian court.

It could be argued that this is just a rhetorical effect, another example of the way in which a culture of performance, and, in turn, of voyeurism, shaped

---

45 Eur. Fr. 403 tells us about Phthonos, which clearly dwells somewhere in the human body, and similarly, in [Xen.] *Kyn.* 12.21, Arete is immortal and ubiquitous, both discussed by Dover 1974, 142.

46 Lys. 6.22 and Lys. 6.27.

47 Lys. 6.32.

48 And. 1. 113.

49 For the tragic lines, see Kannicht and Snell, 1981, fr. 296 who refer forward to fr. 455.

50 Padel 1992.

events in the law courts, among other democratic processes.[51] Scholars have argued that this trend was part of a broader change 'in which the viewer moved from being a direct participant to being an outside observer, from being actively interrogated by works of art to being a voyeur of a process of discussion taking place in an imaginary world'.[52] And, indeed, the cursory references to supernatural interference in these lawcourt speeches do cast the defendant as an actor in drama; they do prompt us (and the dikasts?) to imagine the experience of the defendant in order to make a judgement on it. And yet, even as this occurs, it seems to be taken for granted that the experience that it invokes—of direct, involuntary communication with the gods—is one that the audience will not find shocking or difficult to contemplate. However, the reports of these divine interventions raise questions, in turn, for the way we model Greek religion, and the relationships we depict between mortal and supernatural: if we picture Greek religion in terms of a network of relationships, where should we place the gods?

Some evidence from the oracle of Dodona may provide some further insight: this comprises a number of questions that indicate that a consultant wanted to inquire about a subject, but without revealing its details.[53] The phrasing of the first example suggests that the matter in question may have been discussed elsewhere explicitly—perhaps orally during the process of the consultation.

1. Lhôte 112; SGDI 1580; Karapanos 1878: 77, 14, and pl. 36, 6; fourth to third century BCE (Lhôte)

> Ἠ συμπείθον[τι]
> αὐτῶι ὑπὲρ [το-]
> ῦ πράγματος, ὅ[ν-]
> τινά κα τρόπο[ν
> [φα]ίν<η>ται <δ>[ό] -
> κιμον, βέλτιο[ν]
> καὶ ἄμεινον
> Πυστακίωνι <ἐ> –
> σσεῖται
> Lhôte l. 5: [δ]ῠ̣νᾳται (?) ἄλ-

51 See Wilson 1991 on the shared role of spectator, citizen, dikast; Goldhill and Osborne 1999 on performance and democracy.
52 Elsner 2006, 91; he explores the cultural trends that prompted changes in artistic media in the later fifth and early fourth centuries.
53 For examination of individual consultation at Dodona, see Eidinow 2013.

Whether it will be advantageous for Pystakion if he acts as a joint advocate of this matter in whatever way seems best?

But in two other texts, the way the question is expressed suggests that the god can see the contents of the mind of the consultant.

2. *Ep. Chron* 1935: 258, 25; fifth century BCE

ἦ καιαγκα αὐτὸ -
ς ἐπὶ γνώμαι ἔχ –
ηι καὶ χρήηι

Whether... what he has on his mind you also foretell as an oracle

3. Lhôte 67; Parke 4; SEG 15.386; BE 1956: 143; PAE 1952: 301, 6; M-21; beginning of the fifth century BCE (Evangelidis), c.425–400 BCE (Lhôte)

τίνι κα θεõν εὐξάμενος πράξαι
hὰ ἐπὶ νόōι ἔχē;

To which of the gods must he have prayed so as to achieve what he has in mind?

Lhôte 1.9: τίνι {I}

Two different terms are used in these questions— νόος and γνώμη, both with the preposition ἐπὶ. A search of TLG suggests that that neither term is found with this preposition elsewhere, so the phrase and the conception it describes is rare, although we find ποιέειν τι ἐπὶ νόον τινί 'to put into his mind to do' (Hdt. 1.27.3), and ἐπὶ νόον τρέπειν τινί (Hdt. 3.21.3). Although we could translate these phrases using 'into' the mind, a more literal translation suggests 'on', 'upon', 'onto' or 'towards' 'his mind'. The use of these prepositions is intriguing, and, at first sight at least, suggests a model of the mind as an object rather than a space. Whether the god is thought to observe the mind all the time or not is not clear, but the questions show individuals requesting that the god regard, and respond to, information about which they are thinking, and which remains implicit.

The implication seems to be that the god can see a consultant's inquiry or area of inquiry without it being externally expressed—orally or in writing. At first sight, this contrasts with what we see in the forensic corpus where the god observes an action taken in secret, and can deduce the intention behind it; in turn, these both contrast with those further forensic examples where a divine force redirects attention or plants ideas. And yet, between these examples, there is also an important commonality: across all these examples, the deity is invoked in order to participate in mortal deliberation. In some the god is an overseer, in others a director; in some he appears external to the person, in others, he is somehow understood to be internal. Nevertheless, in each case, the person is still understood to be responsible. Mortal and god are described as acting in combination, but their networks of connections confound simple sets of oppositions, not only public vs. private, but also group vs. individual, mortal vs. supernatural, internal vs. external.

5. Conclusion: From Private to Participatory

The distinction 'public/private' as currently used in the study of ancient Greek religion, and the difficulties surrounding that use, are, I have suggested, at least in part, influenced by the model of *polis* religion. In this model, the concept of privacy appears to depend on current formulations of the individual mind—as impermeable, unseeable, and in those senses 'private'—and yet, paradoxically, the *polis* religion model appears to deny that the individual worshipper experienced anything that cannot be described in public terms. With this approach, in which every experience is simply deemed to be 'not different in nature from that of the group's', it is difficult to know what we are to make of the idea of 'private reflection in a private space'.[54]

The *polis* religion model has been challenged by other definitions of 'private/public', and by evidence for individual religious activity. In this paper I have suggested that consideration of a different model for thinking about Greek religion, one that employs a network approach, could be a next step. Rather than examining religious activity primarily at the level of the social group, it would enable and encourage a focus on the activities, interactions and experiences of the individual; the range of physical/social networks in which an individual participates; the dynamic cognitive processes, both group and individual, involved in the creation of the concepts and practices of ancient Greek religion.

This new model for thinking about Greek religion may also need to encompass a new perspective on ancient ideas about 'the self'. Those speaking in court or writing oracle questions appear to perceive themselves as deliberative beings in conjunction with the divine, their conception of their own social, cultural and cognitive networks comprising both mortals and deities. These relations extended not only out into their surrounding social and political environment, but also internally, within their mental states, in particular with regard to certain deliber-

54 Sourvinou-Inwood 2000b, 44.

ative activities. The evidence examined briefly here suggests that the inner mental realm—what we might think of as the private space—of an individual was considered to be not only porous and permeable to supernatural influences, but also, perhaps, visible to divine perceptions.

How common such experiences of the divine were understood to be, how they varied, and in what contexts, needs further exploration, but the evidence assembled here suggests that we need to recast the categories of public/private in ancient Greek religion, not only to take account of the interactions between mortals within a network of relationships, but also the relations with supernatural beings that occurred *within* individuals.

Works Cited

Aleshire, S. (1994). "Towards a Definition of 'State Cult' for Ancient Athens," in R. Hägg, ed., Ancient Greek Cult Practice from the Epigraphical Evidence. Proceedings of the Second International Seminar on Ancient Greek Cult, 1991. Skrifter Utgivna av svenska institutet I Athen, 8, XIII: 9–16. Stockholm.

Allen, D. (2000). "Changing the Authoritative Voice: Lycurgus' 'Against Leocrates'." Classical Antiquity 19.1: 5–33.

Boyer, P. (1992). "Explaining Religious Ideas: Outline of a Cognitive Approach." Numen 39: 27–57.

Bremmer, J. (2010). "Manteis, Magic, Mysteries and Mythography: Messy Margins of Polis Religion?" Kernos 23: 13–35.

Burkert, W. (1995). "Greek Poleis and Civic Cults: Some Further Thoughts," in M. H. Hansen, and K. Raaflaub, eds., Studies in the Ancient Greek Polis. Papers from the Copenhagen Polis Centre 2 (Historia Einzelschriften 95): 201–10. Stuttgart.

Clark, Andy, and David J. Chalmers. (1998). "The Extended Mind." Analysis 58: 7–19.

Cole, S. G. (1995). "Civic Cult and Civic Identity," in M. H. Hansen, ed., Sources for the Ancient Greek City State: Symposium August, 24–27 1994, Volume 2 of Acts of the Copenhagen Polis Centre: 292–325. Copenhagen.

Cottingham, J. (2008). Cartesian Reflections: Essays on Descartes's Philosophy. New York.

Damasio, A. R. (1994). Descartes' Error: Emotion, Reason, and the Human Brain. New York.

Davies, J.K. (1988). "Religion and the State," in Cambridge Ancient History 4^2: 368–88. Cambridge.

Dover, K. (1974). Greek Popular Morality in the Time of Plato and Aristotle. Oxford.

Eidinow, E. (2014) "Ancient Greek Religion: 'Embedded'... and Embodied," in C. Taylor and K. Vlassopoulos, eds. Communities and Networks in the Ancient Greek World. Oxford.

Eidinow, E. (2013). "Oracular Consultation, Fate, and the Concept of the Individual," in V. Rosenberger, ed., Divination in the Ancient World: Religious Options and the Individual. Stuttgart.

Eidinow, E. (2011a). "Networks and Narratives: A Model for Ancient Greek Religion." Kernos 24: 9–38.

Eidinow, E. (2011b). Fate Luck and Fortune: Antiquity and its Legacy. London.

Eidinow, E. (2010). "Witchcraft on Trial: Patterns of Persecution in Classical Athens." Past and Present 208: 9–35.
Eidinow, E. (2007). Oracles, Curses, and Risk Among the Ancient Greeks. Oxford (Rev. ppbk 2013).
Elsner, J. (2006). "Reflections on the 'Greek Revolution': From Changes in Viewing to the Transformation of Subjectivity," in S. Goldhill and R. Osborne (eds.) Rethinking Revolutions Through Ancient Greece: 68–95. Cambridge.
Feaver, D. D. (1957). "The Priesthoods of Athens." YCS 15: 123–58.
Goldhill, S. and Osborne, R. eds. (1999). Performance Culture and Athenian Democracy. Cambridge.
Granovetter, M. (1973). "The Strength of Weak Ties." American Journal of Sociology 78: 1360–1380.
Hansen, M. H. and Nielsen, T. H., eds. (2004). An Inventory of Archaic and Classical Poleis. Oxford.
Hutchins E. (1995). Cognition in the Wild. Cambridge, MA.
Jameson, M. H. (1997)."Religion in the Athenian Democracy," in I. Morris and K. Raaflaub, eds., Democracy 2500? Questions and Challenges: 171–95. Dubuque, Iowa.
Kannicht, R. and Snell, B. (1981). Tragicorum Graecorum Fragmenta vol. 2. Gottingen.
Kindt, J. (2012). Rethinking Greek Religion. Cambridge.
Kirshner, D. and Whitson, A. (1997). Situated Cognition: Social, Semiotic and Psychological Perspectives. Mahwah, NJ.
LiPuma, E. (1998). "Modernity and Forms of Personhood in Melanesia," in M. Lambek and A. Strathern, eds., Bodies and Persons: Comparative Perspectives from Africa and Melanesia: 53–79. Cambridge.
Luhrmann, T. (2011). "Toward an Anthropological Theory of Mind." Suomen Antropologi: Journal of the Finnish Anthropological Society 36(4): 5–13.
Marchant, E. C. (1923). Xenophon in Seven Volumes. London/Cambridge, MA.
MacDowell, D. (2010). Demosthenes the Orator. Oxford.
Padel, R. (1992). In and Out of the Mind: Greek Images of the Tragic Self. Princeton.
Parker, R. (2011). On Greek Religion. Ithaca/London.
Parker, R. (2005). Polytheism and Society at Athens. Oxford.
Parker, R. (1996). Athenian Religion: A History. Oxford.
Purvis, A. (2003). Singular Dedications: Founders and Innovators of Private Cults in Classical Greece. Volume 1 of Studies in Classics. New York/London.
Robbins, P. and Aydede M. (2008). The Cambridge Handbook of Situated Cognition. Cambridge.
Rorty, A. O. (1992). "Descartes on Thinking with the Body," in J. Cottingham, ed., The Cambridge Companion to Descartes: 371–392, Cambridge.
Solomon, M. (2006). "Situated Cognition," in P. Thagard, Philosophy of Psychology and Cognitive Science: A Volume of the Handbook of the Philosophy of Science Series: 413–428. Amsterdam.
Sourvinou-Inwood, C. (2000a). "What is Polis Religion?" in R. Buxton, ed., Oxford Readings in Greek Religion: 13–37. Oxford.
Sourvinou-Inwood, C. (2000b). "Further Aspects of Polis Religion," in R. Buxton, ed., Oxford Readings in Greek Religion: 38–55. Oxford.
Subotsky, E. (2010). Magic and the Mind: Mechanisms, Functions, and Development of Magical Thinking and Behavior. Oxford.

Todd, S. (1993). The Shape of Athenian Law. Oxford.
Todd, S. (2000). Lysias. Volume 2 of The Oratory of Classical Greece Series. Austin, TX.
Varela, F., Thompson, E. and Rosch E. (1991). The Embodied Mind: Cognitive Science and Human Experience. Cambridge, MA.
Versnel, H. S. (2011). Coping With the Gods. Leiden.
White, Harrison C. (2008). Identity and Control: How Social Formations Emerge. Princeton.
Wilson, P. J. (1991). "Demosthenes 21 (Against Meidias): Democratic Abuse." Proceedings of the Cambrdige Philological Society 37: 164–95.
Wilson, R. (2004). Boundaries of the Mind: The Individual in the Fragile Sciences. Cambridge.
Woolf, G. (1997). "Polis religion and its Alternatives in the Roman Provinces," in H. Cancik and J. Rüpke, eds., Romische Reichsreligion und Provinzialreligion: 71–84. Tübingen.
Zaidman, L. B. and Schmidt Pantel, P. (1992). Religion in the Ancient Greek City. Translated by Paul Cartledge. New York.

Elisabeth Begemann

4. *Ista tua pulchra libertas*: The Construction of a Private Cult of Liberty on the Palatine

Abstract: Upon his return from exile, the Roman orator Cicero fought for the restitution of his house and grounds that had been dedicated to the goddess *libertas* in his absence. The reversion of the dedication has special meaning due to the high visibility of the site in the city center: in establishing a shrine to deified liberty, the dedicant Clodius marks Cicero as a tyrant over whom liberty had triumphed. By the rhetoric employed, Cicero, however, suggests to his audience that the cult has no meaning for the political community, but for Clodius only, that it is a private cult, illegitimately erected in public space, and can therefore be moved without offending the deity. The paper considers the question of public and private spheres in the context of prominent politicians in the late Roman republic.

Introduction

When the Roman orator Marcus Tullius Cicero (106–43 BC) returned to Rome from exile in 57 BC, he strongly felt that full restitution could only be achieved with full restitution also of his house and grounds on the Palatine hill.[1] But since his political opponent Publius Clodius Pulcher (93 – 52 BC) had not been idle in the meantime, this meant evicting a squatter who could prove difficult (as far as religious sentiment and propriety goes) to evict: the *dea libertas* whose shrine Clodius had had dedicated on the site. The *oratio de domo sua* deals with the problems arising from this dedication on Cicero's former land. In this chapter I will argue that Cicero in his speech before the pontiffs employed a rhetoric to suggest, rather than to say, that the dedication was not only inappropriate because Clodius had no leave of the people to do so,[2] but also because the cult of Liberty was not one that concerned the *res publica* as a whole but always remained a private, Clodian cult.

---

1 Cic. *dom.* 100.

2 *Dom.* 127, *cf. Att.* 4.2.3, with reference to the *lex Papiria de dedicationibus*, *cf.* Tatum 1993; Orlin 1997, 170 f.

To speak of a "private" cult, we must initially, of course, clarify what is meant by the two terms "public" and "private" to mark the perimeter within which the following discussion moves. Cicero says in *rep*. 1.39:

> *Est igitur, inquit Africanus, res publica res populi, populus autem non omnis hominum coetus quoquo modo congregatus, sed coetus multitudinis iuris consensu et utilitatis communione sociatus.*
>
> Scipio says, The republic is the property of the people. But a people is not any collection of human beings brought together in any sort of way, but an assemblage of people in large numbers associated in an agreement with respect to justice and a partnership for the common good.[3]

For Cicero, the term *publicus* thus relates to what concerns the community as a whole. He stresses the elements "consensus", "law" and "utility for the common good". My own use of the term draws on Cicero's definition, as it is used to signify the sphere that concerns the community, the *populus*.[4] The man acting publicly denotes the man acting for and in the interest of the *res publica*. That is the magistrate, a chosen, elected member of the people to act for the people, an officeholder, on the one hand, on the other the man who serves her best interests and puts all personal interests secondary to the commonwealth.[5]

The term "private" denotes the opposite. A private person is the one who holds no office, who has no sanction of the people to act on its behalf. His actions do not bind the community at large. "Private" denotes actions, things, persons and concerns outside the communal, political context, even where those actions, things, persons, and concerns take place in, or touch, a "public", i.e. highly visible and communal, and most of all, political, sphere.[6]

---

3 Tr. Keyes, with modifications.

4 *Cf.* also Mommsen 1886, 300.

5 The terms are not necessarily exclusive, because we also find, in Cicero, that a man may act as *privatus*, i.e. without office and charge of the people, for the *res publica*, i.e. in her best interests and defending her traditions – Cicero himself after the death of Caesar is a notable case in this context, Scipio Nasica is another, *cf. off.* 1.76. Of course, "the best interest of the *res publica*" is a very fluid term and meant something else to Cicero than it did to Antonius, one thing for Scipio, another to Gracchus. To refer to it is a defensive act, meant to excuse and legitimize actions of non-office holders and their claim to shape the policies of the *res publica* without election of the senate or the people.

6 E.g. speaking in the forum. A non-office holder could only do that if he is called upon by a magistrate to do so, the magistrate as the elected member of the *populus* speaking on its behalf, therefore acknowledging that whatever the non-office holder has to say is of interest and importance to the people, *cf.* Mommsen 1871, 142. That excludes, to a degree, *laudationes funebris*,

In terms of the following argument, a "private" cult of Liberty would be the cult of the *dea libertas* by an individual, family, or exclusive group of persons;[7] it has no bearing on the community at large, it is not subsidized by the *res publica*, and the community is not bound to it, meaning that the veneration and placation of the deity is the business of the person or persons who initiated or inherited the cult, not the *res publica*. However, a "public" cult of Liberty would be of great concern to the community, to uphold the *pax deum* between the community with *libertas* would fall to the entire populus, the entire *populus* be bound to it, and the entire *populus* count as *libertas*' worshippers. The question is, then, what of the cult of *libertas* on the Palatine? Was it a cult that was to be counted among those that concerned the entire community? Or did the ruins of the house of Cicero "only" provide space for personal worship?

1. Cicero's House on the Palatine: Visibility and the Public Sphere

When Cicero bought his house on the Palatine hill with a fine view over the Roman forum in 62 BC for 3.5 million sesterces, there was much grumbling.[8] Rome was not ready to live easy with such a prominent place for a *homo novus* in the heart of the community.[9] For Cicero, however, the site must have seemed ideal: "proximity to the earliest demarcated public spaces (Forum, Regia, Comitium) signaled social prestige, which, in turn, soon made it necessary for aristocratic families to dwell as near as possible to these locations."[10] His move to the Palatine was purely political. Cicero moved, "in order that those who came to pay their court to him might not have the trouble of a long walk"[11] and he took much pride in the fact that his house was open at all hours to visitors and none was ever turned away.[12] And despite the (apparently) steep price, he never felt it a bad investment, although he had to borrow most of the money.[13] He rather understood the house to underscore the political standing

these are "public" in the sense that the *populus* had just lost an important member who deserves to be remembered with praise by the community.

7 *Cf. leg.* 2.19.

8 Cic. *fam.* 5.6.2; *Att.* 1.16.10.

9 Gildenhard 2011, 301. *Cf.* Wiseman 2013.

10 Beck 2009, 365.

11 Plut. *Cic.* 8.3.

12 Cic. *Sull.* 26, *Planc.* 66, *Att.* 6.2.5, *Phil.* 8.31; advising his brother: *ad Q. fr.* 1.1.25.

13 Cic. *Att.* 1.13.6; Aul. Gell. 12.12.

and *auctoritas* of its owner.[14] It is immediately understandable why no other house would do for the *homo novus:* He bought it after his consulate, in full view of the forum and open to visitors night and day.[15] The claim that no one was ever turned away served to underline his constant availability to all things public and political, his continuous partaking in Roman affairs.[16]

Not only was the house in full view of the Roman city center,[17] it also had a certain tradition. According to Velleius, the house had originally belonged to the tribune M. Drusus, who was also consciously aware of its utility and the need to be on public display:[18]

> When he was building his house on the Palatine on the site where now stands the house that once belonged to Cicero, and later to Censorinus, and that now belongs to Statilius Sisenna, the architect offered to build it in such a way that he would be free from the public gaze, safe from all espionage, and that no one could look down into it. Livius replied, "If you possess the skill you must build my house in such a way that whatever I do shall be seen by all."[19]

Kate Cooper points to the importance for the Roman elite of occupying physical space that clearly marked their social and political standing: "The private establishment of a dominus involved many elements that were crucial to his ability to attain high standing among his peers, leading in the best of circumstances to public office. Foremost, it was critical to have at his disposal a physical space, the *domus*, appointed in a way that would impress his peers and show himself and his family to advantage."[20] While physical space did not make the man, it certainly sustained him.[21] As a distinguished consular, Cicero felt that now was the right time to visually proclaim his central standing within Rome's political landscape, a conclusion to which the unusual honors voted on him after the Catilinarian affair would have helped him come.[22] The house itself served as "a reflection of Cicero's successful consulship and his position at the heart of Rome. [...] Everyone could see Cicero and his palpable material success. Cicero, in turn, could look out over his 'children' in the Forum."[23] Its importance was underlined

14 *Cf.* Cic. *off.* 1.139.
15 *Fam.* 5.6.2. *Cf.* Allen 1944, 4. Krause 2004, 34 f. Coarelli 2012, 318.
16 *Cf.* Beck 2009, 366. Treggiari 1998.
17 Cic. *dom.* 103. *Cf.* Allen 1944, 2. Wiseman 2012, 658.
18 *Cf.* Cooper 2007.
19 Vell. 2.14.3.
20 Cooper 2007, 5.
21 Wallace-Hadrill 1988.
22 Title of *pater patriae:* Plut. *Cic.* 23.3; *supplicatio:* Cic. *Phil.* 14.24.
23 Hales 2000, 45.

by the fact that Cicero, the *homo novus*, could not point to any monuments – road, statue or building – on display in public space that spoke of the history of his family within the *res publica.*[24] Cicero had learned early on in his political career, how much better the Romans understood visual language[25] than the spoken word.[26] In moving to the Palatine, the most fashionable corner of Rome,[27] Cicero applied this lesson to communicate his position and his role within the *res publica.*[28]

The house itself was situated in the northeast[29] corner of the Palatine hill, looking towards the forum and capitol. Both *atrium Vestae* and the house of the *pontifex maximus* were close by; the location was imbued with political and religious connotations. In *de domo sua,* Cicero repeatedly refers to the situation and high visibility of his house: it was in *conspectu prope totius urbis,*[30] *in pulcherrimo urbis loco,*[31] and *in urbis clarissimo loco.*[32]

Clodius, too, lived on the Palatine. His own house was not far from that of Cicero: the two were neighbors.[33] Clodius understood the value of living close to the political center as well as Cicero did: "the very location of the house [...] gave it an air of authority",[34] enhancing the status and the political significance of the owner. That authority would be further underlined if Clodius, as Cerutti assumes, inherited a "family mansion" on the Palatine, not needing to purchase the land.[35] If we follow Coarelli,[36] the house would also, though less prominently, look towards the forum, marking another prominent *domus* in the Roman cityscape.

Again, not everyone was happy with Cicero's purchase. Clodius seems to have been particularly irked by his new neighbor. Was it the pride of the scion

---

24 *Cf.* Itgenshorst 2005, 125 ff.

25 *Cf.* Hölscher 1987.

26 *Planc.* 66.

27 Fellow dwellers on the Palatine include Caesar (*Att.* 2.24.3), Metellus Celer (*Cael.* 59), Hortensius (Suet. *Aug.* 72.1, later Augustus) and, of course, Clodius.

28 *Cf.* Cic. *off.* 1.139. Berg 1997, 122.

29 Wiseman 2012, 658.

30 *Dom.* 100.

31 *Dom.* 103.

32 *Dom.* 132.

33 Next-door neighbors after the return of Cicero and the restitution of his property, *har. resp.* 33.

34 Berg 1997, 126.

35 He was able to build a wall across his sister's *vestibulum,* which effectively blocked her entrance, *Mil.* 75. Cerutti 1997, 421 identifies her as the wife of Lucullus rather than the notorious Clodia who was married to the late Metellus Celer. In the same vein Pepi 1995, 85. However, Berg 1997, 128 dates Clodius' purchase of his house (formerly that of Flaccus) to "61 or 60 BC".

36 Coarelli 2012, 318.

of an old patrician house or just the grudge he held since Cicero testified against him in the Bona Dea trial? In any case, as soon as Cicero was safely out of the way, conveniently exiled to Thessalonike, Clodius had the property confiscated,[37] columns and doors carried away as booty,[38] the house burnt down[39] and generally demolished:[40] Cicero was not to return here!

But Cicero did return and re-claimed his former property. After pestering Atticus and whoever else he counted as his friends and allies the one day, and falling into deep depressions the other,[41] he returned to Italian soil after eighteen months of forced absence. Pompey had finally recognized the value of Cicero's continuous (though occasionally grudging) *gratia* as a counterweight in a city that seemed to spin out of control.[42] Cicero celebrated the occasion with the two orations *post reditum cum gratia*, one addressed to the senate, the other to the people. These he followed up with the demand that his grounds be restored, and his house be rebuilt for him. The importance he attributed to both had not changed – they were still a symbol of his role in Roman politics, now probably more so than ever.[43] Clodius understood that and had taken his own measures to prevent Cicero from returning into his own by dedicating a part of the area to the goddess *libertas* (or, in Cicero's interpretation, *licentia*).[44] The dedication was meant to keep Cicero out: land that has once been turned over to the gods would always be in their possession and uninhabitable to humans.[45]

Although we quickly run into the considerable obstacle that whatever we "know" and say of Clodius is ultimately based on what Cicero said of him[46] – and he is hardly an objective and impartial witness –, but assuming that Cicero did not (or rather: could not) make things up it seems that Clodius was as aware as Cicero of the visual and emotional opportunities the site offered. Not only was

37 *Dom.* 51.
38 *Dom.* 60, 113. *Pis.* 26, 52. *Sest.* 54.
39 *Dom.* 62. *har. resp.* 15; Plut. *Cic.* 33.1.
40 Vell. 2.45; App. *bell. civ.* 2.15.
41 The third book in the collection of letters to Atticus show a thorough psychogram of Cicero in exile.
42 *P. red. in Sen.* 5 *dom.* 30. *Cf.* Benner 1987, 56; Will 1991, 84.
43 Cic. *dom.* 100, *cf.* Hales 2000, 46: "The confiscation of Cicero's property was [...] effectively *damnatio* of the *memoria* that Cicero had stored up of his achievements in Rome. [...] If the house is destroyed, the memory is erased."
44 *Licentia: dom.* 131. The dedication of the altar and statue of *libertas* cannot be dated for certain. Berg 1997, 133 n. 60 sees it "in the nature of a prank [...] carried out when Cicero's return began to look likely".
45 *Dig.* 1.8.3.
46 *Cf.* Rundell 1979.

there the vicinity to the political center, but an emotional and religious landscape with the *atrium Vestae*, the Mater Magna temple, and the hut of Romulus nearby, all of them highly charged locations within Rome that stood for the city's origin, continuity and protection. Putting himself in such a context, Cicero visually claimed that he was a fully accepted member of the Roman aristocracy, a guarantor of the *res publica*'s very survival, the *conservator rei publicae*, as men and gods agreed.[47]

Cicero's house was adjacent to the *porticus Catuli*, decorated with the spoils of Q. Catulus' Cimbrian campaign[48] and erected on a plot of land that had once belonged to M. Flaccus, before Flaccus was sentenced by the senate, the land confiscated and the house razed to the ground.[49] That Clodius did the same to (parts of) Cicero's house and elongated the porticus Catuli to include parts of the *domus Tullii* may be presented by Cicero as an attempt by the tribune to live large,[50] but everyone understood the semantics behind the act. Because Clodius did to Cicero's house what had been done to Flaccus', he proclaims Cicero's actions as just as contrary to the welfare of the *res publica* as Flaccus' had been, and that the Roman public needed to triumph over the space of its enemy again.[51] The high visibility of the site underscored the point Clodius was trying to make, a point Cicero well understood and desperately needed to rectify. He was not the tyrant who put his own will before the well-being of the state and the people. He only ever wanted what was best for the *res publica*. It was Clodius who was the real tyrant, who mocked the Roman republic by putting up the shrine of the *oppressa libertate Libertas*, the suppressor of liberty, the Clodian *Libertas*.[52]

2. The Accusation of Tyranny: *Libertas* as the War Cry of the Late Republic

Clodius' choice of deity is no accident. "*Libertas* was a political catchword in late Republican Rome"[53] and as much employed by Clodius as by Cicero,[54] by M. Bru-

47 *Dom.* 26. *Vat.* 7 and *Phil.* 2.51; *conservator urbis Mil.* 73, *Att.* 9.10.3; *conservator patriae Pis.* 23.
48 Val. Max. 6.3.1.
49 *Dom.* 102.
50 *Dom.* 115.
51 *Cf. dom.* 61. Stroh 2010.
52 *Dom.* 116.
53 Allen 1944, 1.
54 Cic. *Phil.* 3 *passim*. *Cf.* Manuwald 2007, 306.

tus[55] as by Octavian.[56] Each party claimed the deliverance of the *res publica* from the tyranny of their political opponents for themselves. Clodius was no exception: he termed Cicero a tyrant early on.[57] In pushing through the law that those should be punished who killed or had killed Roman citizens without judgment by the people,[58] he paints Cicero as not acting on behalf of the Roman republic, but on his own whim, just like a tyrant would do.

Building and dedicating a shrine to *Libertas* concurs because it has precedent, which Cicero cites in *de domo:* he mentions numerous cases where the suppression of internal foes was followed by the destruction of their property.[59] In tearing down parts[60] of the house on the Palatine and dedicating others to Liberty, Clodius claims that he is dealing with Cicero as the forefathers had dealt with other tyrants, and in the best interest of a free people.[61]

But is Cicero the tyrant with whom the people should be concerned? It was not exactly difficult for Cicero to turn the tables and stick the label unto Clodius, as he does throughout the speech *de domo sua*, by painting Clodius in the most unbecoming and erratic colors possible: Clodius is not fit to interact with the gods,[62] Clodius is *superstitiosus,*[63] Clodius acted without legal justification,[64] he enacted a *privilegium* on Cicero,[65] he acted without religious justification,[66] all in all, he acted as a madman, not as a Roman. Cicero's case was eased, of course, by the common knowledge of Clodius' habit of engaging *collegia* to further his own ends[67] – in Cicero's generalizing interpretation, to turn to violence and force to have his will.[68] It is Clodius, not Cicero, who repeatedly acts with violence against the *res publica*, who does not care about divine *ius* or the will of the gods, who bound and gagged the *res publica*,[69] who accused the senators

55 *Cf.* Gosling 1986, 588.
56 Aug. *gest.* 1.
57 Cic. *Att.* 1.16.10.
58 Cass. Dio 38.14.4; Vell. 2.45.1.
59 Cic. *dom.* 101.
60 Berg 1997, 130.
61 Following Roller 2010.
62 *Dom.* 104.
63 *Dom.* 103, 105.
64 *Dom.* 127. On the question of whether Clodius had legal justification to dedicate parts of Cicero's house *cf.* Tatum 1993, Stroh 2004, Wiseman 2012.
65 *Dom.* 23. 43. 57. 110. 131.
66 *Dom.* 108.
67 *Cf.* Benner 1987 on Clodius' patronage of the *plebs.*
68 E.g. *dom.* 5.
69 *Dom.* 2.

of *inconstantia*,[70] who threatens the state, who lashes out against the Roman people[71] – and who concedes himself that the Roman state cannot do without Cicero (willfully ignoring that of course *Clodius'* statement is to be taken ironically)![72] The presentation culminates in a familiar portrayal: while Clodius' gangs threaten Rome and have to be forcefully driven out,[73] Cicero himself is the peaceful *togatus* who saves[74] and cares for[75] his compatriots.

The contrast between the violent tribune of the *plebs* versus the peaceful consular is established early on and persists throughout the speech. In doing so, Cicero opens up a contrast between the man who acts only on his own will and whim (Clodius) and the man who subjects himself entirely to the wants and needs of the *res publica* (Cicero himself). He uses this forceful imagery throughout the oration before the pontiffs: Clodius gets upright politicians out of the way,[76] he plots against the hero of the Roman people,[77] he turns a deaf ear to the pleading of senate, the *boni* and all Italy,[78] and so on and so forth. Against this foil of the tyrant who sets his own will absolute is set the figure of Cicero himself who is recalled by the entire community,[79] who serves her best interests,[80] who is synonymous with the *res publica* herself.[81] With him returns abundance, peace, tranquility, the rule of the law and the unity of the senate and the people;[82] all of Italy prospers, therefore all of Italy clamored for his return.[83] Most importantly, Clodius clearly does not care at all about the gods' will: a *frequens senatus* saw its decision to recall Cicero approved not only by the positive reaction of the people, but, more importantly, by the approving nod of the immortal gods[84] – the only dissenting voice was that of Clodius. Can *he* interpret the will of the gods for the Romans?

---

70 *Dom.* 3.
71 *Dom.* 2.
72 *Dom.* 4 f.
73 *Dom.* 5.
74 *Cat.* I-IV.
75 *Dom.* 6.
76 Cicero and Cato, *dom.* 21 f.
77 Pompey, *dom.* 13. 129.
78 *Dom.* 26, 55.
79 *Dom.* 76, 142.
80 *Dom.* 26, 64.
81 *Dom.* 141.
82 *Dom.* 17.
83 *Dom.* 26, 30.
84 *Dom.* 14 f.

The question of whether Clodius could know divine will and therefore in fact make a valid dedication is vital from the very beginning: it has bearing on Cicero's entire argumentation.[85] Cicero's portrayal of the tribune as *ille castissimus sacerdos superstitiosus*[86] clearly says that Clodius cannot take care of Roman *sacra*.[87] The Bona Dea scandal is rehashed,[88] his various transgressions revisited, and the "superstitious belief" that blasphemy is punished by actual blindness sent off into the realm of myth and the theatre.[89]

Cicero does not say, however, that Clodius did not dedicate a cult at all, he acknowledged that there was a *monumentum* dedicated to *libertas* where (part of) his house once stood. Cicero does not indicate whether any (regular) cult took place at the site, though that is possible, if not plausible.[90] Cicero's silence on this account may point to the very fact that the *monumentum* was frequented by more people than just Clodius. How many people worshipped at the shrine we will never know, because our sources never mention the acceptance of the cult within Ciceronian Rome. If Liberty's worshippers can indeed be reduced to one, Cicero's suggestion is much aided: if only Clodius is interested in the shrine, and the Roman people neither involved in nor attracted by the cult, it suddenly becomes a very private cult, and therefore movable.[91]

Concerning the "shrine" of *libertas*, Cicero also never mentions there being anything more than the image of the supposed deity *libertas*. Though a number of scholars speak of an *aedes libertatis* as a matter of fact, Wiseman rightly points out that "Cicero nowhere mentions a temple".[92] Though *aedes* is a word employed frequently throughout *de domo sua*, it is mostly used to refer to Cicero's own house.[93] The missing *aedes* makes the entire Clodian construction much

---

85 Gildenhard 2011, 306 ff. points to the oddness of Cicero's interpretation of the pontiffs' role: he ascribes to them not questions of correct procedure only, but *religiones interpretari*, i.e., to judge the case judicially, acting "quite extraneous to their specific expertise" as mediators of divine will, interpreting and "translating" it, rather than issuing responses on procedural questions.

86 *Dom.* 103.

87 *Dom.* 104.

88 Lennon 2010.

89 *Dom.* 105. Note again the rhetorical use of visibility with reference to Claudius Caecus and the mentally blind Clodius: a twofold inability of cognition.

90 *HR* 33 again refers to Clodius, and only Clodius, practicing his cult.

91 *Dom.* 121. *Cf.* Wissowa 1897, 1875 ff.

92 Wiseman 2012, 659, against Picard 1965, Tatum 1999 and Krause 2001. Berg 1997 also assumes there to have been a temple.

93 Already noted by Stroh 2004, 320 n. 40, though *templum* and *delubrum* are used by Cicero in general terms and cannot apply to the *libertas* monument on the Palatine. See n. 92.

more tentative; a (transient)[94] altar is also only mentioned in passing,[95] so that essentially, the *monumentum* consists of the statue of a woman put up within an *ambulatio* that had already been there. Though the pontiffs, as residents of Rome, will have known better, we see only the image of the Greek harlot within the *porticus Catuli* – apart from the figures of Clodius and the hapless Natta who is called upon to dedicate the *delubrum nefandum*,[96] the site lies empty and silent.

Reading *de domo sua* carefully, we hit the unfortunate snag that nowhere in his speech does Cicero actually argue that the cult of Liberty as instituted by Clodius was his private cult – the terminology is not there. Neither *privatus* nor *separatim* are terms used in context.[97] Cicero could not use them: Clodius in 58 acted as a Roman magistrate, he was quite (or actually way too much) active in Roman politics, he was not *privatus*.[98] Neither did Cicero need to use the term *privatus* with reference to Clodius: it would have disrupted his portrayal of Clodius as the tyrant, the blend par excellence of public and private in politics: the non-elected office-holder.[99] Cicero had other ways of making quite clear that the dedication of shrine and statue had meaning for Clodius only and had no bearing on the *res publica*, but was forced on the Roman people, a depraved cult.

He does so mainly by reference to the use of violence. If indeed Clodius had held office according to Roman traditions, there would have been no need for violence[100] – Cicero rather suggests that whatever Clodius enacted could only be done because the people were afraid. That his "rule" is without consent is insinuated by Cicero's repeatedly stating that even his followers had deserted him:[101] Clodius acts so erratically that not even his cronies are able to stick with him anymore. This applies also to the dedication of the Liberty cult, since only Clodius and Natta were present[102] and the imagery with which Cicero

94 Note the parallel sentence structure of *dom* 140: by aligning an *ara* set up *in litore deserto* (again: avoidance of publicity and the public gaze, in contrast to misdeeds which are for all to see) with the altar put up by Clodius in the portico, Cicero means for his audience to understand the *ara* in question to be another strictly temporary structure. *Cf.* Orlin 1997, 162.

95 *Dom.* 140: *unam aram nefarie consecraret. Cf. dom.* 121, with Wiseman 2012, 660.

96 *Dom.* 132.

97 *Cf. leg.* 2.19 for Cicero's terminology of private cults.

98 Cic. *inv.* 2.30; *cf.* Isid. *orig.* 9.4.30.

99 *Cf.* Arist. *Pol.* 1310b14–26.

100 On tyranny and violence, *cf.* Hofer 2000, 64.

101 E.g. *dom.* 7. 67.

102 *Dom.* 126 with its juxtaposition of *uno adulescente* and *contione fecisti* underlines the lack of witnesses to the action.

describes the scene does not only imply faulty procedure, but also a priest who is so unsure of what he is doing and so afraid (of what he is doing? of Clodius?) that one almost commiserates.[103]

But why would a tyrant dedicate a statue of Liberty and worship the very goddess he (in Cicero's interpretation and understanding) expelled from Rome? Cicero says that Clodius did so to mock the people: put up in full sight of the political center an image of what they no longer have to ensure they understand that they now live under the rule of one,[104] after she evicted the very man who saved Rome from servitude under Catiline.[105] The cult of Liberty is a mock cult, a) because liberty is absent from Rome;[106] b) because Clodius is not fit to enact proper *religio* in Rome, as witnessed by his behavior during the Bona Dea rites and his willful ignorance or acceptance of the auspices;[107] and c) because he had no sanction of the people to dedicate the shrine.[108] Therefore, it cannot apply to the Roman people in general and is not binding, and since Clodius' actions in attaining the site were illegal, so is his dedication of the *libertas* shrine.[109] But does the fact that the dedication was illegal and put up in mockery of the actual political situation (as seen by Cicero) in Rome make the *libertas* cult Clodius' personal cult?

3. That Beautiful Liberty: The (In)Appropriateness of a Deity

In considering the cult instituted by Clodius as a private cult of (only) P. Clodius Pulcher, it almost does not matter that Cicero nowhere refers to it as a "private cult". He has other means of getting his meaning across, by referring to her as *ista tua libertas pulchra* – "that beautiful liberty of yours".[110] The epithet is important: it is not just any liberty, it is *libertas pulchra*, "Pulcher" being the cognomen of the Claudian family to which the tribune of 58 bc belonged.[111] Cicero had reminded the audience of the name by citing Clodius' reading of a letter ad-

103 *Dom.* 134 f.
104 *Dom.* 110.
105 *Dom.* 111.
106 *Cf. leg.* 28.
107 *Dom.* 40. 105.
108 *Dom.* 51. 106. 127 f.
109 *Dom.* 128. *Cf.* Tatum 1993, 327.
110 *Dom.* 108.
111 *Cf.* Wiseman 1970 on the relevance of the name.

dressed to him by Caesar, which was headed *Caesar Pulchro.*[112] Accordingly, the cult is not just any cult, it is a specific cult, that of the *Claudii Pulchri* – or just one errant member of them.[113] The sentence structure underlines the intended meaning: Cicero sets *tua pulchra libertas* against his own family gods, creating an echo of the events in the human sphere by events in the divine sphere, while stressing the importance these deities have for the *domus:*[114]

> What is more sacred, what more inviolably hedged about by every kind of sanctity, than the home of every individual citizen? Within its circle are his altars, his hearths, his household gods, his religions, his observances, his ritual; it is a sanctuary so holy in the eyes of all, that it were sacrilege [*fas*] to tear an owner therefrom.

Though the *lares* and *penates* were certainly mobile deities, they must not be removed against their will: Roman history told everyone as much.[115] And as the Clodian Liberty acts just as tyrannically towards Cicero as Clodius did, driving him and his deities out of the house, she is quite fit to be the deity of choice for Clodius, considering her origins, which Cicero dwells on with some relish:[116]

> But where did you find your Liberty? After making careful inquiry, I learn that rumour has it that she was a certain courtesan of Tanagra, a marble statue of whom stood upon a tomb not far from the city. A certain nobleman, not unconnected with our punctilious priest of liberty, had carried this statue off to adorn the entertainment he intended to give as aedile; [...] he took the statue of the courtesan from its pedestal and presented it to Clodius, that it might symbolize the liberty of Clodius and his like rather than that of the state.

The Clodian Liberty is inappropriate in more than one way: she is inacceptable on the social level (a *meretrix*, i.e. a slave or freedwoman), as a foreigner (from Greek Tanagra), on the religious level (due to her origin as a grave marker, i.e. polluted by death) and on the ethical level, since she is stolen goods. But she suits Clodius, as even his brother Appius concedes: her being the image "more of his own than of public liberty" underlines his brother's position as the tyrant, unintended by Appius, but strongly suggested by Cicero's phrasing.

Clodius is described by Cicero as a demented[117] and fanatical[118] man, mad[119] and morally depraved.[120] His deity of choice suits him. Although for most of his

112 *Dom.* 22.

113 Berg 1997, 132.

114 *Dom.* 108. In putting up the *libertas* shrine, Clodius once again aggressively invades sacred space to the detriment of the *res publica, cf. Att.* 1.12.3.

115 *Cf.* Dion. Hal. 1.67; Wissowa 1887 on the movability of household deities.

116 *Dom.* 111f.

117 *Dom.* 2. 76.

oration he refers to her as *libertas*, in *dom.* 131 he calls her *licentia*,[121] for what else could a tribune such as Clodius revere, whom else could he put up a shrine to, since his whole career has – in Cicero's version of events – been one long list of sexual and violent transgressions.[122] Considering the continued suggestions of unacceptable sexual behavior throughout the oration, the description is a further variation of the theme, speaking of deviant behavior unbecoming to a member of the upper class and certainly most improper in a cultic context.

Where such a deity is worshipped, she is fit to be worshipped by only one person – Clodius himself. By painting the cult of *libertas pulchra* as synonymous with *licentia*, Cicero turns the intended message on its head: what Clodius wanted understood as symbol and thanks offering for deliverance from tyranny for the whole polity, Cicero makes out to be the very epitome of self-interested, ruthless behavior, binding the *res publica* to a wanton deity that will, in effect, remove law and order from the community, an offense to the immortals. By calling her *libertas pulchra* Cicero makes clear that it is a Clodian deity, in accord with the tribune's own licentious behavior and criminal act of driving Cicero from Rome, just as *libertas pulchra* now drives him from his house.[123]

In turning to Cicero's description of the dedication of the cult site, we find more evidence that Cicero wanted his audience to understand that the cult in question was strictly Clodian, by stating first that no man and certainly no divinity ever wanted his property, out of gratitude to the man who had saved the city and her temples from burning during the Catilinarian conspiracy.[124] The only one who desired it was *ista tua pulchra libertas*, to carry into Cicero's house the *religio* that Clodius had once driven out of the house of the *pontifex maximus*.[125] Cicero again paints the image of the tyrannical tribune and his deity in the most glaring colors, referring once more to Bona Dea ("Did you install in my house the deity you have already offended?", *dom.* 110) before looking into the origins of the statue, the reasons for putting up said shrine, and finally the procedure of dedication.

118 *Dom.* 105.
119 Ibid.
120 *Dom.* 23. *Cf.* Lennon 2010 on the element of ritual impurity in *de domo sua*.
121 And again in *leg.* 2.42.
122 *Cf.* Leach 2001 on the matter.
123 The use of *sepulcrum* in this context refers back to the origin of the statue of *libertas* as coming from the grave of a *meretrix*, *cf.* Lennon 2010, 436; Rüpke 2007, 59. Cic. *dom.* 100.
124 *Dom.* 108.
125 *Dom.* 104.

Let us listen to Cicero. For how did Clodius attain the statue? His brother gave it to him. Why did he feel the need to set up a shrine? Well, Cicero had already said that every house is "hedged about with every kind of sanctity": Clodius also introduces his own gods into his home, as his aim was clearly not to erect a cult site for the Roman people (what could be more offensive? He had already driven liberty out of Rome!),[126] but to expand his mansion – after all, did he not kill Seius to incorporate his and Cicero's grounds into his own house?[127] That the building even expanded unto public grounds (the *porticus Catuli*) merely serves to underline the picture of the tyrant who cares neither about laws nor property.[128] And finally, who dedicated the statue for him? A priest of high standing? No, his brother-in-law, who had been asked by his sister (Clodius' wife) and forced by his mother[129] – an intimate, "familial" ceremony rather than one creating a greater public. What could be a more personal, Clodian cult?

In turning to his wife's recently elected brother, Clodius forsook the weightier authority that comes with the experience of older priests.[130] For my argument, the question of how Natta dedicated the site is irrelevant, though Cicero emphasizes that he did not do so correctly. Much more important is the question of how Cicero speaks of what he dedicated:

> If you had deliberated, if you had felt bound to expiate or institute anything within your domestic cult, you would have turned to a *pontifex* like everyone else according to the ancient custom: but when you introduced by vile and unheard-of means a new cult in the middle of the city, you did not think to turn to the city's *sacerdotes?*[131]

On the surface, the point Cicero is making is that Clodius acted without the approval and authority of the priestly college as well as of the people of Rome in putting up a new cult on the Palatine. But the reference to *religio domestica* is curious – why mention it? And, more poignantly, why mention it in such a way as to suggest that Clodius did something wrong when clearly he had done exactly what Cicero describes as the right, because ancient, procedure: he turned to a priest (*pontifex*) to introduce a new element to his domestic cult. Clodius did just that: and, what is more, he turned to a family member to do so, to his brother-in-law. He did everything right, then – *if* the cult of *libertas*

126 *Dom.* 110.
127 *Dom.* 115. *Cf.* Wiseman 2013, 260.
128 *Dom.* 114.
129 *Dom.* 118.
130 Ibid.
131 *Dom.* 132.

pulchra is a strictly domestic cult. Clodius wanted it understood that it was not, that it was a cult established for the entire *res publica*. To counter the claim, Cicero suggests that Clodius instituted a personal cult and only got the idea to proclaim it public later on, when Cicero's return was imminent,[132] and therefore should have asked the entire pontifical college and the assembled people before foisting a new cult on them. It is in Cicero's interpretation only Clodius' status as tyrant of the *res publica* that makes this cult matter for all of Rome: just as his house expands to incorporate Cicero's own and the *porticus Catuli*, so his cult expands to bind the entire populace.

4. From Private to Public: Building the *domus Clodiana* and the Cult of *Licentia*

In his description of how *libertas pulchra* came to the Palatine and the very naming of her as *libertas pulchra*, Cicero continually suggests (though he does not say it) that what the pontiffs have to give judgment on is actually a private, strictly Clodian, cult. It was not any deity, much less one with importance to the Roman republic who set up camp in Cicero's ruin, but a Greek harlot who was to keep the "licentious tribune" company and drove Cicero's household gods out. That this happened unjustly he can claim by pointing to the *lex Clodia de exsilio Ciceronis* as being a *privilegium*, a law directed at a specific person and therefore not in accordance with ancestral law and illegal.[133] But if this law did not hold up,[134] neither did anything that followed: Clodius had no right to tear down Cicero's house, to plunder his property, to sell what was left of the site and to expand his own house onto formerly Ciceronian grounds. If all that had happened to Cicero's house after he left Rome had no legal basis, than legally (so he argues) the site is still his and the household gods never moved and are still there (he brought only Minerva to the temple of Jupiter).[135] And considering the blatant visibility of the site, Cicero must insist that his house and grounds be returned to him and *libertas pulchra* evicted.

Cicero paints the picture of an extensive, grandiose Clodian *domus* in the middle of the Roman city on the Palatine. The reconstruction of the site depends

---

132 *Cf.* Berg 1997, 133; Bergemann 1992, 76 *vs.* Stroh 2004, 320 n. 41.

133 *Cf.* Coleman-Norton 1950.

134 It was repealed by the Senate prior to Cicero's return: Cic. *red. in Sen.* 27, *red. ad Quir.* 17; *dom.* 75. 87; Cass. Dio 39.8.2.

135 Cic. *leg.* 2.42.

strongly on Cicero's description in *dom.* 115 f.[136] Without going into detail, it is clear that the houses of the antagonists and the portico were in close vicinity to one another. The *domus* of Seius was adjacent to one[137] or both[138] buildings. Clodius was in any case able to connect his own land to that of Cicero via Seius' grounds.[139] Cicero also gives the reason why Clodius would do so: "he wanted to live large and in luxury by connecting two great and noble houses!"[140] By joining his own house to those of Seius and Cicero and incorporating the *porticus Catuli*, Clodius' Palatine home must have been monumental indeed! Overlooking the political center and facing the religious one, the Roman public well understood the visual message:[141] the scion of one of Rome's oldest *gentes* proclaimed himself as central to Rome's politics and *religio* with his cult of *libertas pulchra* as were forum and Capitol. His Palatine home marks the very center of Roman politics[142] – that at least would be Cicero's reading, once again evoking the figure of the tyrant.

What then of the shrine of *libertas pulchra?* From what Cicero says, her sanctuary was part of the *porticus* that was to figure as *amplissimum peristylum* to Clodius' palace.[143] Behind it, "Clodius created a magnificent dwelling area for himself" by joining his own house to that of Seius and Cicero, incorporating also the Catulus portico.[144] The enlarged portico would overlook the forum, facing *urbis [...] celeberrimae et maximae partes*,[145] providing "a shady walkway from which the populace looked into a spacious peristyle that was both an entrance court for Clodius and a glorification of Liberty whose image reigned here."[146] The building complex was supposed to matter to the entire community as the cult most closely connected with one of the leading politicians and advocate of freedom (or tyrant, as Cicero would have it).[147] The cult, however, is personal: by repeated reference to Clodius' house and his grandiose building

136 *Cf.* Berg 1997, Cerutti 1997, Krause 2004, Coarelli 2012, Wiseman 2013.
137 Berg 1997, 128.
138 Krause 2004, 42.
139 *Dom.* 115.
140 *Dom.* 115. *Cf.* Patterson 2010, 222.
141 *Cf.* Hölscher 1987 on the semantics of visuality.
142 Octavian/Augustus saw the advantages of the site as well, *cf.* Wulf-Rheidt 2012.
143 *Dom.* 116.
144 *Cf. dom.* 115.
145 *Dom.* 146.
146 Berg 1997, 132.
147 The cult and temple of Apollo on the Palatine follows the same pattern, underlining, as did the supposed Clodian palace, the centrality and the transgression of private and public in the combination of private home and temple building, *cf.* Wulf-Rheidt 2012.

schemes, the suggestion becomes so strong that the congregated pontiffs cannot have failed to pick up on it. And if it is a personal cult, with no bearing on the *res publica* at large, the state cannot be bound to it – the cult site can easily be moved.[148]

Unfortunately, in describing the building project on the Palatine as a private enterprise that robbed both private individuals (the houses of Cicero and Seius) and the public (*porticus Catuli*) of their possessions, and ascribing *libertas pulchra* a central space within this building complex, Cicero does not shut the Clodian divinity in – he unleashes her on the public. The Clodian deity who should have her place within the *domus* is let out by the open design of the *porticus* architecture, and threatens to wreak as much havoc on the *res publica* as the violent tribune Clodius himself.[149] The figure of the foreign harlot that became a Clodian deity is worthy of his company, they complement one another. Lennon already noted the repeated suggestions of illicit sex in the oration that taint everything and everyone Clodius comes in contact with.[150] Though *libertas pulchra* does not become *licentia* until the later treatise *de legibus*,[151] she is already introduced[152] and contrasted with the very *libertas populi* she supposedly represents: not only does she not stay put in her sanctuary, she cannot even hide her true colors. Cicero warns the pontifical college to not allow *libertas pulchra* houseroom on the Palatine now, to not allow her to enter the Roman public from the comparable privacy of the Clodian *domus*.

Although the houses of the upper Roman class were always in-between public and private, and some Roman politicians, like Cicero, were not only acutely aware of, but fostering that notion, with regard to the Clodian *domus* Cicero would clearly like to draw a much stricter line and keep *libertas pulchra*, i.e., *licentia*, within the house. It was up to the pontifical college to make sure she did, and left Cicero's house in the process, where she clearly did not belong.

That he succeeded was due to legal rather than religious considerations. His house and grounds were returned to him, and the cult site of *libertas pulchra* removed in the process, based on the consideration that *si neque populi iussu neque plebis scitu is qui se dedicasse diceret nominatim ei rei praefectus esset neque populi iussu aut plebis scitu id facere iussus esset videri, posse sine religion eam partem areae mihi restitui* – "if neither by order of the people nor vote of the *plebs* the party alleging that he had dedicated had been appointed by name to

---

148 *Dom.* 121.

149 *Dom.* 105.

150 Lennon 2010.

151 *Leg.* 42.

152 *Dom.* 131, note also *dom.* 47 where *licentia* is directly attributed to the tribune Clodius.

that function, nor by order of the people or vote of the *plebs* had been commanded to do so, we are of opinion that the part of the site in question may be restored to [M. Tullius] without violence to religion".[153] The legal problem is central to the speech.[154] The suggestion that the liberty cult is strictly Clodian is nothing more than subtle rhetorical maneuvering to suggest images and reasons to the audience that may, unconsciously, move them to agree with the orator. Throughout the speech, Cicero had to acknowledge that the cult of *libertas* on the Palatine was a public cult, meant for, and probably accepted by, the Roman community.[155] He could, however, shift the focus ever so slightly to allow his audience to consider the main actor: Clodius the tyrant who wants the whole *res publica* to worship his personal deity, a dead whore from Tanagra.

In the political fighting of the late republic, the war cry "freedom" was heard on all sides. Clodius went further in that he also wanted the people to see. Cicero's house on the Palatine occupied a prominent space – as did the shrine of *libertas*. Though the shrine itself was much smaller than the former consular home, it was joined by the extended *porticus Catuli* to the house of Clodius himself,[156] becoming, in effect, part of both public property (the portico) and the house of Clodius, who thus became linked in the perception of his fellow citizens to the shrine: Clodius stood for *libertas*, and he did so in full view of the city. That the shrine stood on the very site that before had belonged to a consular who had Roman citizens killed without a trial, and whose house was partly left standing in ruins,[157] marked said consular – Cicero – as the tyrant over whom Liberty had triumphed.[158] Clodius understood and spoke the language of symbolism just as well as Cicero did.

In joining his house to the *porticus Catuli* and the shrine of Liberty, Clodius did what Cicero had done before with the purchase of his home on the Palatine hill: he consciously blurs the lines between public and private. Cicero had to extend more effort, living in the public eye and propagating the symbolism and tradition of the house, supported by the claim that he never closed his doors to anyone. Clodius had it easier in that the portico was already there and now became attached to his own house. Unfortunately, however, that also made it possible for the master of rhetoric to draw on the same imagery and incorporate both portico

153 Cic. *Att.* 4.2.3.
154 Stroh 2004.
155 *Cf.* Gildenhard 2011, 302: "Cicero's task was to undo sacred reality".
156 *Dom.* 116.
157 Berg 1997, 130.
158 Against Hales 2000, who emphasizes the eradication of memory by destroying the *domus* of Cicero.

(wrongfully) and *libertas* shrine into the Clodian complex, making it private – and, in effect, no business of the Roman people.

5. From Public to Private: The Avoidance of an Obvious Argument

Cicero's house and grounds were restored to him, and the rebuilding of the Palatine home took place, on a somewhat smaller scale than before. But the episode rankled. That his memory was to be erased from the Roman cityscape, that the visual reminder of his position within the *res publica* was to be turned into a shameful memorial was hard to swallow even with the passage of time.[159]

A source of pride, however, was his oration before the pontiffs.[160] He addresses the pontiffs as guardians of Roman *religiones* and as citizens, exhorting them to consider what is best for the future of the *res publica*, asking them to give judgment on a site within the city where cult had been introduced. He does not ask them to judge the cult, though he suggests[161] that the cult in question is hardly appropriate and deserving of worship. He was invited to, and presents the case as a court matter,[162] and the pontiffs' decision was made based on the fact that Clodius had no leave of the people to institute a new cult in their name, i.e. based on legal concerns, not religious ones.

Throughout the speech, Cicero ever so slyly suggests and hints that the cult in question was not one that concerned the *res publica* at large, i.e. that it was not a public cult, but a strictly private one, a cult only of Clodius himself. Cicero only suggests it, however. He never says it outright and it is not part of his formal argumentation. Why not? Would such an argument not help his case immensely? Would an argumentation and a decision based on these criteria not be the simplest way by far to achieve his ends? Why did he leave that treasure trove untapped?

The simple, and therefore most likely, answer, is that Cicero could not do so. To suggest to his audience that the cult of *libertas* was only a Clodian cult was the most he could do. To say it out loud would be to negate reality. He could lament the inappropriateness of the deity in question and her origins, he could tell them whom he really thought they worshipped ("It is license you venerate, not

---

159 Hales 2000, 45.
160 *Att.* 4.2.2. *Cf.* also Gildenhard 2011, 302 and Stroh 2004 for an evaluation of the speech.
161 *Dom.* 111, 131.
162 Gildenhard 2011, 302. Stroh 2004, 8.

freedom!"), he could associate the deity closely with the "depraved madman" that had driven him into exile and dedicated the image and altar to *libertas* – but he could do no more than that.

The *lex Clodia* included a passage that allowed for the dedication of a cult site on Cicero's former ground.[163] If we follow Wilfried Stroh,[164] that passage formulated a general clause that permitted the erection of statue, altar or shrine, but did not name Clodius as the person to take that dedication upon himself.[165] Surely no insurmountable problem, unless a stickler like Cicero comes along, saying, "you personally had no leave of the people to do so!" Since the land in question, including monument and altar to *libertas*, had been turned over to the public (and was further beautified by a portico)[166] and was situated in a prominent and busy part of the city, it will soon have developed popular appeal. And why not? The Romans took pride in the *libera res publica* – to worship *libertas* as a deity was no stretch!

The matter hinges on the question if Clodius was lawfully elected tribune or not – Cicero says no, of course.[167] If he was never tribune, whatever he did in office is not legally binding, including the dedication. On the other hand, if his transfer to the *plebs* and consequent election as tribune was legal, then he was a regular officeholder and acted as *publicus*, not *privatus* when he exiled Cicero and put up the altar to *libertas*. If he instituted said cult as a tribune on land that has been turned over to the public, we are dealing with a public cult. But if he instituted the cult as Clodius on land that he sought to integrate into his own monumental building complex,[168] the cult remains private – and Cicero does everything to keep the land (rhetorically) out of the hands of the *populus:* Clodius bribes, Clodius lies, Clodius murders to get that land for himself![169]

In Cicero, things tend to be very black and white. There are Cicero and the *boni* on the one hand: the good; and Clodius and his gang of hirelings on the other: the very, very bad. But if Clodius had no support within the populace,

---

163 *Dom.* 51. 106. *Cf.* Wiseman 2012, 658 with references.

164 Stroh 2011.

165 Stroh argues that Cicero based his arguments on that omission: *quis eras* tu *qui dedicabas?* and *sed quaero quae lex lata sit ut* tu *aedis meas consecrares, ubi* tibi *haec potestas data sit, quo iure* <tu> *feceris, dom.* 127 and 128.

166 Berg 1997, 132.

167 *Dom.* 34.

168 Note that Cicero was so successful in painting a grandiose *domus Clodii* in his oration that even today we see the cult of liberty rather within the tribune's house than on public ground, and see before our eyes a Clodian mansion on the Palatine hill, for which we have no other evidence but Cicero's word alone, *cf.* Pepi 1995, Berg 1997, Cerutti 1997.

169 *Dom.* 114. 115. 129.

how did he ever get elected? And why was the rebuilding of the house on the Palatine repeatedly interrupted by violence, if the people were happy to see the land back in human hands?[170]

Truth is that we cannot draw the lines as strictly as Cicero wants us to believe they were. And while he keeps asserting that the cult of *libertas* (i.e., *licentia*) was strictly Clodian, it is much more likely that it had popular appeal that made it necessary for the pontifical college to decide on the matter in order to restore the property to Cicero: a political and juridical decision that found in favor of the consular, and gave the signal that the dismantling of the shrine was to proceed unhindered – which, in fact, it did not.[171] Instead, we read of repeated attempts of what Cicero called "Clodius' hirelings"[172] to interrupt the rebuilding of his home, but which might also have been attempts of former worshippers at the shrine to restore the deity to her property. In hindering them, did Cicero not in fact drive *libertas* away?

In my reading of the sources, Cicero successfully suggested to his audience (both *pontifices* and later readers) that the cult of *libertas* was a strictly Clodian, private cult. He was unable to say so out loud, as it contradicted the situation in Rome, firstly, because Clodius had acted as a magistrate, a public figure, not a private person; and secondly, because the cult was accepted within Rome.

In deciding to rebuild a smaller version of his Palatium,[173] Cicero will have taken this kind of public mood into account and confined himself to a highly visible building that was less ostentatious in that it was smaller, thus trying to avoid the accusation that Clodius and his friends still made: that he, Cicero, had driven *libertas* from Rome.[174]

Works cited

Allen Jr., Walter (1939). "The Location of Cicero's House on the Palatine Hill", *CJ* 35: 134–143.

Allen Jr., Walter (1944). "Cicero's House and Libertas." *TPAPhA* 75: 1–9.

Beck, Hans (2009). "From Poplicola to Augustus: Senatorial Houses in Roman Political Culture." *Phoenix* 63: 361–384.

Benner, Herbert (1987). *Die Politik des P. Clodius Pucher. Untersuchung zur Denaturierung des Clientelwesens in der ausgehenden römischen Republik.* Stuttgart.

170 *Att.* 4.2.3.

171 *Att.* 4.2.3; 3.2.

172 *Att.* 4.3.3.

173 *Att.* 4.5.2.

174 *Att.* 1.16.10, with Allen 1944.

Berg, Beverly (1997). "Cicero's Palatine Home and Clodius' Shrine of Liberty." *Latomus* 8: 122–143.
Bergemann, Claudia (1992). *Politik und Religion im spätrepublikanischen Rom.* Stuttgart.
Cerutti, Steven M. (1997). "The Location of the Houses of Cicero and Clodius and the Porticus Catuli on the Palatine Hill in Rome." *AJPh* 118: 417–426.
Coarelli, Filippo (2012). *Palatium. Il Palatino dalle Origini all'Imperio.* Roma: 303–336.
Coleman-Norton, P.R. (1950). "Cicero's Contribution to the Text of the Twelve Tables", *CJ* 46: 127–134.
Cooper, Kate (2007). "Closely Watched Households. Visibility, Exposure and Private Power in the Roman *domus*", *Past & Present* 197: 3–33.
Gelzer, Matthias (1969). *Cicero. Ein biographischer Versuch.* Wiesbaden.
Gildenhard, Ingo (2011). *Creative Eloquence. The Construction of Reality in Cicero's Speeches.* Oxford.
Gosling, Anne (1986). "Octavian, Brutus and Apollo: A Note on Opportunist Propaganda", *AJPh* 107: 586–589.
Hales, Shelley (2000). "At Home With Cicero", *Greece & Rome* 41: 44–55.
Hofer, Marc (2000). *Tyrannen, Aristokraten, Demokraten: Untersuchungen zu Staat und Herrschaft im griechischen Sizilien von Phalaris bis zum Aufstieg von Dionysios I.* Bern.
Hölscher, Tonio (1987). *Römische Bildsprache als semantisches System.* Heidelberg.
Itgenshorst, Tanja (2005). *Tota illa pompa. Der Triumph in der römischen Republik.* Göttingen.
Krause, Clemens (2001). "In conspectu totius urbis (Cic. dom. 100). Il tempio della libertà e il quartiere alto del Palatino", *Eutopia:* 169–201.
Krause, Clemens (2004). "Die *Domus* Tiberiana – Vom Wohnquartier zum Kaiserpalast", in Adolf Hoffman and Ulrike Wulf, eds., *Die Kaiserpaläste auf dem Palatin in Rom.* Mainz: 32–58.
Leach, Eleanor W. (2001). "Gendering Clodius", *CW* 94: 335–359.
Lennon, Jack (2010). "Pollution and Ritual Impurity in Cicero's *de domo sua*", *CQ* 60: 427–445.
Manuwald, Gesine (2007). *Cicero, Philippics 3–9 in Two Volumes.* Vol. 1: Introduction, Text and Translation. Vol. 2: Commentary. Berlin, New York.
Mommsen, Theodor (1871). *Römisches Staatsrecht I.* Handbuch der Römischen Alterthümer 1. Eds. Joachim Marquardt and Theodor Mommsen. Leipzig.
Mommsen, Theodor (1886). *Römisches Staatsrecht III.1.* Handbuch der Römischen Alterthümer 1. Eds. Joachim Marquardt and Theodor Mommsen. Leipzig.
Orlin, Eric M. (1997). *Temples, Religion and Politics in the Roman Republic.* Leiden.
Patterson, John R. (2010). "The City of Rome Revisited: From Mid-Republic to Mid-Empire", *JRS* 100: 210–232.
Pepi, I. (1995). "*domus:* P. Clodius Pulcher", *LTUR* 2, 85–86.
Picard, G. Ch. (1965). "L'aedes Libertatis de Clodius au Palatin", *REL* 44: 229–237.
Roller, Matthew (2010). "Demolished Houses, Monumentality and Memory in Roman Culture", *Classical Antiquity* 29: 117–180.
Rüpke, Jörg (2007). *Historische Religionswissenschaft. Eine Einführung.* Religionswissenschaft heute 5. Stuttgart.
Rundell, W.M.F. (1979). "Cicero and Clodius. The Question of Credibility", *Historia* 28: 301–328.

Stroh, Wilfried (2004). "De Domo Sua: Legal Problem and Structure", in Jonathan Powell and Jeremy Paterson, eds., *Cicero the Advocate*, Oxford: 313–370.
Stroh, Wilfried (2010). "Cicero und die römische Religion". *Memorabilia* 6: 1–19.
Tatum, W. Jeffrey (1993). "The lex Papiria de Dedicationibus", *CPh* 88: 319–328.
Tatum, W. Jeffrey (1999). *The Patrician Tribune. Publius Clodius Pulcher.* Chapel Hill.
Treggiari, Susan (1998). "Home and Forum: Cicero between ›Public‹ and ›Private‹", *TAPhA* 128: 1–23.
Wallace-Hadrill, Andrew (1988). "The Social Structure of the Roman House", *PBSR* 56: 43–97.
Wiseman, T.P. (1970). "Pulcher Claudius", *HSCPh* 74: 207–221.
Wiseman, T.P. (2012). "Where did they live (e.g., Cicero, Octavius, Augustus)?" *JRA* 25: 656–672.
Wiseman, T.P. (2013). "The Palatine, from Evander to Elagabalus", *JRS* 103: 234–268.
Wissowa, Georg (1887). "Die Überlieferung über die römischen Penaten", *Hermes* 22: 29–57.
Wissowa, Georg (1897). "Lares", *Ausführliches Lexikon der griechischen und römischen Mythologie.* Ed. Wilhelm H. Roscher, vol. 2.2, 1868–1897.
Wulf-Rheidt, Ulrike (2012). "Augustus und das Gespür für den richtigen Ort. Die Situierung der ersten Kaiserresidenz auf dem Palatin in Rom", in F. Arnold, A. Busch and R. Haensch, eds., *Orte der Herrschaft. Charakteristika von antiken Machtzentren.* Rahden: 33–40.

William Van Andringa

5. “M. Tullius … aedem Fortunae August (ae) solo et peq(unia) sua”

Private foundation and Public Cult in a Roman Colony

Abstract: The case of the well-documented temple of Fortuna Augusta in Pompeii presents scholars with an opportunity to consider the privately financed foundation of a temple built to house the public cult of Fortuna Augusta in the Augustan era. As indicated by the dedicatory inscription, the temple was built *solo et pequnia sua* by M. Tullius, a prominent member of the local aristocracy. The epigraphic formula in the inscription can be related to a precise location: the *aedes* was erected on private ground whereas the altar was built on a public street. Regarding the local history of Pompeii, one must stress the strategy employed in the Augustan era by a member of the local aristocracy to bring the private and public spheres closer. If we reflect on the dedicatory inscriptions from the end of the Republic, it seems that from the Augustan period onwards, the élites identified themselves with the state rather than merely acting on behalf of it: that is the meaning of *solo et pecunia sua*.

1. Introduction

Admittedly very little information on the subject of temple foundations in Roman colonies and cities can be found in literary or epigraphic sources.[1] However, it is well known that on principle cult places were defined by Roman law as extrapatrimonial property belonging to the gods and thus stood apart from the domain of appropriation and exchange reserved for humans.[2] As is stated in the *Institutes* of Gaius, “what is under divine law cannot be private property” (2.2). The divisions between divine and human law were articulated according to this principle. Human law distinguishes between public and private, whereas sacred law divides the consecrated spaces into three categories: the *loca sacra* which refers to the places and things dedicated to the gods, the *loca religiosa*, a term that designates the tombs and places struck by lightning, and finally

1 In this respect, the *lex aedis Furfensis* (*CIL* IX, 3513 = *ILS* 4906) is quite an exceptional document, cf. Laffi 1978.

2 Thomas 2002, 1433f., De Souza 2004, Estienne 2008. See also Mommsen, Marquardt 1889, 174f.

the *loca sancta*, a category that concerns the divine protection of town walls in particular (Gaius, *Inst.* 2.9). According to this definition sacred or religious places do not fall into the legal category of public property. Yet ancient legal texts underline the fact that sanctuaries, like public places, are classified as a type of inalienable property controlled by the city-state. In other words, the public sanctuary is neither defined by the plot where it stands, nor by its founder or dedicator - this could be the city, the magistrates or an individual - but by the status of the cult as defined by the community. In the Roman Empire and its cities a distinction was made between rites and ceremonies performed at public expense on behalf of the people – *quae publico sumptu pro populo* – and private ones, celebrated on behalf of individual persons, households, or family lineages: *pro singulis hominibus, familiis, gentibus* (Festus 284 L).

It was within this general framework that temples for public ceremonies, officially inscribed in the calendar of a Roman colony, were founded (*Roman Statutes* no. 25, chapters 64, 70 and 71). A temple or an altar could be erected on demand by the city-state or by a private person who was willing and able to finance the monument (*pecunia sua*).

Sometimes the benefactor mentioned that the *aedes* dedicated for a public cult was in fact built on private land: *solo et pequnia sua*. The meaning of this peculiar epigraphic formula, which abounded from the Augustan period, is the focus of this chapter. Since we are familiar with the names of some of the benefactors or magistrates responsible for the construction and restoration of the urban temples in ancient Pompeii and since we have good archaeological knowledge of the sanctuaries in this urban setting, the city offers itself as a prime site for the investigation of the aforementioned formula. I would like to focus on one well-documented example, namely that of the temple of Fortuna Augusta. As the dedicatory inscription of the temple indicates that it was constructed *solo et pequnia sua* and since a recent archaeological survey has provided a good working knowledge of the history of the building, the Fortuna Augusta Temple represents a particularly suitable case for historical analysis.[3] Based on the this example I claim that the epigraphic formula attributed to the monument was not used by chance but selected intentionally. By founding a temple dedicated to public ceremonies on private ground, the benefactor marked not only his devotion to the state but also managed to highlight the strong influence of the local élite in the construction of public cults and the celebration of *publica sacra*.

3 Van Andringa 2009, 56f. Recent archaeological reports are available on : http://cefr.revues.org/355 ; http://cefr.revues.org/974.

2. The temple of Fortuna Augusta at Pompeii

The pseudo-peripteral Corinthian temple of Fortuna Augusta at Pompeii was built by Marcus Tullius, an eminent member of the local aristocracy, in the last years of the first century BC during the reign of Augustus. It was located at an important intersection to the north of the Forum (**fig. 1 and 2**). The excavation in 1823-24 revealed a series of nine inscriptions documenting the precise context of the temple's founding (*CIL* X, 820 *sq.*): we know that M. Tullius built the *aedes* on his land and at his own expense. However, the available evidence also suggests that at least from AD 3 onwards the cult of Fortuna Augusta was organized by public authorities when the city council appointed the first *Ministri Fortunae Augustae*, responsible for the organization of the cult (*CIL* X, 824). This information has now been completed by some recent archaeological observations, allowing us to study the use of private and public spaces in the different construction phases of the temple and the annexes dedicated to the *Ministri*. The construction process of the Fortuna Augusta temple began with the demolition of the houses formerly situated on the plot and was concluded with the final dedication of the temple which took place in a densely urbanized area close to the Forum. As always the archaeological evidence consists of much data outlining the ways the spaces were occupied and *the architectural choices that were made* before and during the construction of the temple. In this case, archaeology doesn't only provide us with new historical facts, but also confronts us with a plethora of issues that suggest the importance of renewed scholarly reflection on the question of urban temple foundations.

Among the inscriptions found in the *cella* is the commemorative stone (*titulus*), which was installed above the cult statue of Fortuna (*CIL* X, 820):

> *M(arcus) Tullius M(arci) f(ilius), d(uum)v(ir) i(ure) d(icundo) ter(tium), quinq(uennalis), augur, tr(ibunus) mil(itum) / a pop(ulo) aedem Fortunae August(ae) solo et peq(unia) sua.*
>
> Marcus Tullius, son of Marcus, duumvir with judicial power three times,quinquennial, augur, military tribune by popular demand, (built) the Temple of Fortuna Augusta on his own land and at his own expense.

We know from this dedicatory inscription that the founder of the temple, M. Tullius, was the holder of many important municipal and religious offices and was elected *duumvir iure dicundo* three times. Later he held the highest local office of *quinquennalis*. In addition, he was augur and was awarded the honorific title of *tribunus militum a populo* (military tribune by recommendation of the people), a

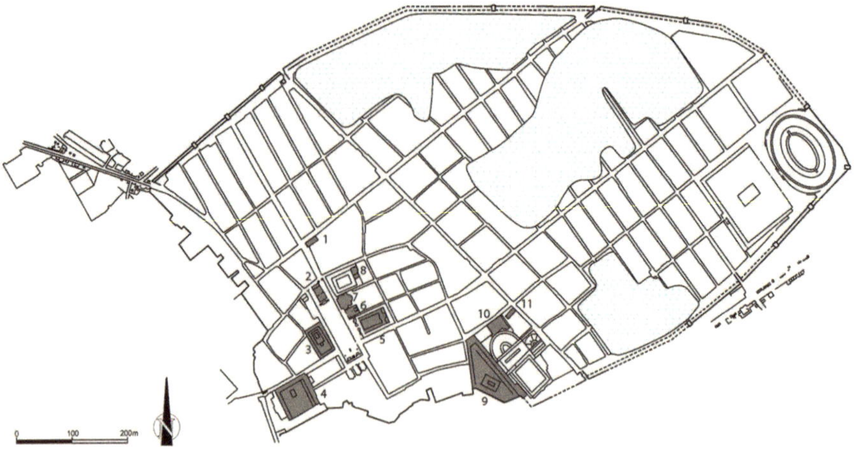

Fig. 1: Sanctuaries of Pompeii (DAO: Carole Chevalier): 1. Temple of Fortuna Augusta, 2. Capitolium, 3. Temple of Apollo, 4. Temple of Venus, 5. Porticus of Concordia Augusta and Pietas, 6. Temple of Augustus, 7. Sanctuary of the Domus Divina (?), 8. Temple of Mercurius (?), 9. Temple of Minerva, 10. Temple of Isis, 11. Temple of Asclepius.

Fig. 2: The temple of Fortuna Augusta from the West (photograph: Johannes Laiho).

designation that made him reach the equestrian order.[4] The Emperor's bestowing of the title of *tribunus militum a populo* indicates a closer acquaintances between Augustus and Tullius. It is likely that this relationship motivated the strong ideological and political focus of the temple and played a significant role in the selection of the cult. The goddess installed on the property of Tullius was indeed Fortuna Augusta, the goddess who accompanied imperial action with *Felicitas*. P. Zanker emphasized that the construction of the temple in the years preceding AD 3 has to be related to the special favour given to imperial Fortuna in Rome. The exceptional status of the goddess is reflected by the dedication of the altar of Fortuna Redux at the Porta Capena in 19 BC, as well as by the celebration of Augustus' triumphal return from the eastern part of the Empire and the consecration of the altar of Pax Augusta following his journey to the West in 9 BC .[5] Admittedly, the meaning of the cult at Pompeii is somewhat distinct, for Fortuna is not *Redux* or *Augusti*, the special protector of Augustus, but *Augusta*, a name that could express the proximity between the goddess and the ambitious political action of Augustus. In addition *Augusta* should not be considered a mere divine epithet because Fortuna Augusta was clearly conceived as a new cult founded in the Augustan period, in the precise context of the establishment of the Principate.[6]

In the case of the Fortuna temple in Pompeii, the meaning of the formula *aedem solo et pequnia sua* partially reveals itself through the remains of the temple and its location in the area. The boundaries precisely correspond to the borders of Tullius' property (even if the North-West angle was built on the pavement). At the same time the *aedes* mentioned in the inscription acts as the podium of the temple, supporting the *pronaos* and the *cella*, where the goddess used to stand in her majesty.[7] As in the case of the temple of Furfo (*CIL* IX, 3513), the *aedes* in the Fortuna temple appears not to have included the altar. Once the masonry of the podium was built, a frontal staircase was added and the altar was installed on a white limestone platform extending onto the street. Since the temple was entirely decorated with white Luni marble, the designers must have consciously chosen to use a different stone for the platform of the altar. It was the fact that the platform of the altar had been deliberately built in a public space that made this monument truly original. In order to separate the temple from the busy street a high-quality iron fence was erected around the platform.

---

4 Nicolet 1967.

5 Zanker 1993.

6 See Gradel 2002 : 103-106.

7 On the term *aedes*, see De Ruggiero, *Dizionario Epigrafico, s.v. aedes*, 150f. Not to mention that *aedes* has very often the general meaning of temple, see Dubourdieu, Scheid, 2000, 66-71.

The fence had two entrances, one on each side. The two corners facing the street were protected from the traffic by two bumper stones. This intentional act of placing the altar by an open street was certainly related to the public status of the cult. Locating the altar on the side of a street created a public site for the Fortuna cult and stressed the rapprochement of public and private spheres. The *aedes* was constructed *solo et pequnia sua*, while the altar was erected on public ground. This very peculiar layout must have been the result of negotiations between the benefactor and the *ordo decurionum*.

After the space of the *cella* had been sanctified during a ceremony called *consecratio*, the statues of the gods and the cult partners could be installed.[8] They were arranged according to specific rules, which reflected the divine hierarchy and symbolised the relationship between the goddess, the emperor and the benefactor.[9] The podium built against the interior back wall of the temple served as the pedestal for the now missing statue of Fortuna. The statue of the tutelary goddess occupied an axial position in the temple raised above the floor in a position of majesty. On each side one can find two niches that held life-sized statues of mortals that were dedicated to Fortuna Augusta.[10] One statue depicts the temple's benefactor M. Tullius, while the other represents Emperor Augustus (*CIL* X, 823). These statues were not the primary addressess of the cult; they belonged to the *ornamenta* of the temple and were meant to pay homage to these two great men. Fortuna Augusta was clearly a cult created especially for the Pompeian community. Its emergence marked a particular moment in local history at which the city began to forge a close relationship with the new imperial power through a member of its elite.

Based on the inscription on another statue base found in the *cella* we know that from AD 3 onwards a four-member collegium was in charge of organizing the cult activities (*CIL* X, 824):

> *Agathemerus Vetti / Suavis Caesiae Prim(a)e / Pothus Numitori / Anteros Lacutulani / minist(ri) prim(i) Fortun(ae) Aug(ustae) iuss(u) / M(arci) Stai Rufi Cn(aei) Melissaei d(uum)v(irorum) i(ure) d(icundo) / P(ublio) Silio L(ucio) Volusio Saturn(ino) co(n)s(ulibus).*

---

8 The act of dedication is known by several inscriptions (Furfo, Salone, Narbonne). When the temple is completed, the magistrate under the dictation of the pontiff, expresses publicly the transfer of the good to the god (by holding the jambs of the door); he defines then the status of goods allocated to the sanctuary and the ritual rules. The temple or at least a part of it is then sacred: Macrobe, *Sat.* 3, 3, 2 and Festus, p. 424 L.

9 For the status of images in the Roman temples, see Steuernagel 2010 and Estienne 2010.

10 On the images of mortals dedicated to the gods, Veyne 1962, 87f. On the relations established by means of temple-sharing, Price 1984, 146-156 and more recently Steuernagel 2010 and Estienne 2010, also Van Andringa 2012 for the variety of local combinations.

Agathemerus, slave of Vettius; Suavis, slave of Caesia Prima; Pothus, slave of Numitor; Anteros, slave of Lacutulanus, the first attendants (ministri) of Augustan Fortune, by command of Marcus Staius Rufus and Gnaeus Melissaeus, duumvirs with judicial power, in the consulship of Publius Silius and Lucius Volusius Saturninus.

According to the rules of their association (a *lex Fortunae Augustae ministrorum* is mentioned by *CIL* X, 825), the *ministri* were required to perform sacrifices and to dedicate statues to the temple upon the accession of a new emperor. These ministers were recruited among the slaves or freedmen of the town's most influential families. They can be identified as the *apparitores* named by the city in the *lex Ursonensis*.[11] It is also very likely that the aforementioned *ministri* lived in the attached residential building situated on Tullius' private property, just beside the temple. Several trenches made at the foot of the podium have confirmed that, despite modern disturbances of the soil, the temple construction and the use of the attached house occurred concurrently. We know from an inscription found next to the temple that while the temple was dedicated to the goddess, the attached building remained in Tullius' private property (*CIL* X, 821):

M. Tulli M. f. / area privata

Private land of Marcus Tullius, son of Marcus.

3. *Solo et Pecunia Sua*: a New Kind of Benefaction?

Keeping in mind the location of the temple and the extent of building activity at Pompeii in the Augustan era one might wonder why M. Tullius did not choose to construct the temple on the eastern side of the Forum where all the divinities related to the imperial power were to be found. The *porticus* of Eumachia dedicated to *Concordia Augusta* and *Pietas*, as well as the *templum Augusti* were both been built in this area. However, the dedicatory inscription suggests that M. Tullius intentionally elected to erect the new temple, or at least the *aedes*, on his own property. It is also crucial to point out that the Augustan aristocracy in Pompeii inaugurated a new era with regards to the private aspect of such foundations.[12] M. Tullius is not the only one to dedicate a religious building *solo et pequnia*

---

11 *Roman Statutes* no. 25, chapter 128.

12 Zanker 1992, see also D'Arms 2003 and Van Andringa 2013, 145-214.

sua.[13] Mamia, a member of one of Pompeii's most prominent families, also built a temple to a *genius* on her private property.

> *Mamia P. f. sacerdos public(a) geni[o -- s]olo et pec[unia sua]*
>
> Mamia, daughter of Publius, public priestess, [built this] to the genius [of the colony/of Augustus] on her own land and at [her own] expense.

The missing part of the inscription does not allow for a precise reading of the text, which could refer to both the *genius Augusti* or the *genius* of the *colonia*.[14] The original location of the stone is not known either. Yet, considering its length, the inscription likely belonged to a monumental building. According to the finds of recent excavations it could have been one of the 'municipal buildings' erected in the Augustan period.[15] We know that before Augustus the area south of the Forum was largely occupied by houses. Hence the kind of benefaction involving private property seems to have been new and not merely a by-product of the intensification of building activity in the Augustan period. In the decades following the foundation of the colony and towards the end of the Republic several preserved dedicatory inscriptions referred to magistrates acting *de decurionum sententia* or *ex d(ecreto) d(ecurionum)*. This strategy corresponded with the regulations regarding games and monuments that were outlined by municipal law (*ILLRP* 648 = *CIL* X, 829 – Baths of Stabiae):

> *C. Uulius C. f., P. Aninius C. f. IIv(iri) i(ure) d(icundo) / laconicum et destrictarium / faciund(a) et porticus et palaestr(am) / reficiunda(s) locarunt ex d(ecreto) d(ecurionum), ex / ea pequnia quod eos e lege / in ludos aut in monumento / consumere oportuit faciun(da) / coerarunt eidemque probaru(nt).*
>
> Gaius Uulius, son of Gaius, and Publius Aninius, son of Gaius, duumvirs with judicial power, contracted out the construction of the sweating-room (*laconicum*) and scraping-room (*destrictarium*) and the rebuilding of the porticoes and the exercise area (*palaestra*), by decree of the town councillors, with that money which by law they were obliged to

---

13 Except Pompeii, the formula is not very often attested. This seems to confirm that the formula was intentional and adapted to a precise kind of benefaction. Temples founded *solo et pecunia sua* are known in Carinola (*CIL* X, 4717), Brescia (*CIL* V, 4266), Albacina (*CIL* XI, 5687), Città di Castello (*CIL* XI, 5928), Ferento (*CIL* XI, 7431), in Spain (CIL II^5, 276), in Dougga (CIL VIII, 1473 = 15522 and VIII, 1493, see Saint Amans 2004), etc. Other monuments were also constructed *solo et pecunia sua* like in Ostia (*crypta and chalcidicum*, *AE* 2005, 301), Spoleto (*basilica*, *CIL* XI, 4819), Mactar (a tomb ?, *AE* 1949, 30), Munigua (*porticus*, *CIL* II, 1074), Barcino (*Balineum*, *CIL* II, 4509), Cartama (unknown building, *CIL* II, 5488).

14 Gradel 2002, 80 proposes the development *genius coloniae*; Zanker 1992, Torelli 1998 and Letta 2003 prefer to understand *genius Augusti*.

15 Kockel, Flecker 2008.

spend either on games or on a monument. They saw to the building work, and also approved it.

At that time, the magistrates dutifully followed the rulings of the local senate, particularly by spending the money which the municipal regulation had allocated to games and monuments. According to the inscriptions, they were consistently in charge of the new construction projects and of their approval (*CIL* X, 819 – Baths of the forum):

L. Caesius C. f., d(uum)v(ir) i(ure) d(icundo), / C. Occius M. f., / L. Niraemius A. f. IIv(iri) / d(e) d(ecurionum) s(ententia) ex peq(unia) publ(ica) / fac(iundum) curar(unt) prob(arunt)q(ue).

Lucius Caesius, son of Gaius, duumvir with judicial power, Gaius Occius, son of Marcus, Lucius Niraemius, son of Aulus, duumvirs, by decree of the town councillors and with public money. They saw to the building work, and also approved it.

Following a similar formula, which undoubtedly repeated the procedure specified in the municipal regulations, other inscriptions inform us about the construction of porticoes (*porticus faciendas coeravit, CIL* X, 794) and a portion of a wall (*murum et plumam faciundum coeraverunt eidemque probaverunt, CIL* X, 937). Sometimes, the source of the funds is mentioned. The magistrates could act by using public money (*ex pequnia publica faciundum curaverunt, CIL* X, 938) but they were also allowed to fund projects through their private income. As the dedicatory inscription of the amphitheatre indicates when a benefactor spent extra money, the act was intended *coloniai honoris caussa*, to honour the colony (*CIL* X, 852):

C. Quinctius C. f. Valgus, / M. Porcius M. f. duovir(i) / quinq(uennales) coloniai honoris / caussa spectacula de sua / peq(unia) fac(iunda) coer(arunt) et coloneis / locum in perpetuom deder(unt).

Gaius Quinctius Valgus, son of Gaius, and Marcus Porcius, son of Marcus, quinquennial duumvirs, for the honour of the colony, saw to the construction of the amphitheatre at their own expense and gave the area to the colonists in perpetuity.

This very conventional procedure that has been well documented throughout Republican Italy,[16] stands in stark contrast to the Augustan period, when the inscriptions more often stressed the personal involvement of the local élite. If we go back to Tullius, the link established between the temple foundation and

16 Examples are numerous : *ILLRP* 519 (Abellae), 521 (Aceruntiae), 522 (Aeclani), 529 (Aletrii), 559, 566 (Castrum Novum), 571 etc.

his own private property is reminiscent of the procedure followed by Octavian/Augustus in the foundation of the temple of Apollo on the Palatine. After the victory of Naulochus in 36 BC Octavian decided to acquire land on the Palatine for a property that he made available for public use (Dio 49.15.5). When lightning struck in the area not long after it was seen as a miracle and a sign from Apollo. While Augustus was augur he decided to build a marble temple at his own expense and on his own land, which was formally dedicated on 9 October 28 BC. We also know from Dio that in AD 3, the house of Augustus was declared to the public for two reasons: first as a sign of recognition of and gratitude for the generosity of the Roman people and, second, because Augustus was Pontifex Maximus and so was supposed to live in a house considered both public and private. Augustus' decision demonstrated devotion to the state and led to the rapprochement of the public and private spheres. This act was then further reinforced by the founding of a temple that housed a public cult on private land.

4. Founding the temple of Fortuna Augusta in the Urban landscape: Private Ground and Public crossroads (fig. 3)

Like Augustus's house on the Palatine, the construction of Tullius's temple was undertaken in the context of the urban development of a Pompeian neighbourhood that was largely the property of Tullius. We have some archaeological evidence regarding the scale of Tullius's urban estate. Firstly, the boundary stone located at the entrance of the attached residential building reveals that this area remained in Tullius' private property. The *Porticus Tulliana* (so called by Della Corte) south of the temple cuts into the walkway, thus linking the temple to the Forum. The portico has to be seen as a monumental entrance to the sacred complex founded by Tullius. It is unclear when Tullius became owner of the area although it is probable that his family settled in the area around the time the colony was founded. However, it is also possible that he purchased the well-situated plot near the Forum in the Augustan period when he became a politically active member of the city. Following the example of Augustus, he allocated part of his private property to a public cult and subsequently built a temple dedicated to a goddess who guaranteed the success of the imperial action. The date of this transfer is known to us thanks to an inscription recording the nomination of the first *ministri Fortunae Augustae* in AD 3 by the city council. This nomination of official attendants proves that the cult of Fortuna belonged to *publica sacra* at the time.

Fig. 3: Aerial view of the temple (photograph: Johannes Laiho).

One other criterion factored into the selection process for a plot of land for temple construction. The building was erected north of the Forum at an important intersection, which was completely modified as a consequence (**fig. 4 and 5**). The construction of the altar directly on the street permanently changed the urban landscape. Before the existence of the temple the street leading to the Forum used to widen at the intersection so as to form a small square. Thanks to recent excavations we know that the enlarged street dates back to the third or even the very beginning of the second century BC. when the town underwent a period of development following the Roman conquest of Campania.

Why the location for the Fortuna Augusta temple was chosen in such a manner that the altar was situated directly on the street, a public space, cannot be understood without paying attention to another important intersection in the city. At said intersection a four-sided arch that bridged the street was built at exactly the same time by another member of the local élite, namely Marcus Holco-

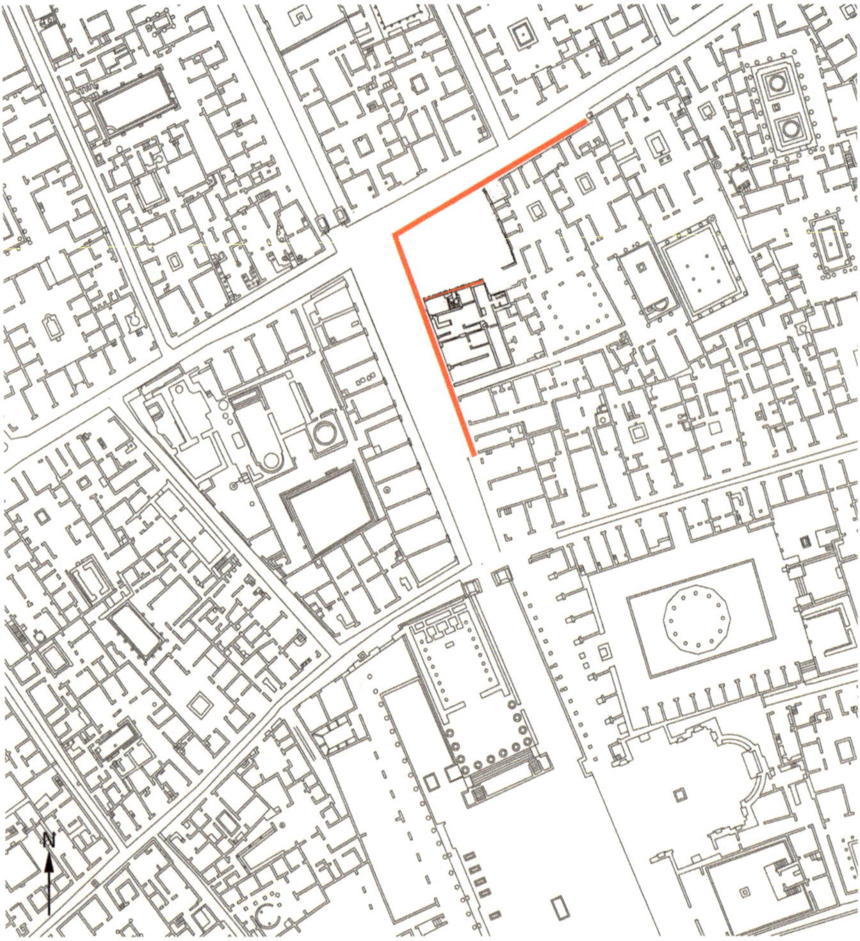

Fig. 4: Map showing the crossroads before the construction of the temple.

nius Rufus, the likely benefactor of the monument.[17] The tetrapylon incorporated a series of statues that portrayed Rufus himself in much the same manner Tullius was depicted in the *cella* of his temple. The similarities of the two projects are striking. Both are built at central intersections that subsequently became enlarged. Furthemore both were ultimately public spaces financed by the local elite. Finally Rufus' tetrapylon was constructed right by the street just like the altar of Fortuna. These monuments highlighted and further manifested a subtle

17 Müller 2011.

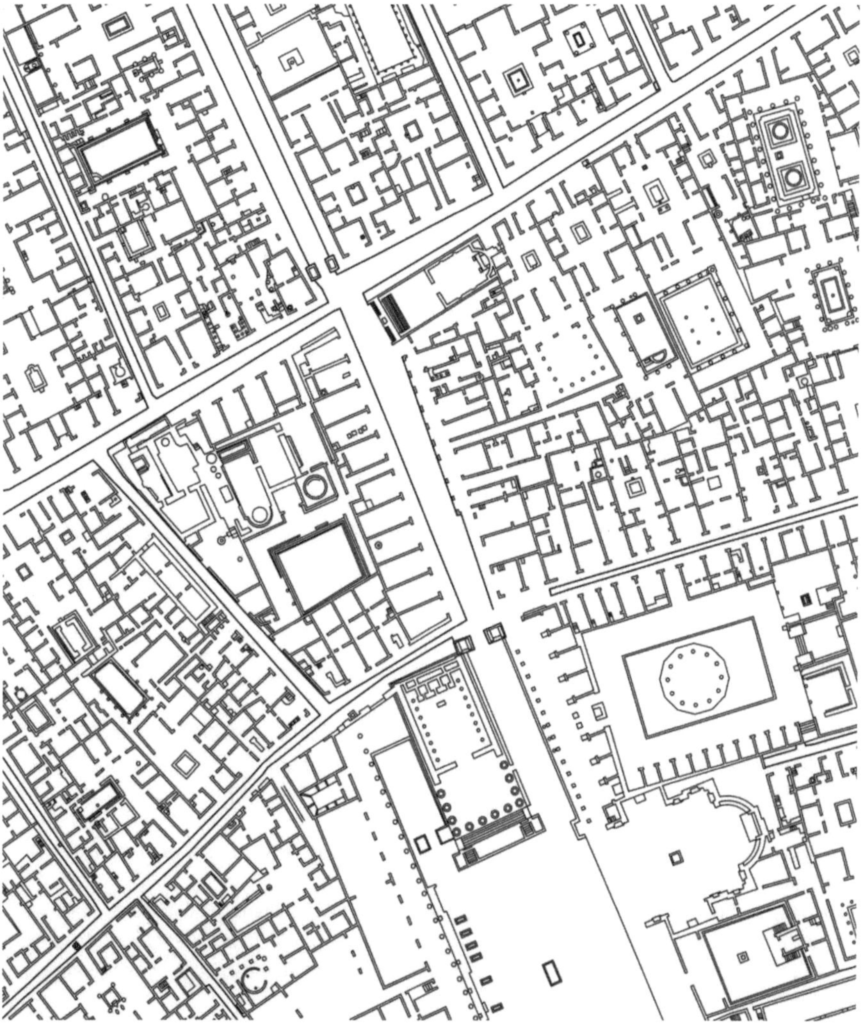

Fig. 5: Map showing the crossroads after the construction of the temple.

dialogue between private and public spaces and a ultimately represented a symbolic *mise-en-scène* expressing the close relations between the benefactors and Augustus. In the urban landscape they established a strong relationship between the local aristocraty and the new imperial power. The two men also had similar political careers. Like Marcus Tullius M. Holconius was the holder of many important municipal and religious offices and was also awatded the honorific title of *tribunus militum a populo*. Clearly the founding of the temple of Fortuna

Augusta and the tetrapylon depended on two conditions: the occupation of public spaces and the aristocratic competition. This behaviour should be understood as a direct consequence of the political changes at Rome.

We find ourselves in AD 3: The *aedes*, fully decorated with white marble from Luni, is completed; the statues are installed; the first attendants, the *ministri*, are nominated, while their residential building remained in Tullius' private property. In the presence of M. Tullius, the magistrate of the city publicly declared the transfer of the temple before defining the status of the goods allocated to the sanctuary and spelling out the ritual rules. At the same time, the *lex Fortunae Augustae ministrorum* was announced, as mentioned in one inscription (*CIL* X, 825). The list of the first four *ministri* from AD 3 shows that the dedication may have taken place the same year, corresponding to the public announcement of the cult. Whether or not these events belong to the local history of Pompeii, one must stress the strategy employed by a member of the local Augustan aristocracy to bring the private and public spheres closer. From the Augustan period onwards elites no longer only worked *for* the state but also identified themselves *with* the state. Such is the meaning of *solo et pecunia sua*.

Works cited

Ando, C., and J. Rüpke, eds (2006). *Religion and law in classical and Christian Rome.* Potsdamer altertumswissenschaftliche Beiträge 15. Stuttgart.

D'Alessio, M. T. (2009). *I culti a Pompei. Divinità, luoghi e frequentatori (VI secolo a.c.–79 d. c.).* Roma.

D'Arms, J. H. (2003). *Romans on the Bay of Naples and other essays on Roman Campania.* Bari.

Estienne, S. (2008). "Éléments pour une définition rituelle des 'espaces consacrés' à Rome," in X. Dupré Raventos, S. Ribichini, S. Verger, eds., *Saturnia Tellus. Definizioni dello spazio consacrato in ambiente etrusco, italic, fenicio-punico, iberico e celtico.* Roma: 687-698.

Estienne, S. (2010). *Simulacra deorum* versus *ornamenta aedium.* The status of divine images in the temples of Rome. In J. Mylonopoulos ed. *Divine Images and Human Imaginations in Ancient Greece and Rome.* Religions in the Graeco-Roman World, 170. Leiden-Boston: 257-271.

De Souza, M. (2004). *La question de la tripartition des catégories du droit divin dans l'Antiquité romaine.* Saint-Étienne.

Kockel, V., Flecker M. (2008). "Forschungen im Südteil des Forums von Pompeji. Ein Vorbericht über die Arbeitkampagnen 2007 und 2008." *RM* 114: 271-303.

Letta, C. (2003). "Novità epigrafiche sul culto del *Genius Augusti* in Italia," in M. G. Angeli Bertinelli, A. Donati, eds., *Serta Antiqua et Mediaevalia VI. Usi e abusi epigrafici. Atti del Colloquio Internazionale di Epigrafia Latina (Genova 20-22 settembre 2001).* Roma: 217-236.

Gradel, I. (2002). *Emperor Worship and Roman Religion*. Oxford Classical Monographs. Oxford.

Mommsen, Th., Marquardt, J. (1889). *Manuel des Antiquités Romaines, T. XII*. Paris.

Müller, K. (2011). *Die Ehrenbögen in Pompeji*. Reichert Verlag.

Nicolet, C. (1967). "Tribuni militum a populo." *Mélanges d'archéologie et d'histoire*, 79: 29-76.

Nock, A. D. (1972). "Synnaos theos." In *Essays on Religion and the Ancient World*. Oxford: 202-251.

Price, S.R.F. (1984). *Rituals and Power. The Roman imperial Cult in Asia Minor*. Cambridge.

Saint-Amans, S. (2004). *Topographie religieuse de Thugga (Dougga), ville romaine d'Afrique proconsulaire (Tunisie)*. Bordeaux.

Steuernagel, D. (2010). "*Synnaos theos*. Images of Roman Emperors in Greek temples." In J. Mylonopoulos ed. *Divine Images and Human Imaginations in Ancient Greece and Rome*. Religions in the Graeco-Roman World, 170. Leiden-Boston : 241-256.

Thomas, Y. (2002). "La valeur des choses. Le droit romain hors de la religion." *Annales HSS* 2002: 1431-62.

Torelli, M. (1998). "Il culto imperial a Pompei," in *I Culti della Campania Antica. Atti del convegno internazionale di studi in ricordo di N. Valenza Mele (Napoli, 1995)*, Roma: 245-270.

Van Andringa, W. (2009). *Quotidien des dieux et des hommes. La vie religieuse dans les cités du Vésuve à l'époque romaine*. Bibliothèque des Écoles françaises d'Athènes et de Rome 337. Rome.

Van Andringa, W. (2012). "Statues in the Temples of Pompeii. Combinations of Gods, Local Definition of Cults and the Memory of the City," in B. Dignas, B. Smith, eds., *Historical and Religious Memory in the Ancient World*. Oxford: 83-115.

Van Andringa, W. (2013). *Pompéi. Mythologie et histoire*. Paris.

Veyne, P. (1962). "Les honneurs posthumes de Flavia Domitilla." *Latomus* 21: 49-98.

Zanker, P. (1992). *Pompei. Società, immagini urbane e forme dell'abitare*. Turin.

Judith Evans Grubbs

6. Making the Private Public: Illegitimacy and Incest in Roman Law

Abstract: The nature of the Roman family, and its relationship to concepts of "public" and "private" in antiquity, are notoriously problematic. This paper examines one aspect of Roman familial relationships and their interplay with more "public" concerns: the situation of illegitimate children in Roman law from the reign of Augustus through the reign of Diocletian, whose legislation marks a change in attitude. After a look at the social and legal condition of illegitimate children in general (both slaveborn *naturales* and freeborn *spurii*), I consider the special case of children born of incestuous marriages. Unlike other illegitimate relationships, incest was considered a matter of religious, and therefore public, concern from the earliest period. Yet until the reign of Diocletian, Roman law appears to have been flexible in regard to individual cases. Diocletian's legislation, both rescripts to imperial officials and his famous edict on close-kin marriages, condemns close-kin marriage as both un-Roman and offensive to the gods of the Romans, uniting concerns with private morals, public safety, and religious piety.

1. Introduction

In their Introduction, the editors of this volume reflect on the broad existence of a distinction between public and private across many cultures of the ancient Mediterranean, but also upon the wide divergence in how and where that distinction was drawn and the interests it served. In the case of the Roman family, the concepts of "public" and "private" are notoriously problematic. Just as studies of the Roman house have shown that domestic space cannot be sharply divided between "private" and "public" functions,[1] so the *familia* that occupied that space participated simultaneously in both the public, civic realm and the intensely private world of sexual and affective relationships, and the "private" con-

1 Andrew Wallace-Hadrill's ground-breaking work (Wallace-Hadrill 1994) has inspired a whole generation of studies of the function and discourse of the Roman *domus*, particularly in regard to the problematic distinction between "public and private," including an on-going research project on "Public and Private in the Roman House" undertaken by scholars at the University of Helsinki (http://blogs.helsinki.fi/romanhouse/research-plan/).

tinually confronted and interacted with the "public."[2] For Romans the family was the nucleus of society, the producer of citizens and soldiers and preserver of ancestral cults and wealth. The *familia* was an autonomous unit headed by the *paterfamilias*, on whom Roman law and mores had bestowed remarkably extensive control over all under his *potestas* (power): his slaves, his legitimate children, even after they had reached adulthood, and in the earlier period of Roman history, his wife.[3] In theory this power even encompassed the so-called *ius vitae ac necis* (or *ius vitae necisque*), the "right of life and death" over his children, although scholars today disagree about the basis of such a power in law.[4] Less dramatic, and much more frequent, manifestations of *patria potestas* included the *paterfamilias*' legal control over all the possessions of those under his power, and the legal requirement that *iustum matrimonium*, legitimate marriage, have the consent of the *paterfamilias* of both partners. The unusual extent to which a *paterfamilias* could control the lives of even his adult children impressed both outsiders and Romans themselves: "for there are almost no other people who have the sort of power over their own children as we do," the jurist (legal expert) Gaius remarked in the second century CE.[5]

Such extensive domestic control, however, was bound to collide with the growing powers of the Roman state in the imperial period, particularly when the emperor himself was styled as *pater patriae*, the "father of the fatherland." Stories (as relayed in the works of later writers) of Roman fathers of the republican period who had put their own sons to death for treason or cowardice, extolled men who subordinated their paternal affection and private needs to the greater public concern of the state.[6] This reflects the realization, with the rise of the first emperor Augustus, that public and private interests could conflict,

2 The word *familia* itself illustrates the fluid nature of Roman concepts of "family" and "household," since it could denote all the inhabitants of a household including slaves, or simply the conglomerate of slaves in a household, or even the "nuclear family" of householders and children. See Saller 1984 and for a clear exposition of the legal side, Gardner 1998.

3 Women who married with *manus* came under their husband's legal power (in this case called *manus*, not *potestas*) but by the reign of Augustus "*manus*-marriage" had largely died out, and most adult women, like their brothers, remained under their father's power even after they married, unless he had died or emancipated them.

4 Harris 1986; Shaw 2001: 56–77; Capogrossi Colognesi 2010: 164–168.

5 Gaius, *Institutes* 1.55: *fere enim nulli alii sunt homines, qui talem in filios suos habent potestatem, qualem nos habemus* (text in Gordon and Robinson 1988; all translations are my own unless otherwise noted).

6 E.g., Lucius Junius Brutus, founder of the Republic: Livy 2.4–5; cf. Valerius Maximus 5.8 on fathers who repudiated (and sometimes killed) sons who acted against the Republic. See Harris 1986: 82–86 and 90.

and that the advent of a monarch whose *auctoritas* and power overrode all others would subject the concerns of *familia* to those of the *res publica*. Imperial law gradually chipped away at the *paterfamilias*' powers, although *patria potestas* itself continued, with some modifications, throughout the imperial period.[7]

The most sweeping intrusion of the *pater patriae* into the affairs of the *paterfamilias* was Augustus's legislation on marriage and adultery: the *lex Julia de maritandis ordinibus* (Julian Law on the Marrying of the Social Orders) of 18 BCE, modified somewhat by the *Lex Papia Poppaea* (Papian-Poppaean Law) of 9 CE, and the *lex Julia de adulteriis* (Julian Law on Adulteries), also of 18 BCE. The marriage laws (known to later legal writers as the *lex Julia et Papia*) mandated that male and female citizens be married and producing children during their most fertile years and penalized those who did not comply with loss of the right to inherit from anyone outside the sixth degree of relationship.[8] With the adultery law the state entered the bedroom: adultery (defined as sexual activity between a married woman and someone other than her husband) became a *crimen publicum*, a "public crime" to be tried by a standing court and punished with exile and partial confiscation of property.[9] Moreover, the now public nature of sexual offenses meant that the right of accusation against accused adulterers was open to all male adult citizens, even those with no bond of kinship or marriage with the accused.[10] Whereas in the Republic, the *paterfamilias* had had full responsibility for punishing those under his control for sexual misbehavior and a husband was entrusted to oversee his wife's chastity, Augustus's law brought the sexual life of Roman women (and of the men they slept with) into the public eye, with the clear implication that Roman men were no longer able to exert control over their private affairs. With Augustus the public interests of the imperial state entered into the private realm of the family – a trend which only intensified in the later Principate and came to a head with the "New Empire" of Diocletian and Constantine.[11]

---

7 For paternal power in the late Roman period, see Arjava 1998.

8 Scholarship on the Augustan laws is extensive and ever-growing; Treggiari 1991: 60–80 provides a succinct summary. For the later history of the marriage law and its eventual repeal in late antiquity, see Evans Grubbs 1995: 103–39. In Roman terms, the 6th degree included second cousins and great-uncles and great-aunts; legacies from those beyond that would be invalid.

9 Treggiari 1991: 277–98; McGinn 1998: 140–247 provides more detail and analysis.

10 The right of *extranei* (those outside the family) to bring an adultery accusation was abolished by Constantine (see Evans Grubbs 1995: 208–16), but otherwise Augustus' adultery law continued throughout late antiquity, as the its inclusion in the Justinianic corpus (D. 48.5; CJ 9.9) shows.

11 To borrow from the title of Barnes 1982. On Constantine's extensive legislation on marriage and the family and involvement in the "private" realm of the family, see Evans Grubbs 1995.

Augustus' legislation was intended to promote marriage and repress extramarital sexual activity by married women. Such goals were firmly in keeping with the widely acknowledged purpose of Roman marriage: the production of legitimate children who would be the heirs of their father and perpetuate his family name (*nomen*). Only children born in *iustum matrimonium* would come under the extensive powers of *patria potestas*; they inherited automatically from their father as *sui heredes* ("his own heirs") if he died intestate and were entitled to at least one-fourth of his estate if he left a will. In addition to taking his *nomen*, they would be responsible for maintaining his cult. It was their name, their property, and their embeddedness within a *familia* that enabled freeborn Romans, both men and women, to take their place in and contribute to Roman society.

But what about illegitimate children, those who were not born within a legally recognized marriage? By definition, illegitimate children had no father and therefore did not come under *patria potestas*, although slaveborn children (all of whom were ipso facto illegitimate, since slaves legally had no kinship relations) would come under the power of their master, who might also be their biological father. Illegitimates took the legal status of their mother.[12] They did not come under the power of their biological father, even if it was known who he was, and they would not inherit from him unless he explicitly left them something in his will. Nor did they come under the legal power of their mother's *paterfamilias*. They were outside the "web of rights and responsibilities" created by paternal authority and familial *pietas*.[13]

Medieval and early modern canon law and civil law (*ius commune*) distinguish between *naturales*, who are the recognized children of concubines and may enjoy some inheritance rights, and *spurii*, who are the abhorred and rightless children of adulterous, incestuous, and promiscuous relationships.[14] This distinction goes back to late Roman law, especially the extensive legislation of Justinian on illegitimate children. It is not found in the classical legal sources. There is, however, a tacit distinction in classical Roman law (c. 100 BCE-235 CE) between *spurii* (also known as *volgo quaesiti*, "commonly conceived") and *naturales*, which adumbrates the postclassical differentiation of the two but without a moral dimension. The classical distinction was made according to legal and social status. In unions that did not fit the Roman definition of *iustum matrimonium*, children took their status from their mother, not their father. *Spurii* were freeborn to a free mother, although often she was a former slave who had

12 D.1.5.19 (Celsus). Ulpian calls this a "law of nature" (D.1.5.24).
13 The expression is that of Rawson 1989: 10.
14 See Kuehn 1997; Wertheimer 2007; Witte 2009: 49–103.

been freed before her child's birth. *Naturales*, on the other hand, were born to enslaved mothers, although their father might be free.[15] The only hint of moral opprobium in regard to illegitimate children in classical law appears in Gaius' use of the word *spurii* to describe the children of "wicked and incestuous marriages." Even there, however, it is the nature of the union that produced them, not the products themselves, that is stigmatized.[16]

This paper discusses the situation of illegitimate children in Roman law, from the reign of Augustus through the reign of Diocletian, whose legislation marks a change in attitude. How were they affected by Roman marriage and inheritance law, which was so geared toward the perpetuation of wealth and status within a publicly recognized marital union? What role, if any, did illegitimates play in Roman society, both within the household and in public life? After a look at the social and legal condition of illegitimate children in general (both slaveborn *naturales* and freeborn *spurii*), I consider the special case of children born of incestuous marriages. Unlike other illegitimate relationships, incest was considered a matter of religious, and therefore public, concern from the earliest period. Moreover, as I will show, because some of the peoples in the eastern provinces had a rather different view of close-kin marriage, their unions, and those who participated in them, could be seen as "un-Roman" and therefore inimical to the continued prosperity of the Roman Empire. By examining Roman social, legal and religious interest in a group that seemingly lay outside the purview of the family, I hope to illuminate one aspect of the complicated interplay between "private" and "public" in the Roman imperial world.

2. *Naturales*

Roman legal sources use the term *naturales* for the offspring of a master and his slavewoman, or for the child of a free man by someone else's slave, or for the child of a freedman born when both he and their mother were still enslaved and therefore unable to form a legitimate marriage.[17] Many slaveborn *naturales*

---

15 The term *naturalis* is also used in the legal sources to designate a man's biological child, as opposed to an adopted one. It is easy to tell from the context which is meant. My definition is closer to Roman usage than Wolff 1945, 24–30, or Niziolek 1975, in that I am concerned with the legal status of the child at birth rather than the type of relationship between the parents. See Evans Grubbs 2014.

16 Gaius *Institutes* 1.64 (*nefarias atque incestas nuptias*). See Rawson 1989: 15; Moreau 2010: 319. But note Papinian at D.50.2.6.*pr.*, on which see at n. 54 below.

17 See Hermann-Otto 1994: 83–84.

were the products of unions between slaveowners and their female slaves. Pre-Christian Roman society had neither religious nor racial scruples against sexual exploitation of slaves (male as well as female) and master-slave sex was unproblematic, as long as the master was male.[18] So there must have been many, many slaves whose father was the owner of their mother.[19] Such children could be the product of rape or sexual exploitation, and the owner/father might have little or no direct contact with his slave children and see them and their mothers solely as marketable objects. However, in some cases a slaveowner (or his son) might develop an affective relationship with a slave of the household and with his children by her. Roman jurists acknowledged that a man might have a personal bond with his *naturalis* child by a slave, one not based on *patria potestas.*[20] Jurists discuss situations where a man had an illegitimate child who was either his own slave or belonged to someone else. Even if the cases are hypothetical, they imply that it was not uncommon for a man to have illegitimate slave children, and that sometimes he would not only free them but even give them property.[21] A man might even adopt his children by his slavewoman after he had freed them, although this would be unlikely – and socially inappropriate – if he were of elite status or already had children by a legal marriage as heirs. Adoption (or rather, in this case, adrogation) was a formal, public recognition of the membership of the adoptee in the free citizen community and his (or, much less likely, her) status as heir and carrier of the family *nomen.*[22]

A slavewoman could also have children by a free man other than her master. The children would be slaveborn and belong to their mother's master, but their father might want to free them and recognize them as his own.[23] Often, however, the child's father was the mother's partner in slavery, her *contubernalis.* Once a slavewoman was freed, any child she bore after manumission would be

---

18 Relationships between a male slave and a female slaveowner *were* problematic, and if the woman was of respectable status, the relationship would fall under the *lex Julia de adulteriis.* See Evans Grubbs 1993.

19 See Scheidel 2009: 284–307; also Betzig 1992.

20 Cf. Wolff 1945: 37 on the "classical conception of the *filius naturalis* as a child belonging to his father's family in the social, although not legal sense."

21 E.g., D.28.6.45 (Paul); D.42.8.17.1 (Julian). See Gardner 1998, 259–60. Cf. D.20.1.8 (Ulpian); D.42.5.38.pr. (*Sententiae Pauli*; not actually by Paul, but an early 4th c. compilation); Treggiari 1979: 193–194.

22 *Adrogatio* is the term for adoption of someone who was legally independent), whereas *adoptio* is used when the adoptee had been under someone else's *potestas.* On Roman adoption, see Gardner 1998: 114–208; on adoption of freedman, Gardner 1989.

23 Note the (hypothetical) case in D.19.5.5 (Paul), where two men each have the *naturalis filius* of the other as a slave and agree to manumit them; one of them does not abide by the agreement.

ingenuus (freeborn) but illegitimate (*spurius*), unless she was legally married. If a couple who had been *contubernales* while still in slavery were both freed, their union became *iustum matrimonium*, assuming there were no other legal impediments. Children born after that point were legitimate and came under their father's *potestas.*[24] But those born while their mother was enslaved remained slaves themselves. If they were also later freed, they would be known as the *filii naturales* of their freedman father.

Despite the legal fiction that slaveborn children had no father, jurists recognized that the enslaved did have family relationships, "and so we speak of parents and children and brothers even of slaves: but servile kin relationships are not of concern to the laws."[25] And once freed, slaveborn children were expected to have the same respect for their freed parents as freeborn people did. Illegitimate children, like legitimate ones, could not summon their *naturale*s parents to court.[26] Moreover, Roman incest rules applied to servile and freed relationships. "Thus a *naturalis* father is not able to marry his illegimate (*volgo quaesita*) daughter, since in contracting marriage one must look to natural law (*naturale ius*) and modesty (*pudor*); it is against modesty to marry one's own daughter."[27] Pomponius adds that the ban on *libertini* marrying their sisters or mothers "was introduced by *mores*, not laws (*leges*)."[28] *Mores*, in this case, refer to traditional Roman customs and norms, perhaps as opposed to those of other peoples, for whom close-kin marriage was an accepted practice. Thus an intrinsically private relationship (in this case, father-daughter marriage, even between those with no legal kinship bond) was forbidden not because it was illegal but because it was considered unnatural and offensive to Roman society at large.

24 CJ 6.55.7 (Diocletian and Maximian to Aemiliana, 294); cf. CJ 8.46.8.

25 D.38.10.10.5 (Paul).

26 D.2.4.6 (Sententiae Pauli). Cf. D.2.4.4.3 (Ulpian). Cf. D.2.4.10.10 (Ulpian).

27 D.23.2.14.2 (Paul). Here the father, a former slave, is called *naturalis*, but the child is *volgo quaesita*, not *naturalis*, because she was freeborn; cf. also CJ 6.55.6 (294), where a *spurius* son of a free woman and a slave has a *naturalis* father. See also D.23.2.54 (Scaevola): "And it makes no difference whether relationship (*cognatio*) derives from legal marriage or not: for it is forbidden to marry even a *volgo quaesita* sister."

28 D.23.2.8. See Moreau 2002: 265–267.

3. *Spurii (volgo quaesiti)*

The terms *spurii* and *volgo* (or *vulgo*) *quaesiti* are used as synonyms in the legal sources to designate the free, illegitimate children born of a free mother in a relationship that did not fall under the Roman definition of *iustum matrimonium.*[29] The jurist Modestinus says that *volgo quaesiti* either "are unable to demonstrate who their father is, or can do so but have one whom they are not permitted to have." Both he and the jurist Gaius derive the term *spurii* from the Greek word for seed, indicating indiscriminate "sowing" of seed outside of legitimate marriage; Gaius offers as an alternative derivation "*quasi sine patre filii*" ("as if children without a father").[30]

Although they had no *paterfamilias* and so, unlike legitimate children, had no paternal inheritance, under Roman law *spurii* did have certain rights and responsibilities in regard to their relationship with their mother. The mother of *volgo quaesiti* was responsible for supporting them and could be forced to do so if she refused. They also had to support her.[31] A *volgo quaesitus* could not bring his mother to court.[32] From the time of Hadrian, *spurii* had intestate inheritance rights (as cognates) from their mother, though they would still rank below their mother's agnate relatives (e.g., her siblings, her father's siblings, and her brothers' children) in order of succession.[33] And mothers of illegitimate children (*vulgo quaesiti*) were able to benefit from the *senatusconsultum Tertullianum* (also under Hadrian), which gave them succession rights to their children who died intestate.[34] Later in the second century, the *senatusconsultum Orphitianum*, enacted in 178 under Marcus Aurelius and Commodus, gave a woman's children first claim as her heirs if she died intestate, and explicitly applied to her *vulgo*

29 This would include children of adultery, but we hear almost nothing about such children outside of satire (see Syme 1960; Rawson 1989: 16–17).

30 D.1.5.23 (Modestinus); Gaius, *Institutes* I.64, explicitly in regard to children of incestuous unions. For discussion of terms, see Rawson 1989: 14–15.

31 D.25.3.5.4 (Ulpian).

32 D.2.4.4.3 (Ulpian); Cf. D.2.4.6 (Sententiae Pauli), n.26 above.

33 See Gardner 1998: 20–34 on succession of cognates (blood relatives within six degrees of kinship) under the Praetor's Edict. Gardner 1998: 252–256 dates this change in inheritance according to praetorian law to the reign of Hadrian; it cannot be later, since the Praetor's Edict reached its final form under Hadrian.

34 *Sc. Tertullianum:* D.38.17.2.1 (Ulpian); Gardner 1998: 256. This applied only to mothers with the *ius liberorum* ("right of children"), given under the Augustan marriage law to citizen women who had borne three or more children. Evidently illegitimate children also counted for the *ius liberorum* (Rawson 1989: 25). Before the *SC Tertullianum*, mothers had been able to inherit only as cognates at best. See Gardner 1998: 228–231.

quaesiti children also.[35] *Volgo quaesiti* could also bring an action *de inofficioso testamento* ("on undutiful will") against their mother's will if they felt unfairly treated, and could even inherit on intestacy from their maternal grandmother. If they died intestate themselves, their mother and siblings from the same mother had a right to inherit from them.[36]

Certainly, some discrimination against *spurii* did exist, beyond their lack of a legal father. As mentioned above, until the second century they could not inherit from their mother if she died intestate. Until the reign of Marcus Aurelius, the birth declarations of *spurii* could not be recorded in the *album professionum liberorum* or kept in the Tabularium of the Temple of Saturn in the Forum, in accordance with the *lex Aelia Sentia* (on manumissions) and the Augustan marriage legislation.[37] (This did not prevent the mothers of illegitimate citizen children from having a written record made of their children's birth, however.[38]) Under the emperor Trajan's alimentary scheme to encourage needy Italian families to rear their children, *spurii* received support as well as legitimate children, but far fewer of them were supported and at a lower rate. These *spurii* were the freeborn children of free unmarried mothers, not slaveborn *naturales*; the Trajanic *alimenta* were for freeborn children only.[39]

35 *SC Orphitianum:* D.38.17.1.2 (Ulpian); Justinian, *Institutes* 3.4.3; Gardner 1998: 231–233.
36 Inheritance rights as cognates under praetorian rules of succession: D.38.8.2 (Gaius; see Gardner 1998, 252–6). Undutiful will: D.5.2.29.1 (Opinions of Ulpian). Inheritance from maternal grandmother: D.38.8.8 (Modestinus). Inheritance from intestate *spurii:* D.38.8.4 (Rules of Ulpian). (The Opinions and the Rules of Ulpian are not by Ulpian but were attributed to him.)
37 See P. Mich. iii.169 = vii.169 (= *FIRA* III.4; 145 CE): Sempronia Gemella of Karanis in Egypt makes a *testatio* of the birth of her illegitimate twin boys, *quia lex Aelia Sentia et Papia Poppaea spurios spuriasve in albo profiteri vetat* ("because the Aelian-Sentian Law and the Papian-Poppaean Law forbid *spurii* to be declared in the album").
38 The literature on Roman birth declarations is enormous: see Schulz 1942 and 1943; and more recently Geraci 2001; Sánchez-Moreno Ellart 2002 and 2004. Texts of these declarations (wax tablets from Roman Egypt) in *CPL* 148–164 and Sánchez-Moreno Ellart 2004: 113–165, who challenges the usual explanation that this means illegitimates had no "official" birth declaration whereas legitimates did: rather, he holds, *spurii* simply could not be recorded in the *album* until Marcus Aurelius' reign.
39 In the Alimentary Tablet of Veleia (*ILS* 6675), there are two *spurii* (one boy, one girl) along with 292 *legitimi* (245 boys and 47 girls). Legitimate girls and the illegitimate boy received the same monthly allowance, which was less than that of legitimate boys but more than that of the illegitimate girl. Woolf 1990: 207–208 explains the differentiation as due to the "greater status" of males and legitimates; Jongman 2002: 52–53 says the distinction "emphasized traditional Roman values of citizenship." Cf. Tomlin 2000 on an alimentary foundation from early 3rd c. Spain, which also distinguishes between *legitimi* and *spurii*.

The term "*spurius*" appears in documentary sources from early imperial Italy, where instead of the usual "filiation" identifying paternity, illegitimate children are identified as "Sp. f." (*Spurii filius/a*), "son (or daughter) of Spurius." "Spurius" is thus a fictitious paternal *nomen* indicating lack of a legal father. Beryl Rawson found 184 sons and daughters of "*Spurius*" in 175 funerary inscriptions from the city of Rome alone, mostly dating to the first century CE, and dozens more are known from outside Rome.[40] In most of these cases the mother of a "child of Spurius" was a freedwoman, freed before her partner in slavery (*contubernalis*).

Such funerary commemorations belong to the world of the private, but children of "Spurius" also appear in public documents, where pseudo-filiation denotes freeborn but illegitimate status. Wax tablets from Pompeii and Herculaneum show that living persons identified *Spurius* as their father for social and legal purposes. The most famous of these is the woman "who claims to be Petronia Sp. f. Iusta" (Justa), whose case is known from a cache of eighteen tablets found at Herculaneum. Justa was the daughter of a freedwoman Petronia Vitalis, who had been jointly owned by Petronius Stephanus and his wife Calatoria Themis.[41] Calatoria Themis claimed that Justa had been slaveborn before her mother was freed, and so was her freedwoman also; Justa, on the contrary, claimed that she was freeborn, having been born after her mother's manumission, and she used the filiation "*Spurii filia*" to identify herself as such.

For "children of Spurius" like Justa, the pseudo-patronymic *spurius* indicated not moral depravity, but free birth, something much more important than legitimacy. This is why mothers of *spurii* in Roman Egypt made written records of their children's birth, even before *spurii* were allowed to be registered in the *album*.[42] It was this *ingenuitas* (free birth), that gave *spurii* a higher place in

40 Rawson 1989: 29–38; her survey includes only *spurii* in *CIL* VI. Lintott 2002, 562 suggests the abbreviation "Sp." found on inscriptions (see below) may be "a corrupt extension of '*s.p.*' = '*sine patre*'."

41 TH (= Tabulae Herculanenses) XIV in Arangio-Ruiz 1959: 223–245. See Lintott 2002; Metzger 2000; Weaver 1991: 166–172 and 1997: 69–71. There is much that is unclear about this case; we do not even know its outcome.

42 See n.37 above on P.Mich. iii.169. Note also SB 5217 (= *FIRA* III.6, 148 CE), an *epikrisis* (status examination) where the freedwoman Julia Primilla states that she bore Gaius Julius Diogenes, son of Spurius, and Julia Isarous, daughter of Spurius, "from unlawful marriage" (see Phang 2001: 44–45); similarly in P.Oxy. xii.1451 (175 CE), Trunnia declares the birth of her children, Lucius Trunnius Lucillianus, son of Spurius, and Trunnia Marcella, daughter of Spurius, also born "from unlawful marriage." Their fathers were probably serving in the military when their children were born and so not legally able to marry their mothers. I do not here consider the *apatores* ("fatherless ones") of Roman Egypt, on whom see recently Malouta 2009; he concludes

the Roman legal hierarchy than slaveborn *naturales*. *Ingenuitas* enabled *spuriae* daughters to marry up and *spurii* sons to enter public life and take on civic duties that slaveborn *naturales* could not.

4. *Spurii* in Public Life

Athough illegitimacy did not connote moral unfitness, it could suggest a lack of social suitability, at least among the "more honorable" (*honestiores*) classes. *Naturales*, because they were slave-born, were *humiliores* and because of their libertine condition were barred from holding public offices like that of decurion.[43] The one position open to them was that of Augustalis.[44] *Spurii*, on the other hand, were freeborn, but they also had a liminal status in Roman society, since their mothers were usually former slaves and they themselves lacked a *paterfamilias*, and therefore would probably not have paternal resources on which to draw.[45] The ambiguous position of *spurii* in public life is illustrated by juristic and imperial decisions regarding their suitability for service on local town councils (*curiae*), whose members were *honestiores*.[46] The jurist Neratius, writing under Hadrian, when considering how the *origo* (hometown, place of origin) of someone "who does not have a legitimate (*iustus*) father" would be determined, decided it would follow that of his mother. Since the *origo* of a person of curial status determined where he or she would be liable for performing civic services (*munera*), Neratius' statement implies that even illegitimates were liable to civic duties, if their mother belonged to the municipal elite.[47] Sev-

---

that they often occupied "a midding social position" and their designation as fatherless "did not seem to taint [them] in a way that was especially damaging" (Malouta 2009: 138).

43 Freedmen were ineligible to serve as decurions and could be punished with *infamia* if they usurped curial status: see CJ 9.21.1 (Tetrarchy, prob. 300); Mouritsen 2011: 248. In this case, however, the *naturalis* father had been "restored to free birth" and thus became eligible. Freeborn sons of freedmen could become decurions and the descendants of freedmen may have comprised a substantial proportion of members of the curial class in imperial Italy (Gordon 1931; Garnsey 1975; but now see Mouritsen 2011: 261–263).

44 Mouritsen 2011: 249–278.

45 Unless their biological father provided for them in his will, as did sometimes happen (see above).

46 On the legal distinction between *honestiores* and *humiliores* ("more humble"), see Garnsey 1970.

47 D.50.1.9; see Garnsey 1974: 237–238. Although women could not be decurions, they could be liable for *munera* (Evans Grubbs 2002: 74–80) and Neratius indicates that this liability could be passed on to their illegitimate children.

eral decades later, a rescript of Marcus Aurelius and Lucius Verus to the governor of Bithynia declared that "there is no doubt that *spurii* can be co-opted into the order (of decurions), but if someone has a legitimate competitor, that one ought to be preferred."[48] Thus illegitimacy was acceptable if the *curia* needed to be filled, but clearly less desirable than legitimate birth. In one case, Septimius Severus ruled that a man born while his father was still in slavery but when his mother was free was not forbidden to become a decurion.[49] Such a person would certainly be illegitimate, since there could not be legal marriage between slave and free, and legally speaking, he would be fatherless. The eligibility of a freeborn child of a free woman and a slave comes up again in a rescript of Diocletian and Maximian to a certain Posidonius: "Someone conceived from a free woman and a slave is considered as *spurius* and cannot be presented as the son of a decurion, even though his natural (*naturalis*) father, after being manumitted and restored to free birth status, held the office (of decurion)."[50] Because the man was illegitimate, he did not have a father, and so could not call himself the "son" of anyone, although his father was clearly known and had even held public office. His father's time in slavery did not preclude the *spurius* son from becoming a decurion himself, but legitimate sons of decurions would be preferred to him.

These rulings by emperors suggest that questions were raised repeatedly in the second and third centuries about the eligibility of illegitmate children of free women for municipal office.[51] This was a time when the *curia* was becoming a more "closed" institution, in which vacancies were usually filled by the sons of decurions or those "adlected" by the *curia*, with little new blood coming in from those not already in the curial order. On the other hand, economic and social conditions in the third century made holding the decurionate and fulfilling the required *munera* (which could carry a heavy financial burden) less attractive, and numbers had to be kept up. Thus those who in earlier times would not have

---

48 D.50.2.3.2 (Ulpian). It is not clear from Ulpian's wording whether this is a verbatim quotation from the rescript or Ulpian's summary of it.

49 D.50.2.9 pr (Paul). The mother is described as *libera* (free), not *ingenua* (freeborn), and therefore was no doubt a former slave herself. This was an actual case that came before the emperor, from Paul's Decreta.

50 CJ 6.55.6 (294): *Ex libera conceptus et servo velut spurius habetur nec ut decurionis filius, quamvis pater eius naturalis manumissus et natalibus suis restitutus hunc fuit adeptus honorem, defendi potest.*

51 As Wertheimer 2007: 372 points out.

been considered eligible were now acceptable.[52] Under such circumstances, an illegitimate freeborn child of a free (perhaps freed) woman might not have seemed a bad prospect, if he had acquired the wealth necessary to hold a position on the town council.[53] Papinian extended this (relative) receptiveness to include children of incest: "*Spurii* become decurions; therefore one born from incest will also be able to become one. For the office-holding (*dignitas*) of one who has done nothing wrong ought not to be impeded."[54]

5. *Spurii et nefarii?* Children of incestuous relationships

Not everyone had as liberal an attitude as Papinian, however. The Romans had what Philippe Moreau has aptly called "l'horreur de l'inceste." According to the classical jurist Gaius:

> Therefore if someone has contracted an unholy and incestuous marriage (*nefarias atque incestas nuptias*), he appears to have neither wife nor children. And thus those who are born from this sexual union seem indeed to have a mother, but certainly not a father, and for this reason they are not in his power. They are like those whom their mother has conceived promiscuously, for those are also understood not to have a father, since he [i.e. his identity] is also uncertain. Therefore they are usually called spurious children (*spurii filii*), as if conceived "from scattered seed" (Greek *sporaden*) or as if [they are] children without a father.[55]

---

52 See Garnsey 1974. Cf. D.50.2.12 (Callistratus) and D.50.2.3.3 (Ulpian) and D.27.1.15.6 (Modestinus) for other examples of eligible candidates who in earlier times might not have been acceptable.

53 We do not know whether the 2nd- and 3rd-century decisions represent a new policy toward *spurii* in the town councils, prompted by a shortage of eligible candidates, or simply reiterate an older position. They do provide a precedent for measures taken later by 5th and 6th century emperors allowing men of curial status who had no legitimate children to make their illegimate offspring heirs, provided the children became decurions (if male) or married decurions (if female): see Novels 22.1 (442) and 22.2.11 (443) of Theodosius II; Evans Grubbs 2014.

54 D.50.2.6.pr. (Papinian); Moreau 2010: 321. If Papinian, who according to the *Historia Augusta* was an *adfinis* (relation by marriage) of the emperor Septimius Severus (*Caracalla* chapter VIII), was from Syria (as Severus' wife Julia Domna was), as some have thought, then Papinian could be seen as expressing a more relaxed eastern attitude toward close-kin relationships. While this idea is attractive, it cannot be proven.

55 Gaius, *Institutes* 1.6; Moreau 2002, esp. 29–85. The word *incestum* broader semantic range in Latin than "incest" in English; it means "unchastity," particularly that with religious implications, and was applied to the illicit sexual activity of Vestal Virgins as well. Here I am speaking only of the term's use in regard to close-kin sexual relations.

Incestuous unions are "unholy" or "sacreligious": they are *nefas*, against the divine order of things, and in need of religious expiation (*piaculum*).[56] The adjectives *nefariae* and *incestae* recur in later legal references to incestuous marriages, whereas such religiously laden language is not used in describing other non-legal unions.

The Roman definition of incest included unions between parent and child (or grandparent and grandchild), between siblings or half-siblings (even if one was illegitimate; see above); step-parents and step-children, and parents and adopted children.[57] Marriage between aunt and nephew and between maternal uncle and niece was incestuous under Roman law; marriage to a brother's daughter had once been also, but in 49 CE the emperor Claudius had the law changed so that he could marry his niece Agrippina. Both Tacitus and Suetonius note that despite Claudius' encouragement, almost no other Romans responded to the dispensation of the new law, indicating that the emperor had changed the law, but not *mores*.[58]

These rules applied only to Roman citizens, both in Italy and in the provinces. Indeed, for the Romans their stricter definition of what qualified as incest was something that distinguished them from other peoples, a mark of separation from "the other."[59] In the first two centuries of the Empire, those who were not Roman citizens could continue to follow their local marriage practices, which might run counter to Roman ideas of incest. For instance, marriage between siblings or half-siblings was not uncommon in some areas of the eastern Mediterranean under Roman domination. In Roman Egypt, considerable evidence for brother-sister marriage, including between full siblings, can be found in census returns, private correspondence, and even a record of a divorce agreement between two formerly married siblings.[60] Marriage between half-siblings was

---

56 Moreau 2002: 41–59.

57 Gaius, *Institutes* 1.59 and 1.61; marriage between adoptive siblings was possible if one of them had been emancipated from paternal power. With an illegitimate (*volgo quaesita*) sister: D.23.2.54 (Scaevola). Marriage between step-siblings was allowed: D.23.2.34.2 (Papinian). For a thorough treatment of the law of incest, see Puliatti 2001.

58 Gaius, *Institutes* 1.62; Tacitus, *Annales* 12.6–7; Suetonius, *Divus Claudius* 26.3.

59 See Moreau 2002: 87–105 for the range of attitudes toward the close-kin alliances of other peoples like the Greeks (who allowed marriage between half-siblings) or the Egyptians (who allowed full sibling marriage) or the Persians (who allowed parent-child marriage); whether horrified or tolerant, all Roman commentators note that such practices are not Roman.

60 The literature on close-kin marriage in Egypt is vast; see Huebner 2007 and Rowlandson and Takahashi 2009 for bibliography. For brother-sister marriages in the census returns, see Bagnall and Frier 1994, 127–34. P. Kronion 52 records the divorce of a sibling couple (trans. in Rowlandson 1998: 130–131). Remijsen and Clarysse 2008 and Rowlandson and Takahashi 2009 (who in-legal in the Greek world, and further east in Persia.[61] It is worth noting that the Roman government felt no need to force non-citizens to accept their religious and social taboo on incest – it was only the marriage of Roman *citizens* with close kin that was a problem. The private lives of non-citizen provincials was not a concern.

Incestuous unions between Roman citizens had none of the legal effects of *iustum matrimonium*, and the partners were liable under the adultery law of Augustus. Exceptions were made if the participants did not know that what they were doing was wrong and thought they were legally married. Three such cases came to the attention of Marcus Aurelius and Lucius Verus and were recorded by the Severan jurist Papinian.[62] These rulings do not mention any children of the union, and in fact there are few references to the children of incest (as opposed to the alleged incestuous partners) in classical sources outside of mythology. When the partners knew what they were doing was wrong, they would make efforts to prevent having a child. Domitian is said to have forced his niece, with whom he was having an incestuous affair, to have an abortion.[63] If a child was born, the parents would probably do away with it by exposure or infanticide.

Another rescript of Marcus Aurelius and Lucius Verus to a woman named Flavia Tertulla does concern the status of children of an incestuous union that had been considered legitimate marriage by all concerned:

> We are moved by the length of time in which you, ignorant of the law, were in a marriage with your maternal uncle, and by the fact that you were placed in marriage by your grandmother, and by the number of your children. And therefore, since all these things add up together, we confirm the status of your children (*liberi*) acquired within this marriage, which was contracted forty years ago, just as if they had been conceived legitimately (*perinde atque si legitime concepti fuissent*).[64]

---

clude an Appendix of definite and probable examples) argue against the conclusion of Huebner 2007 that almost all of the apparent cases of sibling marriage in Roman Egypt are really instances of adoption and marriage to the adopter's biological child. It is certainly possible, however, that some of the cases of sibling marriage in the papyri do reflect a strategy of adoption and marriage; see further Huebner 2013.

61 Rowlandson and Takahashi 2009: 106–108; for Persia, see Chadwick 1979. Moreau 2002: 93–94 notes also the favorable attitude toward uncle-niece marriage among Jews, and suggests that L. Vitellius, the senator who proposed lifting the Roman ban on paternal uncle-niece marriage so that Claudius and Agrippina could marry, was thinking of contemporary Herodian examples.

62 See D.48.5.39.4–6 (Papinian); Moreau 2002: 354–5.

63 Suetonius, *Domitianus* 22; Pliny, *Epistle* 4.11.6.

64 D.23.2.57.a (Marcian); Moreau 2010: 321–323.

Since Flavia Tertulla's marriage to her mother's brother was arranged by her grandmother, her *paterfamilias*, who normally would have been responsible for arranging his children's marriages, must have been dead. The marriage was contracted sometime in the 120's, under Hadrian, since the rescript dates to the period 161–169. Decades later, Tertulla learned that her marriage was invalid and her children were illegitimate. What precipitated her petition to the emperors is unknown: perhaps her husband had recently died and the children's right to inherit from him had been challenged on the grounds of their parents' kinship. While neither condoning the union nor legitimating the children, the emperors took into consideration Tertulla's lack of responsibility for the marriage, her legal ignorance, and her child-bearing – which showed that she had fulfilled the purpose of marriage and obeyed the Augustan law. They decided that for practical purposes (i.e. inheritance), her children should have the same rights they would have had if they had been born in a legal marriage.

Tertulla's *nomen*, Flavia, indicates that she was a Roman citizen; her family may have received citizenship under the Flavian emperors (69–96 CE). Perhaps one of her antecedents (maybe her grandfather) had been in the auxiliaries and received citizenship upon discharge.[65] She may have lived in a province where uncle-niece marriage was acceptable and not uncommon, and have been following provincial practice.[66] But as a Roman citizen – wherever she lived – Tertulla had to marry in accordance with Roman law. In Egypt, Pardalas, the *idiologos* (chief financial official) in the first or early second century, confiscated the property of married siblings who were Roman citizens.[67] Along with the privileges of citizenship came the restrictions of Roman marriage law, and consequently the intrusion of Roman public officials into the private lives of enfranchised provincials.

The Constitutio Antoniniana (Edict of Caracalla) of 212, granting Roman citizenship to virtually all free inhabitants of the Empire, meant that these restrictions applied throughout the provinces, including Egypt and elsewhere in the eastern Mediterranean where endogamous marriages were customary. Continued mention of sibling marriage in official declarations in Egypt in the two decades after the Edict suggests that there was a sort of amnesty for those who had mar-

---

65 Moreau 2002: 356–357, suggests she was related to Q. Flavius Tertullus, suffect consul in 133 and proconsul of Asia in 148–149. If so, this would be a case of endogamy in the senatorial class. But cf. Millar 1977: 547–548.

66 Note the case of another grandmother, Sempronia Urbica of Simitthus in what is now Tunisia, who arranged a marriage between her daughter and her deceased husband's nephew: *AE* (*L'Année Épigraphique*) 1998, 1576–78, discussed by Corbier 2005.

67 *Gnomon of the Idiologos* 23 (in Sel. Pap. II.206, pp. 46–47).

ried before 212. After that, papyrus documentation of close-kin marriages in Egypt dies out, evidently in response to the requirements of Roman law.[68]

Lack of documentation, however, does not mean such unions no longer took place, simply that the participants no longer mentioned their existence in contexts that might draw official attention. Indeed, imperial laws from the late third century and into the Byzantine period show that unions considered incestuous under Roman law did not entirely disappear in the eastern Empire. A rescript (*epistula*) of Diocletian and Maximian to an official, Flavius Flavianus, said that those who mistakenly contracted incestuous marriages would receive imperial *clementia* and not be punished if they broke up their "wicked" or "sacrilegious" marriage (*nefarias nuptias*).[69] This is in line with the attitude of earlier law toward incestuous marriages undertaken through ignorance; the characterization of such unions as "wicked" recalls Gaius' description. But it also may signal a more active repugnance toward incest than that found in classical law. Virtually all free people were now Roman citizens, and therefore their marriage practices were of concern: "*nefariae nuptiae*" would alienate the gods and cause them to remove their support.

Moreover, another rescript of Diocletian and Maximian specifically punished the children of incestuous marriages. Addressed to an imperial official, Honoratus, the rescript prohibited children "who were born from incestuous marriage" (*incestum matrimonium*) from becoming judges, advocates, or procurators (legal representatives) or from having any "profession" except, if necessary, that of decurion.[70] As with other rulings of the second and third century that allowed *spurii* to serve as decurions, this concession was made in response to a need for more citizens eligible for the decurionate, whose members were responsible for an increasingly burdensome array of services. Sons of incestuous marriages who do

---

68 See Montevecchi 1979, who cites several papyri, including P.Oxy. xliii.3096 (dated 223/4), that suggest that brother-sister marriages that took place before 212 were still in existence afterwards. Cf. Moreau 2002: 109. On the Constitutio Antoniniana, see Modrzejewski 1990 and Buraselis 1995.

69 This text is not in the Codex Justinianus but appears in the *Mosaicarum et Romanarum Legum Collatio* VI.5–6 (in *FIRA* II.560–1), where it is said to have been in both the Codex Hermogenianus (dated 291) and the Codex Gregorianus (dated 287). On this problem see Corcoran 1996: 34–35 and Frakes 2011: 270. The recipient is probably to be identified with a Flavius Flavianus who was governor of Numidia under Diocletian and Maximian, but not necessarily at the time he received the rescript (Corcoran 1996: 125).

70 Text from Corcoran 2000, 4: *Iudicem, causidicum et procuratorem omnes, qui incesto matrimonio nati fuerint, fieri prohibemus et omni modo nullam professionem recipere nisi tantum [taxeotalem vel] curialem si necessitas accedat.* The reference to "taxeotic" duties is probably a Justinianic interpolation: see Corcoran 2000: 15–17.

follow the forbidden professions, or are asked to represent someone in court as patron, will receive the penalty for sacrilege, which at this period would probably mean deportation. (Daughters would not be affected, since they could not serve in any office or profession.)

This rescript is not included in modern editions of the Codex Justinianus, but is found in several manuscripts of epitomes of the Code and seems to have appeared originally in it. Most manuscripts attribute this text to Justinian, but one names Diocletian and Maximian as the emperors, and the wording has several features of the Tetrarchic period.[71] The rescript's equation of incestuous marriages, and their offspring, with sacrilege is reminiscent of the description of such unions as offensive to the gods in those emperors' edict of 295 (see below).[72] On the other hand, Justinian himself legislated extensively on illegitimacy, and whereas his treatment of *naturales* born of high-ranking men and low-born women was more generous than that of previous imperial law (especially the legislation of Constantine and his successors), his attitude toward *spurii* born of incestuous unions was very negative, especially in his later *novellae* ("new laws").[73] But the negative attitude toward incestuous unions found in the rescript to Honoratus is in keeping with other rescripts of Tetrarchic date on practices perceived as non-Roman, and I am inclined to accept its attribution to Diocletian. The rescript's wording indicates that it was sent to an official, not a private petitioner, but it is not known what office the recipient held; he may have been Titius Honoratus, prefect (governor) of Egypt in 291–2, who perhaps had come across cases of incestuous marriage in his province. In any case it was likely prompted by a particular case or cases in an eastern Mediterranean province.[74]

A few years later imperial repugnance toward incestuous marriages found expression in a long and sternly-worded edict against all illegal close-kin unions.[75] The edict, enacted in 295 at Damascus in the names of Diocletian and

71 This is the interpretation of Corcoran 2000, who thoroughly discusses the manuscript evidence, the textual problems, and the import of this rescript. He dates it to c.290 (Corcoran 2000: 24).

72 Corcoran 2000: 15; but see Moreau 2002: 213 n.74.

73 Moreau 2002: 185–6 and 365–6 and Moreau 2010: 327–8, who attributes this rescript to Justinian. On Justinian's legislation on *naturales*, see n.91 and Evans Grubbs 2014.

74 Corcoran 2000: 5–8.

75 Preserved in full in the *Mosaicarum et Romanarum Legum Collatio* VI.4 (in *FIRA* II.558–60), where it is said to have been taken from the 5th book of the Codex Gregorianus, under the title on marriage. Trans. and discussion in Evans Grubbs 2002: 140–143. In 1982 T.D. Barnes suggested that the edict was issued at Damascus by Diocletian's Caesar Galerius (Barnes 1982: 62–63 n. 76). More recently he has argued that Diocletian was indeed the issuer of the edict, but that he issued it from Demessus, in the Danube region, rather than Damascus (Barnes 2005). Al-

Maximian along with their Caesars Galerius and Constantius, condemned those acts "which have been done in a wicked and incestuous [or "unchaste"] way by certain people in the past" (*quae a quibusdam in praeteritum nefarie incesteque commissa sunt*). Forbidden marriages are compared to the matings of "cattle or wild beasts" and must be repressed in order to win the favor of the gods who will see that "all people living under our rule lead a wholly pious and religious and peaceful and chaste life in all respects." Indulgence is granted to those who entered incestuous marriages in the past out of ignorance or inexperience (i.e. youth), but they are told that "the children they have borne from so wicked a union are not legitimate" and that they are barred from succession to the children "to whom they illicitly gave birth".[76] It is only after this long rhetorical diatribe that the law gets around to defining which unions are its target: marriage with direct ascendants and descendants (mothers, grandmothers, daughters and granddaughters, etc.), full and half-siblings, stepdaughters and stepmothers, mothers-in-law and daughters-in-law, and the daughter or granddaughter of one's sister – in other words, the same kin who had always been off-limits as spouses to Roman citizens.[77] For all its unusual length and harshness, the edict promises clemency for those who forsake forbidden unions within eight months of the law's enactment. Moreover, it lays down no penalty for the children of such marriages, who may still have been able to inherit from their parents by will.[78] Illegitimate children of incest could still marry and have legitimate children of their own – assuming they did not marry close kin.

Although as an edict this law had universal application in the Empire, it was particularly aimed at provincials in the eastern Mediterranean. Close-kin marriage is known to have occurred not only in Roman Egypt, but also further east in the Euphrates region, at Dura Europos, and Greek and Roman writers

though Damascus as the place of issuing would better support the argument that it was primarily directed against provincials in the eastern Mediterranean, as an edict it would have had application throughout Diocletian's empire.

76 *Collatio* 6.4.3: . . . *non legitimos se suscepisse liberos, quos tam nefaria coniunctione genuerunt. . . ut liberorum quos inlicite genuerunt successione arceantur.* The edict adds that inability to inherit from their children was also denied to those in incestuous marriages "by Roman laws according to antiquity."

77 Notably, the law does not include marriage with a brother's daughter, which had been legal since Claudius; see at n. 58 above. This is changed in the one-sentence adaptation of the edict in the CJ, because by Justinian's time such marriages had again been banned (by Constantius in 342: CTh 3.12.1).

78 It is not clear from the law if the children could inherit from their father by will. Presumably they could still inherit from their mother, under the *senatusconsultum Orphitianum* passed in 178.

often refer to incestuous unions among the Persian royal families. Since the law was enacted at a time when tensions between the Roman Empire and neighboring Persia were high, the emperors may have been reacting not only to "non-Roman" marriage practices, but to concerns about Persian sympathies among eastern provincials.[79] Maintaining Roman marriage law and Roman family mores and suppressing barbaric, "beast-like" marriages would be essential if the Empire were to retain the divine good will that would enable it to defeat its enemies, who not coincidentally engaged in the same unholy practices the law condemns.

That close-kin marriages continued even after the Edict of Caracalla, in Egypt or elsewhere in the Empire, is not surprising; much later legislation of Justinian and his successor Justin reveals the persistence of the custom in Mesopotamia centuries later.[80] What is different is the law's tone of religious and moral outrage. It can be compared to another Tetrarchic edict, the famous Edict on Maximum Prices known from multiple inscriptions found in the eastern Empire.[81] Like the marriage edict, the preamble to the Price Edict describes the behavior of those subjects whose actions it wishes to check (in this case, merchants who overcharge or stockpile goods in a time of scarcity) as savage and scarcely human.[82] However, the marriage edict stresses the un-Roman nature of the marriage practices it condemns and repeatedly invokes the Roman name and laws, exhorting Roman subjects that "they should recall that they are concerned with *Roman* discipline and laws and they should know that only those marriages that have been permitted by *Roman* law are licit."[83] The edict uses the adjective "*Romanus*" six times to describe Roman laws, Roman gods, the Roman majesty, and

79 See Chadwick 1979: 145 – 153; Evans Grubbs 1995: 100 – 101; Corcoran 2000: 9 – 13. Cf. the rescript against Manicheans sent to the governor of Africa below. Interestingly, the marriage edict does not mention the Persians, even though ancient sources often refer to the incestuous habits of the Persians.

80 Lee 1988; Justinian Novel 154 (535/6 CE).

81 See Corcoran 1996: 205 – 233. I am citing from Lauffer's text found at http://droitromain.upmf-grenoble.fr/. Another comparandum is the law addressed to Julianus, proconsul of Africa, regarding the Manicheans in his province (Collatio XV.3.). Like the marriage edict, the rescript to Julianus is anxious to eliminate practices inimicable to the "ancient religion" (*vetus religio*) and tradition, but appears more concerned with the Persian associations of Manicheanism and the dangers that following "the doctrine of the Persians" might pose to the Empire. This was a rescript (an *epistula*, to be precise) to an official, not an edict.

82 Cf. the Price Edict: . . . *ardet avaritia desaevians, quae sine respectu generis humani*. . . . *hanc debachandi licentiam* . . . with the marriage edict's *cum pecudum ac ferarum promiscuo ritu ad inlicitia conubia* [2] and *nemo audeat infrenatis cupiditatibus oboedire* [3].

83 *Collatio* VI.4.4 . . *ut se ad disciplinam legesque Romanas meminerint pertinere et eas tantum sciant nuptias licitas, quae sunt Romano iure permissae.*

the Roman name. The preamble to the Price Edict, on the other hand, refers only once, at the very beginning, to "*Romana dignitas maiestasque*" but stresses instead the emperors' concern for the "public" and "common" good. Moreover, although the Price Edict begins by mentioning the thanks owed to "the immortal gods" for recent victories against barbarian peoples, its main concern is for the *public* good and the emperors' anger is directed against those whose extortionate business practices harm the people, especially soldiers. Price-gouging is a crime against one's fellow man, the act of one devoid of human feeling. In contrast, the intrinsically private act of close-kin marriage is an offense against the Roman gods, the act of one who is not truly Roman, and endangers the relationship between the Roman people and their gods. Interestingly, although the emperors do not hesitate to call for a capital penalty for price-gougers, those who persist in incestuous marriages "against the honor of the Roman name and the sanctity of the laws" are told only that they will be "struck with a worthy severity."[84]

The edict on close-kin marriage is not the only legislation of Diocletian that explicitly condemns as "un-Roman" certain practices involving private behavior and relationships of the family. Rescripts to individuals speak disapprovingly of the "adoption" of brothers, the expulsion (*apoceruxis*) of a child from the home, and having two wives simultaneously. All were practices impossible under Roman law, but known to occur in the provinces, especially in the East.[85] However, alien as such practices were to traditional Roman family mores, they were not considered abhorrent to the Roman gods.

It is also worth noting that our knowledge of Diocletian's edict on close-kin marriage is due only to its preservation in full in a legal compilation of the fourth or early fifth century, the *Lex Dei* ("Law of God"), more commonly known today as the *Mosaicarum et Romanarum Legum Collatio* ("Comparison of Mosaic and Roman Laws").[86] This strange work, of Christian (or less likely, Jewish) authorship, was an attempt to prove the compatibility of "God's law" with Roman law by juxtaposing rules on the same subjects (e.g. homicide, adultery, magic, and false witness) taken from the Old Testament ("Moses says") and the com-

---

84 Collatio VI.4.8: *Si qua autem contra Romani nominis decus sanctitatemque legum post supra dictum diem deprehendentur admissa, digna severitate plectentur.*

85 Brother adoption: CJ 6.24.7 (Diocletian and Maximian to Zizo, 285). *Apoceruxis:* CJ 8.46.6 (idem to Hermogenes, possibly governor of Asia, 287). Bigamy: CJ 5.5.2 (to Sebastiana, 285). See Corcoran 2000: 8–9 and Evans Grubbs 2011: 388–391.

86 Only one sentence of the edict is preserved in CJ (CJ 5.4.17; cf. *Collatio* VI.4.5), and it simply enumerates the prohibited degrees of kinship, adding in marriage to a brother's daughter, which was not in the edict originally but which again became illegal in 342 (CTh 3.12.1; Constantius to the Phoenician Provincials; see above at n. 77).

mentaries of Roman jurists or rulings of Roman emperors.[87] For Moses' contribution on incest the Collator cites a mélange of passages from Leviticus and Deuteronomy; for Roman law he quotes passages he attributes to the jurists Ulpian, Paul, and Papinian (although they are actually from pseudonymous works), the rescript of Diocletian and Maximian to Flavius Flavianus (mentioned above), and of course the same emperors' long edict.[88] That the Christian Collator found Roman condemnation of incest particularly congruent with both the strictures of "Moses" and his own views is clear from the final section of his title on incestuous marriages, which rains down a litany of curses upon those who sleep with their own relatives.[89]

6. Conclusion

The Tetrarchic period appears to mark a turning-point in the Roman imperial attitude toward illegitimate children, specifically the *spurii* of close-kin marriages. Although incestuous marriages are described in negative terms in classical law, prior to the end of the third century the children of such unions do not seem to have been marked out or penalized any more than other illegitimate children. Apart from Gaius' brief reference to "*nefarias atque incestas nuptias*" and Paul's explanation of the rule against marriage between a (freedman) *pater naturalis* and his illegitimate (*volgo quaesitam*) daughter as contrary to "natural law and modesty" (*naturale ius et pudor*), extant pre-Diocletianic Roman law does not use morally laden terms to describe incestuous relationships.[90] However, this non-judgmental stance may not reflect the views of most Romans in the west, who may have had a more negative view of incest, stemming from religious taboo. Although the Roman "horreur d'inceste" is not new with Diocletian, the confrontation of Roman law with the private mores of previously non-Roman peoples meant that close-kin marriage now had public implications.

From the idea that incestuous, un-Roman marriages bring pollution and the gods' anger, it is a small step to the conclusion that the child produced by such a

---

87 Text of the *Collatio* in *FIRA* II: 544–589; Frakes 2011: 157–201 re-edits the text and provides a translation. On the controversy over the (anonymous) author's religious affiliation and on the date of composition, see Frakes 2011: 124–151.

88 See Frakes 2011: 267–273 on the Collator's sources for Title VI.

89 Frakes 2011: 271–273. He notes that it is unusual for the Collator to add a second biblical passage after the citations from Roman law; in most cases excerpts from the "law of Moses" only preface the much lengthier Roman legal passages.

90 See above.

union is also a source of pollution. Thus Novel 89 of Justinian (539), which significantly improved the inheritance rights of the illegitimate children of masters by their slaves or former slaves (*naturales* = Greek *nothoi* or *phusikoi*), concluded by explicitly excluding "everyone who has come forth from wicked or incestuous or condemnable couplings – we will not call them marriages – such a one is not called *naturalis* nor is he to be reared by the parents nor will he have a share of the present law."[91] When the edict is considered along with the rescript to Honoratus banning the children of incestuous marriages from all public positions except the now onerous one of *curialis*, we may detect a shift from earlier imperial law. More than with previous emperors, under Diocletian we find the equation of the norms of Roman private law, specifically family law, with Roman religion and with the preservation of the public good. In the edict on close-kin marriages, and the rescripts to the officials Flavius Flavianus and Honoratus, Diocletian's legislation brings together concern for religious purity, public welfare, and private behavior in a way not seen earlier in extant imperial law.[92]

Abbreviations

CJ	=	Codex Justinianus (ed. P. Krueger; vol. 2 of the *Corpus Iuris Civilis*).
CIL	=	*Corpus Inscriptionum Latinarum.*
CPL	=	Corpus Papyrorum Latinorum.
D	=	Digest (most easily accessible in Watson 1985).

---

91 Novel 89.15. The Greek text of the Novel actually uses the Latin letters (with Greek endings) of the Latin words *nefarius*, *incestus*, and *damnatus*, signifying how alien the concepts were to Greek. (See at n.16 and 69 on *nefariae atque incestae nuptiae*.) The admonition that a child of forbidden unions is "not to be reared" (*neque alendus est*) is particularly shocking from an emperor who elsewhere banned and penalized the exposure of newborn free and slave children (see Novel 153). Justinian himself had to step back from his condemnation of close-kin unions after learning that Jews in Tyre and the peoples of Mesopotamia and Osrhoene persisted in following their ancestral customs of endogamy (Novel 139 on the Jews of Tyre and Novel 154 on Mesopotamia and Osrhoene; see Evans Grubbs 2011: 390 – 391).

92 And yet, here our incomplete knowledge of pre-Tetrarchic imperial edicts may deceive us. Perhaps a similar collocation of public and private, religious and familial had appeared already in the Edict of Caracalla of 212, which by extending Roman citizenship to virtually all free people in the Empire, had simultaneously extended the purview of Roman marriage law. The exiguous remnants of the decree extant on papyri (P.Giss. 40) indicate that it was occasioned by the emperor's rejoicing (evidently after being saved from an assassination plot allegedly by his brother Geta) and wish to increase the numbers of those who by virtue of their new civic status would worship the gods of the Empire. Would this not also have been a time to enjoin upon the new citizens their duty to obey the laws of the Romans, including their marriage laws?

FIRA	=	*Fontes Iuris Romani Antejustiniani.* Vol. I: *Leges*, ed. S. Riccobono. Vol. II: *Auctores*, ed. J. Baviera. Vol. III: *Negotia*, ed. V. Arangio-Ruiz. Florence: 2nd ed. 1968–1969.
ILS	=	*Inscriptiones Latinae Selectae.*
JRS	=	*Journal of Roman Studies.*
P.Mich	=	*Michigan Papyri.*
P.Oxy.	=	*The Oxyrhynchus Papyri.*
RIDA	=	*Revue internationale des droits de l'antiquité.*
SB	=	*Sammelbuch griechischer Urkunden aus Aegypten.*
Sel. Pap.	=	*Select Papyri.*

Full details of papyri collections can be found in the "Checklist of Editions of Greek, Latin and Coptic Papyri, Ostraca, and Tablets" at http://library.duke.edu/rubenstein/scriptorium/papyrus/texts/clist.html

Works Cited

Arangio-Ruiz, V. (1959). "Testi e Documenti. IV. Tavolette ercolanensi (il Processo di Giusta)." *Bullettino dell'Istituto di diritto romano* (3rd) 1: 223–245.

Arjava, A. (1998). "Paternal power in late antiquity." *JRS* 88: 147–65.

Bagnall, R. and B. Frier (1994). *The Demography of Roman Egypt.* Cambridge, UK.

Barnes, T.D. (1982). *The New Empire of Diocletian and Constantine.* Cambridge, MA.

Barnes, T.D. (2005). "Damascus or Demessus?" *Zeitschrift für Papyrologie und Epigraphik* 151: 266–268.

Betzig, L. (1992). "Roman Polygyny." *Ethnology and Sociobiology* 13: 309–349.

Buraselis, K. (2007). *Theia Dorea: Das Göttlich-Kaiserliche Geschenk Studien zur Politik der Severer und zur Constitutio Antoniniana.* Vienna.

Capogrossi Colognesi, L. (2010). "La famiglia romana, la sua storia e la sua storiografia." *Mélanges de l'École française de Rome* 122: 147–174.

Chadwick, H. (1979). "The Relativity of Moral Codes: Rome and Persia in Late Antiquity," in W.R. Schoedel and R.L. Wilken, eds., *Early Christian Literature and the Classical Intellectual Tradition in honorem Robert M. Grant:* 135–153. Paris.

Corbier, M. (2005). "Family and Kinship in Roman Africa," in M. George, ed., *The Roman Family in the Empire: Rome, Italy, and Beyond:* 255–285. Oxford.

Corcoran, S. (1996). *The Empire of the Tetrarchs: Imperial Pronouncements and Government AD 284–324.* Oxford. Revised paperback edition 2000.

Corcoran, S. (2000). "The Sins of the Fathers: A Neglected Constitution of Diocletian on Incest." *The Journal of Legal History* 21: 1–34.

Evans Grubbs, J. (1993). "'Marriage more shameful than adultery': Slave-Mistress Relationships, 'Mixed Marriages', and late Roman law." *Phoenix* 47: 125–154.

Evans Grubbs, J. (1995). *Law and Family in late Antiquity: The Emperor Constantine's Marriage Legislation.* Oxford.

Evans Grubbs, J. (2002). *Women and the Law in the Roman Empire: A Sourcebook on Marriage, Divorce, and Widowhood.* London and New York.
Evans Grubbs, J. (2011). "Promoting *pietas* through Roman Law" in B. Rawson, ed., *A Companion to Families in the Greek and Roman Worlds:* 377–392. Chichester.
Evans Grubbs, J. (2014). "Illegitimacy and Inheritance Disputes in the Late Roman Empire" in B. Caseau and S. Huebner, eds., *Inheritance, Law and Religions in the Ancient and Mediaeval Worlds:* 25–49. Paris.
Frakes, R. (2011). *Compiling the* Collatio Legum Mosaicarum et Romanarum *in Late Antiquity.* Oxford.
Gardner, J. F. (1989). "The Adoption of Roman freedmen." *Phoenix* 43, 236–57.
Gardner, J. F. (1998). *Family and* Familia *in Roman Law and Life.* Oxford.
Garnsey, P. (1970). *Social Status and Legal Privilege in the Roman Empire.* Oxford.
Garnsey, P. (1974). "Aspects of the Decline of the Urban Aristocracy in the Empire." *Aufsteig und Niedergang der römischen Welt* II.1: 229–52.
Garnsey, P. (1975). "Descendants of Freedmen in Local Politics: some Criteria," in B. Levick, ed., *The Ancient Historian and his Materials:* 167–180. Westmead and Farnborough.
Geraci, G. (2001). "Le dichiarazioni di nascita e di morte a Roma e nelle provincie," *Mélanges de l'École française de Rome* 113: 675–711.
Gordon, M.L. (1931). "The Freedman's Son in Municipal Life." *JRS* 21: 65–77.
Gordon, W.M. and O. Robinson (1988). *The Institutes of Gaius.* Ithaca, NY.
Harris, W.V. (1986). "The Roman Father's Power of Life and Death," in R. Bagnall and W.V. Harris, eds., *Studies in Roman Law in Memory of A. Arthur Schiller:* 81–95. Leiden.
Hermann-Otto, E. (1994). Ex ancilla natus: *Untersuchungen zu den "hausgeborenen" Sklaven und Sklavinnen im Westen des Römischen Kaiserreiches.* Stuttgart.
Huebner, S. (2007). "'Brother-Sister' Marriage in Roman Egypt: a Curiosity of Humankind or a Widespread Family Strategy?" *JRS* 97: 21–49.
(2013). "Adoption and Fosterage in the Ancient Eastern Mediterranean," in J. Evans Grubbs and T. Parkin, eds., *The Oxford Handbook of Childhood and Education in the Classical World:* 510–531. Oxford and New York.
Jongman, W. (2002). "Beneficial Symbols. *Alimenta* and the Infantilization of the Roman Citizen," in W. Jongman and M. Kleijwegt, eds., *After the Past: Essays in Ancient History in Honour of H.W. Pleket:* 47–80. Leiden.
Kuehn, T. (1997). "A Late Medieval Conflict of Laws: Inheritance by Illegitimates in *Ius Commune* and *Ius Proprium.*" *Law and History Review* 15: 243–273.
Lee, A.D. (1988). "Close-Kin Marriage in Late Antique Mesopotamia." *Greek, Roman, and Byzantine Studies* 29: 403–13.
Lintott, A. (2002). "Freedman and Slaves in the Light of Legal Documents from First- Century AD Campania." *Classical Quarterly* 52: 555–565.
Malouta, M. (2009). "Fatherlessness and formal identification in Roman Egypt," in S. Huebner and D. M. Ratzan, eds., *Growing Up Fatherless in Antiquity:* 120–138. Cambridge, UK.
McGinn, T.A.G. (1998). *Prostitution, Sexuality, and the Law in ancient Rome.* Oxford and New York.
Metzger, E. (2000). "The Case of Petronia Iusta." *RIDA* 47: 151–65.
Millar, F. (1977). *The Emperor in the Roman World.* Ithaca. (2nd ed. 1992).

Modrzejewski, J. (1990). "Edit de Caracalla conferant aux habitants de l'Empire le droit de cité romaine (Constitutio Antoniniana)" in idem, *Droit impérial et traditions locales dans l'Égypte romaine:* 478–490. Aldershot and Burlington, VT.
Montevecchi, O. (1979). "Endogamia e cittadinanza romana in Egitto." *Aegyptus* 59: 137–44.
Moreau, P. (2002). *Incestus et prohibitae nuptiae. L'inceste à Rome.* Paris.
Moreau, P. (2010). "Rome: the Invisible Children of Incest" in V. Dasen and T. Späth, eds., *Children, Memory, and Family Identity in Roman Culture:* 311–329. Oxford and New York.
Mouritsen, H. (2011). *The Freedman in the Roman World.* Cambridge, UK.
Niziolek, M. (1975). "Meaning of the Phrase *Liberi Naturales* in Roman Law Sources up to Constantine's Reign." *RIDA* 22: 317–44.
Phang, S.E. (2001). *The Marriage of Roman Soldiers (13 BC-AD 235).* Leiden.
Puliatti, S. (2001). Incesti crimina: *Regime giuridico da Augusto a Giustiniano.* Milan.
Rawson, B. (1989). "*Spurii* and the Roman View of Illegitimacy." *Antichthon* 23: 10–41.
Remijsen, S., and W. Clarysse (2008). "Incest or Adoption? Brother-Sister Marriage in Egypt Revisited." *JRS* 98: 53–61.
Rowlandson, J., ed. (1998). *Women and Society in Greek and Roman Egypt: A Sourcebook.* Cambridge, UK.
Rowlandson, J. and R. Takahashi (2009). "Brother-Sister Marriage and Inheritance Strategies in Greco- Roman Egypt." *JRS* 99 (2009): 104–39.
Saller, R.P. (1984). "*Familia, domus*, and the Roman Conception of the Family." *Phoenix* 38: 336–55.
Sánchez-Moreno Ellart, C. (2002) Professio Liberorum. *Los registros y las declaraciones de nacimentos en Derecho romano.* Madrid.
Sánchez-Moreno Ellart, C. (2004). "Notes on some new Issues concerning the Birth Certificates of Roman Citizens," *Journal of Juristic Papyrology* 34: 107–111.
Scheidel, W. (2009). "Sex and Empire," in I. Morris and W. Scheidel, eds., *The Dynamics of Ancient Empires:* 255–324. Oxford and New York.
Schulz, F. (1942). "Roman Registers of Births and Birth Certificates," *JRS* 32: 78–91.
Schulz, F. (1943). "Roman Registers of Births and Birth Certificates Part II," *JRS* 33: 55–64.
Shaw, B. (2001). "Raising and killing Children: Two Roman Myths," *Mnemosyne* 54: 31–77.
Syme, R. (1960). "Bastards in the Roman Aristocracy." *Proceedings of the American Philosophical Society* 104: 323–327.
Thomas, J.A.C. (1967). "Some Notes on *adrogatio per rescriptum principis.*" *RIDA* 14; 413–427.
Tomlin, R.S.O. (2000). "An Early Third-Century Alimentary Foundation." *Zeitschrift für Papyrologie und Epigraphik* 129: 287–92.
Treggiari, S. M. (1991). *Roman Marriage:* Iusti Coniuges *From the Time of Cicero to the Time of Ulpian.* Oxford.
Wallace-Hadrill, A. (1994). *Houses and Society in Pompeii and Herculaneum.* Princeton University Press.
Watson, A. (1985), ed. *The Digest of Justinian. Latin Text edited by Theodor Mommsen with the aid of Paul Krueger, English translation edited by Alan Watson.* 4 volumes. Philadelphia.
Weaver, P.R.C. (1991). "Children of Freedmen (and Freedwomen)" in B. Rawson, ed., *Marriage, Divorce and Children in Ancient Rome:*166–90. Oxford.
Weaver, P.R.C. (1997). "Children of Junian Latins," in B. Rawson and P. Weaver, eds., *The Roman Family in Italy: Status, Sentiment, Space:* 55–72. Oxford.

Wertheimer, L. (2007). "Continuity and Change in Constructs of Illegitimacy Between the Second and Eighth Centuries." *Historical Reflections/Réflections* 33: 363–393.

Witte, J. Jr. (2009). *The Sins of the Fathers: The Law and Theology of Illegitimacy Reconsidered.* Cambridge, UK.

Wolff, H. J. (1945). "The Background of the Post-Classical Legislation on Illegitimacy." *Seminar* 3: 21–45.

Woolf, G. (1990). "Food, Poverty and Patronage: The significance of the epigraphy of the Roman alimentary schemes in early imperial Italy." *Papers of the British School at Rome* 58: 197–228.

Harry O. Maier

7. Public and Private in Emergent Christian Discourse

Abstract: This paper uses the tools of social geography, specifically the theorization of territoriality as developed by Sack (1986) to observe how emergent Christianity classified, represented and regulated divergent belief by associating it with unregulated domestic life. The essay investigates the territoriality advanced by 1 and 2 Timothy and Titus (the Pastoral Epistles), Irenaeus' account of the household activities of the Valentinian teacher Marcus in local households, and the letters of Ignatius of Antioch to explore this dichotomy and its associations. The visible household was associated in Roman and Greek political discourse with good civic order. The same association appears in this early Christian literature. Christianity associated false and correct/ heretical and orthodox teaching with unregulated domestic life and the properly ordered household, respectively. The result is a configuration that builds on contemporary civic ideals, modulated with the help of Christian beliefs and practices.

1. Introduction

Social geography attends to the role of place, place-based practice, and the imagination of space in human behavior and identity. Spatiality, a subset of social geographical study, is a term that "refers to how space and social relations are made through each other; that is how, space is made through social relations, and how social relations are shaped by the space in which they occur."[1] "Human geography," writes the social geographer David Sack, "include[s] not only the actual locations, extension, and patterns of things, but how these are described and conceived of in different social and intellectual perspectives."[2] It is such a social and human geography this chapter seeks to understand. Scholars have devoted much attention to the role of the household in the organization, growth, and institutional development of early Christianity.[3] The social geographical discussion taken up here moves beyond an empirical discussion of the places early Christian met to consider the ways in which spaces, their mem-

1 Hubbard and Kitchin 2009, 499.

2 Sack 2009, 25.

3 For a survey of scholarship and the present state of research see Gehring 2004, 1–25.

bers, and public and private practices are represented in ancient texts as a means classifying, representing, and regulating teaching. This paper contributes to the discussion of private and public in Greco-Roman antiquity by taking up the social production of space as it relates to representation of true and false teaching in emergent Christianity. I will examine three sites: 1&2 Timothy, Titus (the Pastoral Epistles); Irenaeus' representation of his opponent, Marcus; and Ignatius of Antioch's letters. I aim to show how each of these writers in slightly differing ways creates a spatially oriented discourse centered on household practices and that they wed social space open to public view with right teaching and figure space hidden from scrutiny as the place of incorrect and ultimately heretical teaching.[4] In doing so they were developing an understanding of Christianity consistent with the ideals of their contemporaries, where polis and household join together for a common good, preserved by right religion.

Sack uses the term territoriality to define "the attempt by an individual or group to affect, influence, or control people, phenomena, and relationships, by delimiting and asserting control over a geographical area."[5] He defines geographical area socially as "the extent of activities in space." Such areas become territories when they "are used by some authority to mold, influence, or control activities."[6] A social geographical study of territory attends to how space is defined or classified, communicated to others, and access to it enforced. Sack's interests are in historical human geography, that is, the varying ways in which space is classified, represented, and regulated in different historical contexts. His discussion does not extend to the Christian household, or to notions of private and public in antiquity, but his treatment of territorialism proves useful in three ways. First it alerts us to the rhetorical use of household metaphors and representations of household behavior in the social construction of allies and enemies and of public and private in early Christianity. Next, it points us to how households were contested spaces in early Christianity and competing territories of belief and practice. Finally, it invites consideration of the uses of household ideals associated with the practices of domestic duties and correct uses of space to demarcate, represent and regulate Christ followers.

The development of early Christian territorialism this essay will consider was in part a consequence of the overlapping domains of public and private in Greco-

---

4 In what follows for the sake of simplicity I will refer to "Christianity" and "Christian" although what constitutes either term was under development, a topic of debate in this period (as it is amongst contemporary scholars), and not always inextricable from "Judaism," an equally inchoate term.

5 Sack 2009, 19.

6 Sack 2009, 19.

Roman domestic life. It is now a commonplace in scholarship that modern conceptions of private and public life are anachronistic categories when used to understand the household in the Greek and Roman world. Very broadly speaking in the industrialized west public and private are distinguished by state/non-state, public good/private property, the street/the home, and so on.[7] The ancient world conceived a different demarcation in its articulation of the street/home divide. Kate Cooper has shown, for example, that the public sphere extended from the extramural world of the *civitas* into the shared communal sphere of the intramural *domus*.[8] Daily access by clients and other visitors created spaces with a good deal of social traffic. Andrew Wallace-Hadrill draws on empirical evidence in Herculaneum, Pompeii, and Ostia Antica and in an often quoted phrase invites us to imagine the Roman family not as a household, but a houseful, with daily traffic from clients who dotted the neighborhood or were resident even in the same insula complex.[9] The Roman *domus* was, when considered from a contemporary point of view, both public and private. What distinguished the private from the public was not the threshold, but, again following Cooper, the relative degree of regulation and the reach of public authority as well as public scrutiny into the different zones that were the sites of differing kinds of activities.[10] These observations are most at home in the atrium-style elite Roman household.

When we look beyond the Italian Roman *domus* to the Greek peristyle *oikos* of the eastern Empire the importance of lines of sight and public scrutiny does not diminish. Plutarch, for example, cites for a Greek audience the story of the artisan who for five talents offered to renovate Drusus' house to render it inaccessible to his public view. Drusus replied, "[T]ake ten and make the whole house open to view, that all the citizens may see how I live" (*Precepts of Statecraft* 800F). Unlike the domus, however, in the *oikos* the role of the householder in allowing entry into domestic spaces was more decisive. As Monika Trümper has shown, in that instance, thresholds mark a stronger demarcation that separates inside from outside; gatekeepers in the case of more well-to-do households restrict access to the household. Trümper contrasts the more lavish, multiple-courtyard *oikos* from the single-courtyard one. The former allows one to conceive a sharp demarcation of gendered space and the marking off of relatively private domestic from the more public activities of leading males. This is the material backdrop both for Vitruvius' discussion of female and male life in domestic space as well as Ischomachus' descriptions of the training of his wife in Xeno-

---

7 Des Rosier 2003, viii-x.
8 Cooper 2007, 3–33.
9 Wallace-Hadrill 2003, 4; similarly, Saller 1984, 336–55.
10 Cooper 2007, 15; similarly in this regard, Wallace-Hadrill 1988, 46.

phon's *Oeconomicus.*[11] In modest single-courtyard houses, private and pubic were marked off by time and activities rather than space.[12] For the topic under consideration here, the spaces beyond the threshold as open to public scrutiny, and the spaces that are subject to diminishing level of public scrutiny, proved to be powerful sites for the production and imagination of right and false belief and practice.

It is doubtful that many early Christ followers inhabited even the more modest peristyle household of the Greek east; in the urban world of early Christianity we should expect that they rented modest apartments, or, if they owned shops, they lived above them or in rear quarters.[13] Despite these more modest living situations, however, early Christian literature draws on and develops a territorial discourse that presumes the more extended household setting and set of relations. This is instructive, as we will see, for the socially constructed imagination of right and false teaching: while the empirical settings may in fact be modest, the imagination of group life is of a higher social standing and set of expectations that go along with it. This allowed early Christians to draw upon a larger tradition of political discourse to articulate group ideals. This elevated social imagination, as we will see, is consistent with early Christian strategies to promote and represent Christian public and private life as consistent with the civic and social aims of the contemporary polis and Empire.

2. Rooms with a View: Territorialism in the Pastoral Epistles

"I hope to come to you soon, but I am writing these instructions to you so that, if I am delayed, you may know how one ought to behave in the household of God [ἐν οἴκῳ θεοῦ] which is the church of the living God, the pillar and bulwark of the truth" (1 Tim. 3.14–15). "In a great house [μεγᾶλῃ δὲ οἰκίᾳ] there are not only vessels of gold and silver but also of wood and earth ware, and some for noble use, some for ignoble. If any one purifies himself from what is ignoble, then he will be a vessel for noble use, consecrated and useful for the master of the house [τῷ δεσπότῃ], ready for any good work" (2 Tim. 2.20–21). In the

11 Vitruvius, *arch.* 6.7.2; 6.7.5; 6.10; and Xenophon, *oec.* 7.30–9.19; Trümper's discussion centres on Hellenistic Delos and first century CE Pergamon.

12 Trümper 2003, 37–43.

13 Oakes 2009, 80–97; for economic levels and urban poverty, Meiggitt 1998, 62–78; Friesen and Scheidel 2009, 61–91.

Pastoral Epistles (1&2 Timothy, Titus), pseudonymous letters most probably composed between 90–130 CE most probably in Asia Minor, "Paul" describes the ideally governed and correctly believing church as a rightly ordered household and immoderate behaviors as a sign of false teaching and belief.[14] The letters take the form of instructions to his apostolic delegates, Timothy and Titus, about how to appoint and regulate the churches he has been sent to found and organize. They open up to their first/second century audiences site lines to classify, communicate, and regulate properly conducted private and public life. The Pastorals offer insight into an emergent Christian conceptualization of private and public and the formation of institutional strategies to define and demarcate them. In these letters the rightly functioning and governed church is a strictly organized and demarcated household in which members play out their assigned household roles and in which space is defined by the assignment of domestic duties and obligations.[15] They are especially concerned to delineate and regulate space according to gender identity and domains.[16] The classification of domestic space as "the household of God" is an outcome of an earlier strategy on the part of the historical Paul to adopt the household as an important organizational component in his mission to the Gentiles, as well as household language as a vehicle for self-representation and communal ideals.[17] In the use of household language Paul and his followers echo the use of familial language in contemporary associations to designate fellow members and leaders, and there are examples of household associations with all members of the household as participants.[18] But, whereas for Paul household arrangements were a provisional means toward a larger end, the Pastorals represent a normalization of household structures as definitive of religious identity and practices. This reflects a development that can be seen in an earlier pseudonymous Pauline letter, Ephesians, where "Paul" celebrates his audience as "members of the household of God" (Eph. 2.19), as indeed it is recognizable in the paraenetic use of a Household Rule in Colossians and Ephesians to outline the duties and obligations of differing participants in the household to one another (Col. 3.18–4.1;

14 For authorship and date, Dibelius and Conzelmann 1972, 1–5; Marshall 57–92; 2007, 197–236, who also outlines a situation similarly advanced here, of an ambiguity amongst meetings and leaders the letters seek to clarify.

15 Verner 1983.

16 Kartzow 2009, 209; Zamfir 2013, 85–89.

17 Gehring 2004, 119–210; Adams 2013 does not take this fully enough into account in his arguments.

18 Harland 2009, 63–96 for "brothers," "sisters," "mothers," "fathers," and "papas," "daughters, " "sons" in associations, with inscriptions (88).

Eph. 5.21–6.9; also 1 Pet. 2.18–3.7, similarly late first century). Even if, as Edward Adams has recently argued, not all early Christ followers met in house churches but also gathered at a variety of places such as *tabernae*, *popinae*, *cauponae*, *thermopolii*, barns, gravesites, and so on, it is notable that the household functions as a chief mode of discursive formation of conduct and right belief in much early Christian literature.[19] What can this teach about notions of private and public in an emerging religious movement? When Christianity is conceived with the use of household metaphors and differing interpretations of belief are given territorial demarcations, how do private and public come into play as modes of self-definition and social imagination?

In the Pastoral Epistles, as in the Pauline corpus generally, there is a strong emphasis placed on public sight lines. The Pastorals emphasize visibility.[20] In this regard they also echo associational ideals, especially household associations that prescribe right domestic relations, piety, and virtues as requisites for membership.[21] In the Pastorals, requirements for ecclesial leadership include a well governed household: a bishop "must manage his own household well, keeping his children submissive and respectful in every way; if a man does not know how to manage his own household, how can he care for God's church" (1 Tim. 3.4–5; also v. 12). These are not purely abstract representations of rightly conducted household relations; the text opens up the households of aspiring leaders to public view: bishops/overseers and deacons can be seen by outsiders rightly to govern their households. English translations of 1 Tim. 3.7, such as in the NRSV, that the one who aspires to the office bishop "must be well thought of by outsiders" diminishes the visuality the text implies that he possess "a good public witness by outsiders [μαρτυρίαν καλὴν ἔχειν ἀπὸ τῶν ἔξωθεν]." Although much more institutionalized in orientation, these passages reflect concerns the uncontested Pauline corpus expresses regarding public scrutiny. Paul, for example, exhorted Corinthian Christ followers not to exercise gifts of glossolalia indiscriminately lest the scrutiny of others lead to a bad public reputation: "If ... the

19 Adams 2013, 137–97. Ebner 2012, 190–235 refers to "social networks" between household and city in multiple forms of social gathering contemporary with emergent Christianity. Instead of single social models for organization he prefers what he calls a "messy taxonomy" (199) that captures the role of temples, agora, forum, and households in identity and group formation, especially in domestic associations.

20 Similarly, MacDonald 1996, 63–4; she accounts for this emphasis by a twofold desire to evangelize outsiders and to avoid accusations of secrecy by detractors. This argument furnishes an alternative account of the polemical construction of religious dissent as secret and typical of an unregulated household and right confession as public.

21 Dittenberger 1915–1924, 985 is an example of a domestic association from late second to early first century BCE Philadelphia in Lydia. For discussion, Stowers 1998, 287–301.

whole church assembles and all speak in tongues, and outsiders or unbelievers enter, will they not say that you are mad?" (1 Cor. 14.23). Appearing as it does in a letter suffused with civic discourse, Paul in this passage is inviting his audience to imagine the conduct of his assemblies under the scrutiny of the public eye.

The Pastorals are doubly pseudonymous, that is, even as the author, "Paul" is a literary and rhetorical construct, so also are the recipients of his letters, "Timothy" and "Titus."[22] This double pseudonymity proves effective rhetorically since it frees the author to invent not just author and audience, but also setting and narrative. As the letters unfold, the audience of the letters peers into households to scrutinize their regulation. The letters thus give listeners rooms with a view. The letters represent Timothy and Titus as products of a proper upbringing and hence from right families. Paul remembers Timothy's grandmother Lois and his mother Eunice for their "sincere faith [ἀνυποκρίτου πίστεως]" (2 Tim. 1.5); "from infancy [ἀπὸ βρέφους]" Timothy has known "the sacred writings" (2 Tim. 3.15). He depicts familial relations with Timothy and Titus by representing them as his (beloved/true/faithful) child (1 Tim. 1.2,.18; 2 Tim. 1.2; 2.1; Tit. 1.4). As men who have been properly raised, their conduct fits their age: Timothy is to exhort elder men and women as fathers and mothers, respectively (1 Tim. 5.1), and to honor widows (5.3). Titus is thus in a good position to teach older men, older women, wives, younger men, and slaves (Tit. 2.1–10) to lead a life that "befits sound teaching [τῇ ὑγιαινούσῃ διδασκαλίᾳ]." The letters create a domestic space with a view for recognizing and patterning true belief and practice.

The letters conform to a view of the regulated *oikos* as a necessary part of the properly governed state. Here the *polis* extends beyond the threshold to include household relations and, conversely, from domestic space to the city. 1 Timothy exhorts listeners that "supplications, prayers, intercessions, and thanksgiving be made for all, for emperors and all who are in high position, that we may lead a quiet life, pious and reverent in every way [ἠσύχιον βίον γιάγωμεν ἐν πάσῃ εὐσεβείᾳ καὶ σεμνότητι]" (1 Tim. 2.1–3). Directly following this instruction, the author instructs men how to pray and women to adorn themselves modestly, wives to remain silent, and to fulfill domestic obligations by bearing children (2.8–15). There then follow prescriptions of candidates of bishops and deacons, that these have properly governed households (3.1–13). The author rhetorically designs movement from the polis to the household, from the extramural polis to the intramural *oikos* to show that both work together to achieve a certain kind

22 Marshall 2008, 781–803; similarly, Richards 2002, discusses the fictional narratives as "the epistolary situation" of each letter (97–99, 136–38,1 83–87) acted out by "*dramatis personae*" (68–71, 103–8, 140–44).

of harmony and respectability.[23] When he exhorts women/wives to prefer "pious worship of God [θεοσέβειαν] through good works" to adornment, commands them to silence, forbids them from having "authority over men [αὐθεντεῖν ἀνδρός]" and promises them salvation if they bear children "in faith and love and holiness, with modesty [ἐν πίστει καὶ ἀγάπῃ καὶ ἁγιασμῷ μετὰ σωφροσύνης]" (2.10, 11,12,15) he promotes the view that religion entails both the right management of women by men. In a similar manner, in Tit. 2.1–3.1, the author hierarchically organizes codes of household duties and links them with the public view and ultimately the well being of the state. Titus is to "teach what is consistent with sound doctrine [τῇ ὑγιαινούσῃ διδασκαλίᾳ]" (Tit. 2.1). Older women are to teach young women to fulfill domestic roles faithfully "that the word of God may not be discredited [ἵνα μὴ ὁ λόγος τοῦ θεοῦ βλασφημῆται]" (vs. 4–5). Younger men are to be "models of good deeds, and in your teaching show integrity, gravity, and sound speech that cannot be censured, so that an opponent may be put to shame, having nothing evil to say to us [λόγον ὑγιῆ ἀκατάγνωστον, ἵνα ὁ ἐξ ἐναντίας ἐντραπῇ μηδὲν ἔχων λέγειν περὶ ἡμῶν φαῦλον]" (vs. 7–8). And finally slaves are to be honest and dutiful "so that in everything they may adorn the doctrine of God our Savior [ἵνα τὴν διασκαλίαν τὴν τοῦ σωτῆρος ἡμῶν θεοῦ κοσμῶσιν ἐν πᾶσιν]" (vs. 9–10). When in 3.1 he exhorts the audience "to be submissive to rulers and authorities [ἀρχαῖς ἐξουσίαις ὑποτάσσεσθαι], to be ready and honest for good work" again the movement is from intramural to extramural life and the site lines continually penetrate from the extramural to the intramural household domain. In all of this the author presumes a relatively well-heeled domestic world that probably does not conform to the historical socio-economic realities of his audience.[24] Rhetorically these exhortations and instructions cast listeners, however modest their means, in a "household of God" that represents itself as a more magnificent domestic world – a world with "vessels of gold and silver ... wood and earthenware, ... some for noble use, some for ignoble" (2 Tim. 2.20). The link in these quotations between piety, sound teaching, reverence for authority, and good domestic and public order reflect a strategy of social territorialism: the letters classify, describe and seek to regulate private space and household relations by making them susceptible of public view and hence scrutiny.

---

23 Similarly, Zamfir 2013, 60–159.

24 I thus differ from Kidd 1990, 35–109 and Countryman 1980, 154, who are inclined to read these texts straightforwardly as evidence of a great wealth; rather, they should be read as part of a rhetorical strategy to outline right and wrong behaviours more generally and thereby cast right teaching as also the right management of material resources and benefaction in accordance with good citizenship and proper religious identity.

Such close and (always potentially) public examination of household relations arises because of contest over private space and behaviors. The opposite of the respectability that comes from right regulation and imagined good public testimony are the vices that emerge from a lack of regulation in the private sphere, the place where public scrutiny is weak, even abjured, and where religion reveals its socially erosive qualities. The letters cast its audience in "later times" when people depart from "the faith" and "forbid marriage" (1 Tim. 4.1,3). In 2 Timothy "Paul" again warns that in "the last days" will come social degenerates amongst whom are those, significantly, who "are disobedient to their parents" (2 Tim. 3.2). "Amongst them are those who worm their way into households [οἱ ἐνδύνοντες εἰς τὰς οἰκίας] and capture weak women, burdened with sins and swayed by various impulses, who will listen to anybody and can never arrive at a knowledge of the truth" (3.6–7). Paul instructs Titus to appoint elders to give instructions in "sound doctrine [ἐν τῇ διδασκαλίᾳ τῇ ὑγιαινούσῃ], "for," he continues, "there are many insubordinate people [ἀνυπότακτοι], empty talkers and deceivers...; they must be silenced, since they are turning whole households upside-down [ὅλους οἴκους ἀνατρέπουσιν] by teaching for base gain what they have no right to teach (Tit. 1.10–11). These descriptions have been persuasively linked with an alternative set of Pauline teachings that were circulating amongst the audience of these letters, in which women are being invited by visitors to reject traditional domestic duties in favor of ascetical practices that include renunciation of marriage and sexual intercourse.[25] A measure of support for this interpretation has been found in 1 Tim. 5.13, where the author commands that all women under 60 to (re)marry and warns against enrolling "younger widows" because "they learn to be idlers, gadding about from house to house, and not only idlers but gossips and busybodies, saying what they should not [ἀργαὶ μανθάνουσιν περιερχόμεναι τὰς οἰκίας, οὐ μόνον δὲ ἀργαὶ ἀλλὰ καὶ φλύαροι καὶ περίεργοι, λαλοῦσαι τὰ μὴ δέοντα]" (v. 13). Here it is more than possible that "younger widows" are unmarried women who have become teachers in their own right and who are spreading the message the Pastorals reject.[26] It is arguable, further, that the Pastorals reflect a social situation in

---

25 Macdonald 1983, 34–77; Merz 2004, 218–22, 318–33, 374–5.

26 Dibelius and Conzelmann 1972, 74; Thurston 2003, 172–74; Bassler 2003, 122–46; Davies 1980, 70. Davies also links the Pastorals treatment of the widows with continent women in the apocryphal Acts, where an unfavourable "view from the street" into the household shows that women throw off traditional roles and transgress gendered space, while expressing a form of religious devotion that overthrows civic ideals, and expresses a different formulation of the social order and relation of the household to the state.

which contemporary women were breaking free of traditional domestic and spatially circumscribed roles.[27]

The main interest here is not to gauge the probability of such a historical reconstruction, but to observe the ways in which this alternative account of private, secretive, and mismanaged households contrasts with the rightly regulated one described above. In the Pastorals improper religion and household insubordination are linked with social chaos. Unlike the sound teaching of rightly regulated households, these teachers and their women are chatterboxes. The obedient silent wife of the rightly ordered household can withstand public scrutiny. In this regard the Pastorals share a set of paradoxical social ideals promoted in contemporary domestic discourse: the wife should be at once available for public scrutiny, but such scrutiny should render her invisible. The women the Pastorals pillory are visible and hence fail to measure up to public expectations: these women are gadabouts who, unlike those who rightly confess religion and win the respect of outsiders by their good order, risk bringing the whole household of Christ followers into disrepute. The reverent older woman who is a "teacher of good things" [καλοδιδάσκαλος] (Tit. 2.3), contrasts with these men who not only worm their way into their households and corrupt women but also spread "other teaching [ἑτεροδιδασκαλεῖν]" (1 Tim. 1.3; 6.3). Paul commands Timothy and Titus to set up leadership structures based on households who will faithfully pass on his teachings. Opponents trade in "myths and endless genealogies which promote speculations rather than the divine training" (1 Tim. 1.4), "a morbid craving for controversy and for disputes about words, which produce envy, dissension, slander, base suspicions, and wrangling amongst those who are depraved in mind and bereft of truth" (6.4–5), "godless chatter and contradictions of what is falsely called knowledge: (6.20). They are purveyors of "silly myths and old wives' tales [τοὺς δὲ βεβήλους καὶ γραώδεις μύθους]" (1 Tim. 4.7). Marianne Kartzow argues that these representations of prolix and unregulated speech belong to a larger strategy of feminizing opponents.[28] The households invaded by false teachers display an order that fails to withstand public scrutiny because the men who upset them are incapable of regulating domestic relations much less themselves. They are men "who swerve [ἀστοχήσαντες]" and "turn away into vain babble [ἐξετράπησαν ʒἰς ματαιολογίαν]" (1 Tim. 1.6). Like the prolix speech of the women they affect, they betray all the mismanagement of self that was associated in feminine babbling men.[29]

27 Maier 2013, 188–92; Osiek and MacDonald 2006, 144–63, 194–219.
28 Kartzow 2009, 180–201, building on Gleason 2003, 235–63.
29 For further discussion, Maier 2013, 177–79.

The Pastorals open up the households influenced by false teachers and present them as a socially erosive order whose secret life infects the public order. Here a private life in which marriage is rejected and women are unregulated blocks out the lines of public sight and threatens not only the piety of the household but public insurrection. This is the logic of letters that link submission to governing authority with properly conducted household life. In the ideally governed household of the Pastoral epistles, as in the household of God generally, there is nothing to hide and everything to show, to reveal that the pious Christian household cult and the religion that supports the well being of the state are one and the same. In this regard the letters also replicate a contemporary political discourse in which public and private cult share a similar logic, whereby the magistrate as temporary father of the state is homologous with the father as magistrate of the household.[30] But in these households where home invasion masks the deeper truth of community eroding vices of insurrection, erosion of marriage, and household insubordination, the private as that realm beyond public scrutiny hides secrets that threaten God's household, which, analogous with the political order, also undermines the civic order God has established.

The Pastoral epistles mark out a territoriality that links religion, the private and public aspects of the household, and the civic order. The author classifies the households of those who rightly follow Paul and those who do not as strategy to delimit access by those judged false teachers and to assert control over women who appear to have welcomed them. The letters classify space, represent it, and seek to regulate it through the application of a household discourse that creates public sight lines into Christian households. Right and false teaching create and reflect a household whose life, both public and private, is correctly governed and guarantees a stable civic and ecclesial order.

3. Marcus's Love Potions: Marking Territory in Irenaeus

Irenaeus (c. 130 – c. 200 CE), bishop of Lugdunum in Gaul, continues and significantly develops the territorialism we have discovered in the Pastoral Epistles.[31] Indeed he bases the title of his chief work, *On the Detection and Refutation of Knowl-*

---

30 I am grateful to Clifford Ando for drawing my attention to this analogue. For fuller discussion of the motif of magistrate as father of the state and as father of the household, and its analogues in Pauline thought, Mengestu 2013, 51–90.

31 For further sources of Irenaeus' representation of opponents as heretics, Royalty 2013, 119–76; for Irenaeus' construction of Valentianism, Le Boulluec 1985, 1.113–253.

edge Falsely So Called (here after *Heresies*) on 1 Tim. 6.20, where "Paul" exhorts "Timothy" to avoid "the godless chatter and contradictions of what is falsely called knowledge." Although Irenaeus rarely quotes the Pastoral Epistles, James W. Aageson has shown that he champions and develops an institutionalized vision of Pauline theology enshrined in them.[32] The Pastorals represent Paul's teaching as a "deposit [παραθήκη]" Timothy is to guard and preserve (1 Tim. 6.20–21; 2 Tim. 1.14); Irenaeus (*Heresies* 3.4.1) likens the apostles' teachings as deposits in a bank account – the church. In the Pastorals, Timothy and Titus are to appoint presbyter-bishops and deacons who will rightly govern churches. Irenaeus develops these ideas by linking them: those bishops who can trace their succession from bishops appointed by the apostles, who teach what conforms with their deposit, and thus preserve and pass it on, alone are the guardians and representatives of true Christian teaching (*Heresies* 3.2.2; 3.3.1,3; 4.26.2). The Pastorals accuse opponents of "other teaching [ἑτεροδιδασκάλειν]." Irenaeus uses the term αἱρετικός (*hereticus*) expressly to describe false teachers and impious belief (*Heresies* 2. praef.1; 3.3.4; 3.6.4, 15.2, 23.8; 4.26.2; 5.32.1).

Irenaeus like the Pastorals associates right doctrine with public instruction and heresy with a form of secret teaching he describes as circulating privately away from open view. He emphasizes the public proclamation of the apostles (3.11.7–12.13), who faithfully transmitted the teachings they received from Jesus, first orally and then later in written form (*Heresies* 3.1.1). This he contrasts with that of heretics who confess one thing in church in public but think another in secret, or teach false opinions in private that contradict the truth. The public private distinction is important for Irenaeus' own territorialism, as we will see. In *Heresies* 3.4.3 he describes how Valentinus when he came to Rome confessed one thing in public and another in private. Later in 3.16.8 he warns against those who "appear to be like us, by what they say in public, repeating the same words as we do [*habent extinsecus loquelam similis nobis apparent*]; but inwardly [*intrinsecus*] they are wolves." This he warns is a strategy "to entrap the more simple, and entice them, imitating our phraseology." They wonder, Irenaeus asks, "how it is, that when they hold doctrines similar to ours, we, without cause keep ourselves aloof from their company; and that when they say things, and hold the same doctrine, we call them heretics?" (3.15.2).

Irenaeus puts forward a concrete example in an extended description (1.13.1–15.6) of the behaviors and beliefs of the Valentinian teacher, Marcus, active in his own community in Gaul.[33] From a social geographical perspective it is

32 Aageson, 167–70.

33 Irenaeus' discussion is extant only in Latin, but appears, slightly altered, in Greek in Epiphanius' *Panarion* 34.1 and Hippolytus' *Refutation* 6.39–40; for the Greek text cited here, Rousseau and Doutreleau 1979.

important to note how Irenaeus represents Marcus' activities both in households away from public view and how he associates them with women. Irenaeus' report is undoubtedly based on hearsay, and he caricatures his opponent with commonplace accusations, but it is also likely that Marcus represents a real person in his community and that neither Marcus nor his disciples considered themselves as the outsiders Irenaeus casts them as.[34] The point of Irenaeus' portrait of Marcus is precisely to cast him outside the community and to bring definition where there is apparent ambiguity from Irenaeus' perspective. For the purposes of this discussion, it is important to note how he links Marcus' secret teachings with his activities in households away from public view. This allows him to make the same kind of link with false teaching and private household actions free from public scrutiny we see in the Pastorals.

Irenaeus represents Marcus as a "magician [μᾶγος]" who "compounds philters and love-potions [φίλτρα καὶ ἀγώγιμα]" (1.13.5.1) with which to seduce women who are "covered in fine garments/ well born, and clothed in purple, and of greatest wealth [τὰς εὐπαρύφους, καὶ περιπορφύρους, καὶ πλουσωτάτας = *honestae, et circumpurpuratae, et ditissimae*]" (1.13.3.6–9). Marcus invites them to participate in a nuptial ritual in which they are invited to ecstatic speech and prophesy. A woman, he goes on, having participated in the ritual, "considers herself a prophet [προφητίδα]" and then rewards Marcus "not only by the gift of her possessions [τὴν τῶν ὑπαρχόντων], by means of which he has collected a very large fortune [πλῆθος πολύ], but also by sharing her body" (1.13.3.29,54,55–57). He represents Marcus' rituals as "banquets [δείπνοι]" in which lots are drawn by women to prophesy (1.13.4.20–29). Irenaeus goes on to describe how Marcus, invited by a deacon into his house, seduced his wife and convinced her to travel with him (1.13.5). Finally "when with no small difficulty, the brothers had converted her, she spent her whole time in the exercise of public confession, weeping over and lamenting the defilement which she had received from this magician" (1.13.5.18–23). But Marcus is not alone: "Some of his disciples, too, prowling about [περιπολίζοντες] in the same manner, have led astray many silly women [γυναικάρια], and defiled them" (1.13.6.2,3–4). It is reasonable to assume that Marcus' followers, if not Marcus himself was part of Irenaeus' community. In a telling sentence Irenaeus observes: "But already some of the most faithful women, possessed of the fear of God, and not being deceived (whom nevertheless, he did his best to seduce like the rest by bidding them

34 For the historical Marcus, his presence in Irenaeus' Christian community in Gaul, the ambiguity he represented, and a detailed commentary of the passages that follow see Förster 1999, 54–162.

prophesy), abhorring and execrating him, have withdrawn from such revelry [θιάσου]" (1.13.4.1–8). Some "make public confessions of their sins" he later says, but "others hesitate between the two courses, and incur that which is implied in the proverb, 'neither without nor within' [μήθτε ἔξω, μήτε ἔσω] ...." (1.13.7.12–13).

In these intriguing descriptions Irenaeus deploys a number of commonplaces to cast Marcus and his followers in a dubious light. The teacher invited home by an unsuspecting husband, only to discover himself a cuckold when the teacher seduces his wife, was a commonplace both in Greek and Roman fiction as well as street burlesque.[35] The woman "covered in fine garments, and clothed in purple, and of greatest wealth" who leaves the private household spaces assigned her in the well-regulated household to attend banquets is also at home in a stereotype of luxuriating women as immoral and immodest.[36] The representation of Marcus as a magician who concocts love potions to seduce other men's wives is similarly consistent with these representations.[37] As practitioner of magic Marcus reveals his impiety; the chaotic household is symptomatic of his "bad religion." Irenaeus' report of Marcus and his followers hidden from public view and therefore engaging in impiety destructive of the household order is part of a broader strategy of the whole of *Against Heresies* to classify, represent, and regulate true and false teaching. Irenaeus seeks to bring clarity to what is ambiguous. For, what is not commonplace amongst the descriptions he uses to describe his ecclesial situation is the picture of a woman "μήθτε ἔξω, μήτε ἔσω" an observation that fits in well with the very presence of Marcus amongst the Christians in Gaul, as it is with Irenaeus' other descriptions cited above of those who confess one thing publicly but believe or teach other things secretly.

Irenaeus' representation of this case is an excellent example of strategic territorialization of Christian belief and practice. The distinction between public and secret teaching functions as a means of classifying insiders and outsiders; the representation of a teacher like Marcus and others as believers in "wolves' clothing," or a seducer and magician who circulates in households marks his

---

35 Karris 1973, 549–64; for example, Lucian, *fug.* 18–19; *tim.* 55; *par.* 56; *rh. pr.* 23; Juvenal, *sat.* 9.22–38. For street drama, *oxyrhyncus* 432 (Wiemken 1972, 97–105), probably a more available resource for a largely illiterate audience.

36 For example Juvenal, *sat.* 6.457–60; Petronius, *satyr.* 67; Martial, *ep.* 8.81. For further examples of the stereotype in Greek and Latin literature, Olson 2008, 80–95; Winter 2003, 98–109.

37 For example, Lucian, *Alexander* 42; see Stratton 2013, 125–35; 2006, 102–8 for the stereotype and its uses as part of a larger tradition of polemic, and Stratton 2007, 80–95 for parallels with Irenaeus' account of Marcus. The stereotype appears also in the apocryphal *Acts of Andrew* 5–39; in the *Acts of Paul and Thecla* 3.15 Paul is accused of being a magician who has seduced Thecla.

teaching as sexually motivated and thus a transgression of domestic order; the description of women who have rightly confessed and publicly wept over their false beliefs and practices demonstrates regulation through a possible penitential ritual. It is notable that this story, the only concrete and extended representation of Irenaeus' own community, comes near the start of Irenaeus' five-volume polemic against heresy. At the outset he indicates that his chief concern is to refute the disciples of Valentinus (1.praef.2) and he counts Marcus amongst them (1.13.1). *Against Heresies'* vivid casting of Marcus' nuptial ritual and the private activities of Marcus and religious practices of those women he seduces functions both to create and delimit space, to use public and private as a means of asserting a clear line between right apostolic teaching and heresy. Thus Irenaeus takes ideas and associations of private and public in the Pastorals and extends them for a much more universal application.

4. Household Stewards and Biting Dogs: Creating Public and Private in Ignatius of Antioch

"Everyone whom the Master of the house sends to manage his own house [ὁ οἰκοδεσπότης εἰς ἰδίαν οἰκονομίαν] we must welcome as we would who sent him. It is obvious, therefore, that we must regard the bishops as the Lord himself" (*Eph.* 6.1). "For there are some who are accustomed to carrying about the Name maliciously and deceitfully while doing other things unworthy of God. You must avoid them as wild beasts. For they are mad dogs who bite by stealth [εἰσιν γὰρ κύνες λυσσῶντες, λαθροδή[eisin gar kunes lussontes, lathrodekta]κται]; you must be on your guard against them, for their bite is hard to heal" (*Eph.* 7.1).[38] Ignatius of Antioch, who wrote seven letters to churches in Asia Minor while en route to martyrdom in Rome, perhaps as late as the 130s, offers a formulation in a similar vein to the territoriality and association of right and false teaching with public and private configuration of belief and practice we encounter in the Pastoral Epistles and Irenaeus.[39] More expressly than they, however, Ignatius relates right teaching to allegiance with a local bishop, and forbids meetings in places outside of the bishop's control or knowledge.

38 For the Greek text, Holmes 2007. Translations are my own.
39 For the dating, Holmes 2007, 170, with literature.

Ignatius' letters oppose what he conceives as docetic Christological ideas (*Eph.* 9.1; *Tral.* 9.1–2; 10.1; *Smyrn.* 2.1; 3.1; 4.2; *Philad.* praef.) and "Judaizing" (*Magn,* 8.1; 10.3; *Philad.* 6.1). It lies outside of the focus of this discussion to determine whether or how these two charges are related, or to identify those whom he accuses.[40] Of interest here is the way Ignatius casts the respective topography of those he charges as false teachers and champions for professing rightly. He portrays the former as conducting their meetings in private away out of eye's reach, as it were, of the local bishop. The latter meet publicly, that is with the knowledge of the bishop. Ignatius uses the term αἵρεσις twice (*Eph.* 6.2; Tral. 6.1) to describe those he opposes. In the first passage he commends the Ephesians that their bishop, Onesimus, praises them for their "orderly conduct in God [τὴν ἐν θεῷ εὐταξίαν]" and that "no heresy has found a home among you [ἐν ὑμῖν οὐδεμία αἵρεσις καοικεῖ]." In the second he distinguishes "Christian food [ἡ χριστιανὴ τροφή]" from "every strange plant, which is heresy [ἀλλοτρίας δὲ βοτάνης ..., ἥτις ἐστὶν αἵρεσις]." Elsewhere he exhorts Philadelphian Christ followers to "flee from division and false teaching [τὸν μερισμὸν καὶ τὰς κακοδιδασκαλίας]" and goes on significantly to urge them to remain where the shepherd is and to resist "seemingly trustworthy wolves [λύκοι ἀξιόπιστοι]" (*Philad.* 2.1, 2). He contrasts the division such false teaching brings with the unity of right teaching. Ignatius is the first writer to use the phrase ἡ καθολικὴ ἐκκλησία (*Smyr.* 8.2), significantly in a passage where he urges his audience to flee from divisions (μερισμοί, 8.1) and to meet where the bishop is present (8.2).

Ignatius turns his opponents into those who meet in secret and his allies as those who meet openly with the local bishop, in unity with the presbyters and deacons, who together represent right Christological teaching and alone gather legitimately. He learned that in Ephesus "some from elsewhere have stayed with you" (*Eph.* 9.2). That they meet in households is strongly implied when he states "family corrupters [οἰκοφθόροι]" cannot inherit the kingdom of God (16.1). A further strong measure of support for a household setting for meetings is where Ignatius commands that Christians at Smyrna "not only not welcome, but, if possible, not even meet with them [οὐ μόνον δεῖ ὑμᾶς μὴ παραδέχεσθαι, ἀλλ'εἰ δυνατὸν, μηδὲ συναντᾶν" (*Smyrn.* 4.1). Unlike his opponents who have evidently enjoyed material support at least through hospitality, "no one can boast" Ignatius says, secretly or openly that I was a burden in anything either small or great [τις καυχήσασθαι οὔτε λάθρα οὔτε φανερῶς, ὅτε ἐβάρησά τινα ἐν μικρῷ ἢ ἐν μεγάλῳ]." They are to speak to them "neither in private nor in public [μήτε κατ' ἰδίαν περὶ αὐτῶν λαλεῖν μήτε κοινῇ]" (7.2). It is probable that they conduct

40 For discussion with literature see Maier 2002, 187.

their own house church meetings: on account of their docetic beliefs, Ignatius states, they "abstain [ἀπέχονται]" from the Eucharist and prayers (*Smyrn.* 6.2). Conversely, he instructs them that there can be no baptism or agape without the bishop, and those who do anything without his knowledge "serves the devil" (8.2). Such meetings, he instructs the Magnesians, are invalid (*Magn.* 4.1). Only those meetings known by or directly conducted by the bishop and his co-leaders are legitimate (*Trall.* 2.2; 3.1; *Smyrn.* 8.1; 9.2; *Philad.* 8.2). The Philadelphians are to participate in one Eucharist because Christ's flesh is one, there is one cup, one altar, and one bishops joined in unity with the presbyters and deacons (*Philad.* 4.1). Ignatius exhorts his audiences to meet more often (*Eph.* 13.1); he instructs Polycarp, bishop of Smyrna, to "let the meetings be more numerous" (*Poly.* 4.2).

Ignatius repeatedly charges those who meet in private, that is without the bishop's knowledge, as guilty of deception. They hide or do things in secret (*Eph.* 15.3); they hypocritically deceive the local bishop (*Magn.* 3.2); they bear the name "Christian" only in name and not reality (*Magn.* 4.1). "[T]here are some who are accustomed to carrying about the name deceitfully and wickedly [δόλῳ πονηρῷ] while doing other things unworthy of God" (*Eph.* 7.1). It was God himself who gave Ignatius knowledge of secret divisions in the Philadelphian church when the Spirit filled him with the prophetic pronouncement to do nothing apart from the bishop (*Philad.* 7.2). Together with this secrecy come a host of vices drawn from a wide repertoire of civic ills centering on social ills of "faction [ἔρς, ἐριθεία]" (*Eph.* 8.1; *Philad.* 8.2), "*division* [μερισμός]" (*Philad.* 2.1; 3.1; 7.2; 8.1; *Smyrn.* 7.2), "arrogance, [ὑπερυφάνειν, μεγαλορημοσύνη]" (*Eph.* 5.3; 10.2), "boasting, [καύχησις]" (*Eph.* 18.1), and "conceit [φυσιόειν]" (*Magn.* 12.1; Trall. 7.1). Opposite to these are the virtues of those who worship correctly, who manifest "peace [εἰρήνη]" (*Eph.* 13.2; *Smyrn.* 12.2), and "unity [ἕνωσις]" (*Magn.* 13. 2; *Tral.* 11. 2; *Phld.* 4.1; 7. 2; *Pol.* 1.2; 5. 2); ἑνότης (*Eph.* 4. 2; 5.1; 14.1; *Phld.* 2.2; 3.2; 5.2; *Smyrn.* 12.2); ἑνόειν (*Eph.* inscr.; *Magn.* 6.2; 14. 1). They are to demonstrate "humility [ταπεινόφρονες]" (*Eph.* 10.2), right worship and sacrifice (*Eph.* 5.2; 20.2; *Magn.* 7.2; *Trall.* 7.2; *Philad.* 4.1) and "good order [εὐταξίαν]" (*Eph.* 6.2). In both representations Ignatius reveals himself at home in civic topoi relating to "concord [ὁμονοία]" (*Eph.* 4.1,2; 13.1; *Magn.* 6.1; 15.1; *Trall.* 12.2) and its opposite ἔρις.[41] He deploys a revised household code to instruct Polycarp of his ecclesial responsibilities as bishop of the Smyrnaeans to assure right order and domestic conduct (*Pol.* 4.2–5.2). Under such conditions right Christological confession and proper ecclesial government confirm right household order. Indeed, he reinfor-

---

41 For full discussion, Maier 2005, 307–24; Lotz 2007.

ces that view when he shows care in sending greetings to households in Smyrna. But conversely, although Ignatius does not spell it out as directly, those who manifest deceit, welcome false teachers, conduct meetings outside of the bishop's knowledge, and profess heresy exhibit disorderly household life, hidden from public view, the origin of disunity and faction. It is only as a consequence of this that either false confession could be possible or illegitimate meetings could be convened. Those who upset households upset right belief; households in disarray manifest secrecy, deceit, hypocrisy, and disorderly conduct that ruins unity and harmony.

I have argued elsewhere that Ignatius' letters do not mirror an ecclesiastical set of structures already in existence in the churches they addressed. Rather they seek to create and solidify those structures and use them as a means of asserting and promoting a set of teachings Ignatius endorses.[42] That strategy I argue here can be understood from a social geographical perspective as a form of territorialism. Ignatius draws a portrait of right teaching as public and known and heresy as private and unknown, but in doing so he seeks to lengthen ecclesial sight lines so that they penetrate all houses, not only those of the bishop, to assure that only those rituals he can see (i.e. sanction) are legitimate and all other unknown ones are tainted with secrecy and vice. Based on Ignatius' description of those in Philadelphia who "desired to deceive me after the flesh," whose presence he revealed through a divinely given utterance, it is reasonable to infer that in fact these enjoyed a rather more ambiguous position in the community than Ignatius would have desired. Ignatius describes them as hidden; one could also argue Ignatius was importing a distinction that hitherto was absent. One can adduce the same from Ignatius' need both to rule out meetings apart from those conducted by local bishop or the ones he knows about, as well as his exhortations to make meetings more numerous. Under conditions such as these Ignatius "as a man set on unity" (*Philad.* 8.1) sought to bring a certain level of discord by classifying and sharpening religious confession, representing opponents and allies as belonging respectively to rightly governed and ordered public and private domains, and by regulating meetings in households and house churches. These in turn he links up with a larger civic discourse so that from the sanctuary/house church of the rightly conducted worship issue forth a set of ideals celebrated in the greater polis. From those "altars" not sanctioned by the bishop arise all the community eroding vices that tarnish shared civic life and its best aspirations. Ignatius' letters when considered from a social geographical perspective offer two site lines, one shared by Ignatius and those he

42 Maier 2002, 175–81.

promotes into the well ordered household, and the other represented by his unmasking of disorderly conduct that taints private, allegedly secret, meetings with antisocial vices. What is seen and public is right and what is unseen and hence private is wrong.

5. Conclusion

The Pastoral Epistles, Irenaeus' account of Marcus, and Ignatius of Antioch's letters each in their own way deploy territorial strategies that invoke and create public and private spaces for the circulation of right belief and delimitation of false teaching. By classifying opponents as inhabiting secret, hidden, and unregulated private spaces they are able to associate with them all the vices that lead to the destruction of the polis. To them belongs also a destructive practice of religion these authors classify as "other teaching," "heretical," or "heresy." Central to the classification of them is that their hidden, private, religious practices erode the common good. By contrast, those meetings where leaders practice right teaching are either open to public view, represent the public teaching of the apostles, or display the virtues of a harmonious social order. This religion is public and promotes the ideals of the civic order. The uses of private and public to represent right and wrong teaching becomes a means of regulation, to assure that a public eye is kept on private actions, and to create a status quo. Those spaces kept open to the public view, defined of course as the church's eye, make sure that if there is a private domain in the church they will always stay under the eye of approved leaders.

Works Cited

Aageson, J. (2008). *Paul, the Pastoral Epistles, and the Early Church.* Library of Pauline Studies. Peabody, Mass.

Adams, E. (2013). *The Earliest Christian Meeting Places: Almost exclusively Houses?* The library of New Testament studies, Early Christianity in context 40. London.

Bassler, J. (2003). "Limits and differentiation: the calculus of widows in 1 Timothy 5.3–16," in Amy-Jill Levine, ed., *A Feminist companion to the New Testament and early Christian writings,* 7: 122–46. London.

Cooper, K. (2007). "Closely watched households: visibility, exposure, and private power in the Roman *domus.*" *Past and Present* 197: 3–33.

Countryman, W. (1980). *The rich Christian in the church of the early empire.* New York.

Davies, S. (1980). *The revolt of the widows: the social world of the Apocryphal Acts.* Carbondale.

Des Rosiers, N. (2003). “Introduction,” in Law Commission of Canada, ed., *New Perspectives on the Public-Private Divide*, vii-xviii. Vancouver.
Dibelius, M. and Conzelmann, H. (1972). *A Commentary on the Pastoral Epistles.* Translated by Philip Buttolph and Adela Yarbro. Hermeneia. Philadelphia.
Dittenberger, W. ed. (1915–1924). *Sylloge inscriptionum graecarum.* 3rd ed, 4 vols. Leipzig.
Ebner, M. (2012). *Die Stadt als Lebensraum der ersten Christen. Das Urchristentum in seiner Umwelt I.* Grundrisse zum Neuen Testament 1.1. Göttingen.
Förster, N. (1999). *Marcus magus.* WUNT 114. Tübingen.
Friesen, S. and Walter S. (2009). “The size of the economy and the distribution of income in the Roman Empire.” *JRS* 99: 61–91.
Gehring, R. (2009). *House church and mission: the importance of household structures in early Christianity.* Peabody, Mass.
Gleason, M. (1995). *Making Men: Sophists and self-Representation in ancient Rome.* Princeton.
Harland, P. (2009). *Dynamics of identity in the world of the early Christians.* London.
Holmes, M. (2007). *The apostolic fathers: Greek texts and English translations.* 3rd ed. Grand Rapids.
Hubbard, P. and Kitchin R., eds. (2011). *Key thinkers on space and place.* Los Angeles.
Karris, R. (1973). “The Background and Significance of the Polemic of the Pastoral Epistles.” *Journal of Biblical Literature* 92: 549–64.
Kartzow, M. (2009). *Gossip and gender: othering of speech in the Pastoral Epistles.* BZNW 164. Berlin.
Kidd, R. (1990). *Wealth and beneficence in the Pastoral Epistles.* SBL dissertation series 122. Atlanta.
Le Boulluec, A. (1985). *La notion d’hérésie dans la littérature grecque, IIe-IIIe siècles.*, 2 vols. Etudes augustiniennes. Paris.
Lotz, J.-P. (2007) *Ignatius and concord: the background and use of concord in the letters of Ignatius of Antioch.* Patristic studies 8. New York.
MacDonald, M. (1996). *Early Christian women and pagan opinion: the power of the hysterical woman.* Cambridge.
MacDonald, D. (1983). *The Legend and the apostle: The battle for Paul in story and canon.* Philadelphia.
Maier, H. (2013). *Picturing Paul in empire: imperial image, text and persuasion in Colossians, Ephesians and the Pastoral Epistles.* London.
Maier, H. (2005). “The politics of discord and concord in Paul and Ignatius of Antioch,” in Andrew Gregory and Christopher Tuckett, eds., *The New Testament and the Apostolic Fathers:* 307–24. Oxford.
Maier, H. (2002). *The social setting of the ministry as reflected in the writings of Hermas, Clement and Ignatius.* Studies in Christianity and Judaism / Études sur le christianisme et le judaïsme 12. Waterloo, Ont.
Marshall, I. (1999). *The Pastoral Epistles.* ICC. Edinburgh.
Marshall, J. (2008). “‘I left you in Crete’: narrative deception and social hierarchy in the letter to Titus.” *Journal of Biblical Literature* 127: 781–803.
Meiggit, J. (1998). *Paul, Poverty and Survival.* Studies in the New Testament and its world. Edinburgh.
Mengestu, A. (2013). *God as Father in Paul: Kinship Language and Identity Formation in Early Christianity.* Eugene, OR.

Merz, A. (2004). *Die fictive Selbstauslegung des Paulus. Intertextuelle Studien zur Intention und Rezeption der Pastoralbriefe.* NOTA 52. Göttingen.
Oakes, P. (2009). *Reading Romans in Pompeii: Paul's letter at ground level.* Minneapolis.
Olson, K. (2008). *Dress and the Roman woman: self-presentation and society.* London.
Osiek, C., MacDonald, M. and Tulloch, J. (2006). *A Woman's Place: House Churches in Earliest Christianity.* Minneapolis.
Richards, W. (2002). *Difference and distance in post-pauline Christianity: an epistolary analysis of the Pastoral Epistles.* Studies in Biblical Literature 44. New York.
Rousseau, A. and L. Doutreleau, L. (1979). *Contre les heresies I.* Sources Chretiennes 263, 264. Paris.
Royalty, R. (2013). *The origin of heresy: a history of discourse in second temple Judaism and early Christianity.* London.
Sack, R. D. (2009). *Human territoriality: its theory and history.* Cambridge Studies in Historical Geography. Cambridge.
Saller, R. (1984). "*Familia, domus,* and the Roman Conception of the Family." *Phoenix* 38: 336–55.
Stowers, S. (1998). "A cult from Philadelphia: oikos religion or cultic association?" in A. Malherbe, F. Norris, and J. Thompson, *The early church in its context: essays in honor of Everett Ferguson:* 287–301. Leiden.
Stratton, K. (2013). *Naming the witch: magic, ideology, and stereotype in the ancient world.* New York.
Stratton, K. (2007). "The rhetoric of 'magic' in early Christian discourse: gender, power and the construction of 'heresy,'" in T. Penner and C. vander Stichele, *Mapping Gender in Ancient Religious Discourses:* 89–114. Leiden.
Thurston, B. (2003). "1 Timonty 5.3–6 and leadership of women in the early church," in Amy-Jill Levine, ed., *A Feminist companion to the New Testament and early Christian writings,* 7: 159–74. London.
Trebilco, P. (2007). *Early Christians in Ephesus from Paul to Ignatius.* Grand Rapids, Mich.
Trümper, M. (2003). "Material and social environment of greco-roman households in the east: the case of hellenistic Delos," in D.L. Blach and C. Oseik, eds., *Early Christian families in context: an interdisciplinary dialogue:* 19–43. Grand Rapids.
Verner, D. (1983). *The Houshold of God" The social world of the Pastoral Epistles.* Society of Biblical Literature dissertation series 71. Chico, CA.
Virgili, P. (1989). *Acconciature e maquillage.* Vita e costumi romani antiche 7. Rome 1989.
Wallace-Hadrill, A. (2003). "*Domus* and *insulae* in Rome: families and housefuls," in D.L. Blach and C. Oseik, eds., *Early Christian families in context: an interdisciplinary dialogue:* 3–18. Grand Rapids.
Wallace- Hadrill, A. (1988). "The Social Structure of the Roman House." *Papers of the British School at Rome* 56: 43–97.
Wiemken, H. (1972). *Der griechischen Mimus. Dokumente zur Geschichte des antiken Volks-Theaters.* Bremen.
Winter, B. (2003). *Roman wives, Roman widows: the appearance of new women and the Pauline communities.* Grand Rapids.
Zamfir, K. (2013). *Men and women in the household of God: a contextual approach to roles and ministries in the Pastoral Epistles.* Göttingen.

Rubina Raja

8. Staging "private" religion in Roman "public" Palmyra. The role of the religious dining tickets (banqueting *tesserae*)

Abstract: The so-called banqueting *tesserae*, of which far beyond 1500 pieces are known, present a wonderful corpus of material through which a lot may be learned about the city's religious life. These tiny, for most part clay objects, present the richest source for the city's religious life and until now remain largely unexplored in this respect. There is no extensive evidence for the organisation of religion in Roman-period Palmyra. However, the tesserae offer a glimpse into at least some aspects of the organisation of religious life at Palmyra, since they present evidence pertaining to group construction and identity in specific sacred contexts, namely as invitations to single-standing occasions, the religious banquets. Furthermore the combination of the find spots of the tesserae, mostly from within the parameters of the sanctuaries in the city, and the iconography of the tesserae, showing priests of various cultic groups, tell us about the structure of at least parts of the religious life of Palmyra, not least about the way in which sanctuaries or parts of sanctuaries could be used by a variety of cultic groups at different points in time. This aspect, namely the use of the sanctuaries by various cultic groups, including groups who did not celebrate the main deity or deities of a given sanctuary, is one of central concern to this article. At its core stands the question about definitions of "private" and "public" space in the ancient city and about the variety of uses of such spaces, which we would not be able to access without such evidence as the tesserae.

1. Introduction

Palmyra's special role as a border city has long been recognized (fig. 1). The city was situated between the two mighty empires of Rome and Parthia, halfway between the Euphrates and the Mediterranean Sea. Palmyra's languages, society and religion, its art and architecture speak of a rich and varied heritage.[1] How-

1 General literature on Palmyra: Starcky and Gawlikowski 1985; Will 1992; Millar 1993, 319–36; Kaizer 2002a; Schmidt-Colinet 2005; Sartre and Sartre-Fauriat 2008.

ever, the art of Palmyra has received remarkably little in-depth research, despite its familiarity.[2] Most scholars concerned with the classical world will be acquinted with the images of wide-eyed Palmyrene gods or citizens lined up stiffly, looking back at the viewer; but despite the familiarity of this kind of sculpture, academic ground work is still lacking. This is especially true of the English-speaking world, where the excellent handbook *The Art of Palmyra* by M.A.R. Colledge remains the only work of its kind.[3] Apart from the vast corpus of Palmyrene sculpture, which is currently being collected and studied within *The Palmyra Portrait Project*, there is another crucial category of material from Palmyra, which long has been overlooked in research, namely the so-called banqueting tesserae.[4]

2. The banqueting tesserae from Palmyra

The so-called banqueting tesserae, for the most part small clay tokens with iconography stamped on them, of which far beyond 1500 pieces are known, present a wonderful corpus of material through which we may learn a lot about the city's religious life.[5] In fact one may dare to say that these tiny objects present the richest source for the city's religious life and that they until now remain largely unexplored in this respect. All tesserae then known were published in the comprehensive publication by Ingholt, Seyrig and Starcky in 1955.[6] This publication holds 1132 examples of tesserae from various collections across the world.[7] Furthermore tesserae have been published in various museum catalogues, as well as by Comte Mesnil du Buisson in two volumes, the volume with the illustrations

2 The beautifully illustrated catalogue of the most important exhibition in recent years, *Moi, Zenobie, Reine de Palmyre* (Charles-Gaffiot et al. ed. 2001) contains 30 specialist articles, none of them on sculpture, painting or other visual arts.

3 Colledge 1976.

4 More can be read about the Palmyra Portrait Project on the following webpage: http://projects.au.dk/palmyraportrait/. The corpus currently comprises more than 1800 Palmyrene portraits. The first attempt at a comprehensive publication of the tesserae is Ingholt, Seyrig and Starcky 1955. In 1940 Seyrig, one of greatest scholars of the Roman Near East published one of the first articles which dealt with the tesserae (Seyrig 1940b).

5 There is no literary evidence which speaks of these tesserae and therefore we do also not know what they in fact were termed in antiquity.

6 Ingholt, Seyrig and Starcky 1955. This publication holds several tesserae of the same series. Dunant 1959 added some until then unknown examples.

7 The collections are listed on pages 6–7 in Ingholt, Seyrig and Starcky 1955.

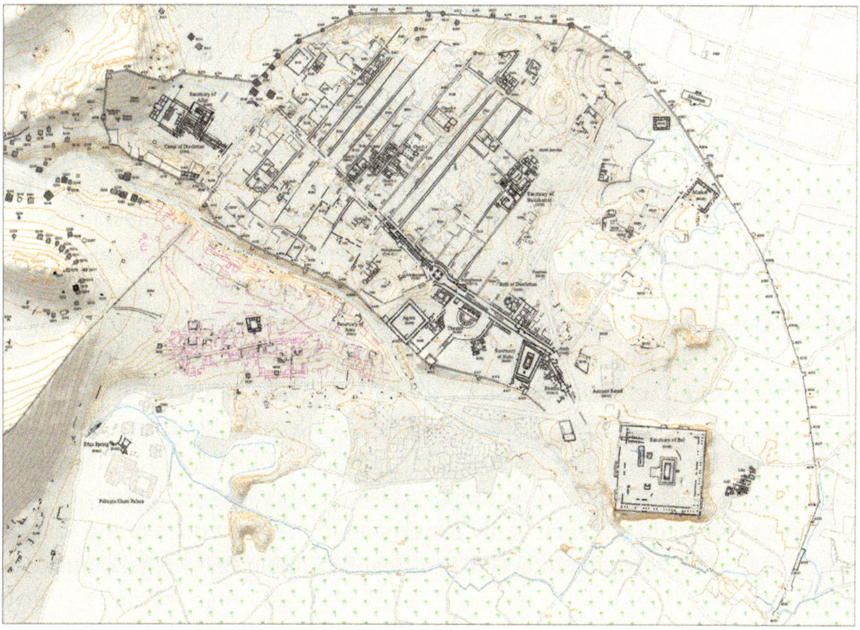

Fig. 1: Plan of Palmyra (Schnädelbach 2010)

having appeared 18 years before the text volume.[8] Although these publications are important, since they have made the material broadly available to scholars, they do not explore to the fullest the implications that these tesserae hold for our understanding of religious life in Palmyra and the way it was organized, including the way in which various groups could act within what might be termed the public, civic, or religious sphere.[9] This chapter represents an attempt to assess the implications of the tesserae for the understanding of the structure of the religious life of Palmyra and to indicate the importance of non-civic religious groups acting in the public spaces of Palmyra.

The banqueting tesserae from Palmyra are plentiful. They were already interpreted by Ingholt, Seyrig and Starcky as religious dining tickets and this inter-

8 Mesnil du Buisson's publication appeared in two volumes. The illustrations were published in one volume in 1944 and the accompanying text volume only appeared in 1962. While the publication is richly illustrated, the text volume in some cases offers some doubtful interpretations.
9 Kaizer has in Kaizer 2002a, 215 and Kaizer 2002b, 155 pointed to the possible implications of the tesserae.

pretation has been widely followed since then.[10] The tesserae were found mainly in and around the banqueting hall in the Sanctuary of Bel in Palmyra, which is the largest sanctuary in the city (fig. 2).[11] The largest number there was found in and around the drainage leading from the banqueting hall. The find spot of these numerous tesserae is one indication that these were not objects that people necessarily took with them after a given event. They could obviously be discarded when they had served their purpose. A few particular find circumstances are documented as well. In the Arsu temple in Palmyra, parts of which were excavated by Will in 1980, a pot with a total of 125 tesserae of a single series was found deposited under floor level within the architectural limits of the sanctuary.[12] It is not possible to say whether these tesserae had already been used or were waiting to be given out for a special occasion. Al As'ad, Briquel-Chatonnet and Yon tend to the conclusion that these tesserae had been collected after distribution and had already been used as entrance tickets already.[13] Other tesserae have been found in other sanctuaries in Palmyra.[14] However, the deity or deities depicted on these tesserae do not necessarily correspond to the main deity of the sanctuary in which they were found.[15] This is a clear indication that the religious banquets may have been held in honour of a different deity than the one to which the given sanctuary was dedicated. Stray finds, also from outside the sanctua-

10 Ingholt, Seyrig and Starcky 1955, 4 and Kaizer 2002a, 22. Also in the new book by Smith 2013, 16 the tesserae are mentioned as being important evidence for "the banquets and other gatherings". However, Smith does not explain which other gatherings these might have been and we do not about such other gatherings. Much remains speculative about the exact use of the tesserae apart from the fact that they were used as entrance tickets for banquets held in the sanctuaries of Palmyra. Also see Ingholt, Seyrig and Starcky 1955 as well as Kaizer 2002 and Smith 2013 for further literature on the tesserae.

11 Ingholt, Seyrig and Starcky 1995, 3–5.

12 Al-As'ad, Briquel-Chatonnet and Yon 2005 for the most comprehensive publication of these as well as Will 1983 for a preliminary publication of the Sanctuary of Arsu. Al-As'ad and Teixidor (1985) for the information on the sanctuary through epigraphic evidence. The existence of this temple was already known through epigraphic evidence: *PAT* 0197 (dated to 132 CE) and through the publication by Drijvers (1995), 34–38 (dating to 144 CE).

13 Al-As'ad, Briquel-Chatonnet and Yon 2005, 6 for considerations about which suggestion is the most likely. They tend to an interpretation of the tesserae as having been distributed for invited guests before the event and now being collected in the vase in which they were found at the point in time when the banquet took place. However, this suggestion is not based on evidence which is conclusive and this is also acknowledged by the authors.

14 See above for the tesserae in the Sanctuary of Bel as well as Ingholt, Seyrig and Starcky 1955 for a list of provenance for the known tesserae. Dunand 1959 for the tesserae from the Sanctuary of Baalshamin.

15 In general Spoer 1905 and Kaizer 2002. Dunand 1959 on the tesserae from the Sanctuary of Baalshamin, where not one single tesserae depict the main deity of the sanctuary.

ries, have been made across the city. Interestingly one of the earlier excavators in Palmyra, the dane Harald Ingholt, built a collection of tesserae during his campaigns there in 1924, 1925 and 1928, which today largely are in the Palmyra collection at the Ny Carlsberg Glyptotek in Copenhagen (fig. 3).[16]

The tesserae were most often made of finely levigated clay.[17] However, examples of glass, lead, bronze and iron are also known. The tesserae, which were made in series, hold a vivid and varied iconographical language, with, however, some standardized patterns, such as almost always depicting one or two reclining priests on a kline on the obverse (fig. 4).[18] Of some series more than a hundred examples exist.[19] More than over a thousand different series can be counted, which indicates that the tesserae were a wide-spread phenomenon in use in Palmyra for a longer period of time.[20] The dating of the tesserae can loosely be situated in the period between the first and the third centuries CE (in 273 CE Palmyra was sacked by the Romans), with a concentration in what seems to be the late second and third centuries CE.[21] However, the exact dating of the tesserae is done on the basis of the fairly few tesserae that carry inscriptions and therefore can be firmly dated.[22] Stylistically it is impossible to date the tesserae firmly since they are quite small objects, measuring between 2 to 5 centimetres in diameter and stylistic developments are impossible to trace.[23] Therefore it also re-

16 Raja, Sørensen and Yon forthcoming.

17 For good photos of a wide variety of examples see Hvidberg-Hansen and Ploug 1993, 169–210.

18 Ingholt, Seyrig and Starcky 1955 for drawings of a variety of types. Also see Al-As'ad, Briquel-Chatonnet and Yon 2005 for further references to tesserae of which more examples have been found.

19 Al-As'ad, Briquel-Chatonnet and Yon 2005, 7 with reference to Ingholt, Seyrig and Starcky 1955, RTP 422 and 429.

20 Ingholt, Seyrig and Starcky 1995, 9 counted 1130 different types. However, it must also be underlined that since it is difficult to pin the exact time span of the tesserae down and that they might have been produced for around two hundred years this would amount to perhaps only around 5 to 6 banquets a year. However, this is a hypothetical calculation based on the assumption that the tesserae indeed were a phenomenon which endured for more than 200 years.

21 Hvidberg-Hansen and Ploug 199, 24 for a dating between the early first century CE and 273 CE. However they do not speak about a concentration of dates in the late second and third centuries CE.

22 Smith 2013, 16 who mentions a number of 633 inscribed tesserae counted in the publication by Ingholt, Seyrig and Starcky 1955. This does not mean that all 633 can be dated precisely, since inscriptions do not necessarily include dates.

23 A study of various symbols and their frequency both in combination with dates and on their own is currently being undertaken by the author. Such a study may contribute to the dating of the tesserae on the grounds of the symbols used over time.

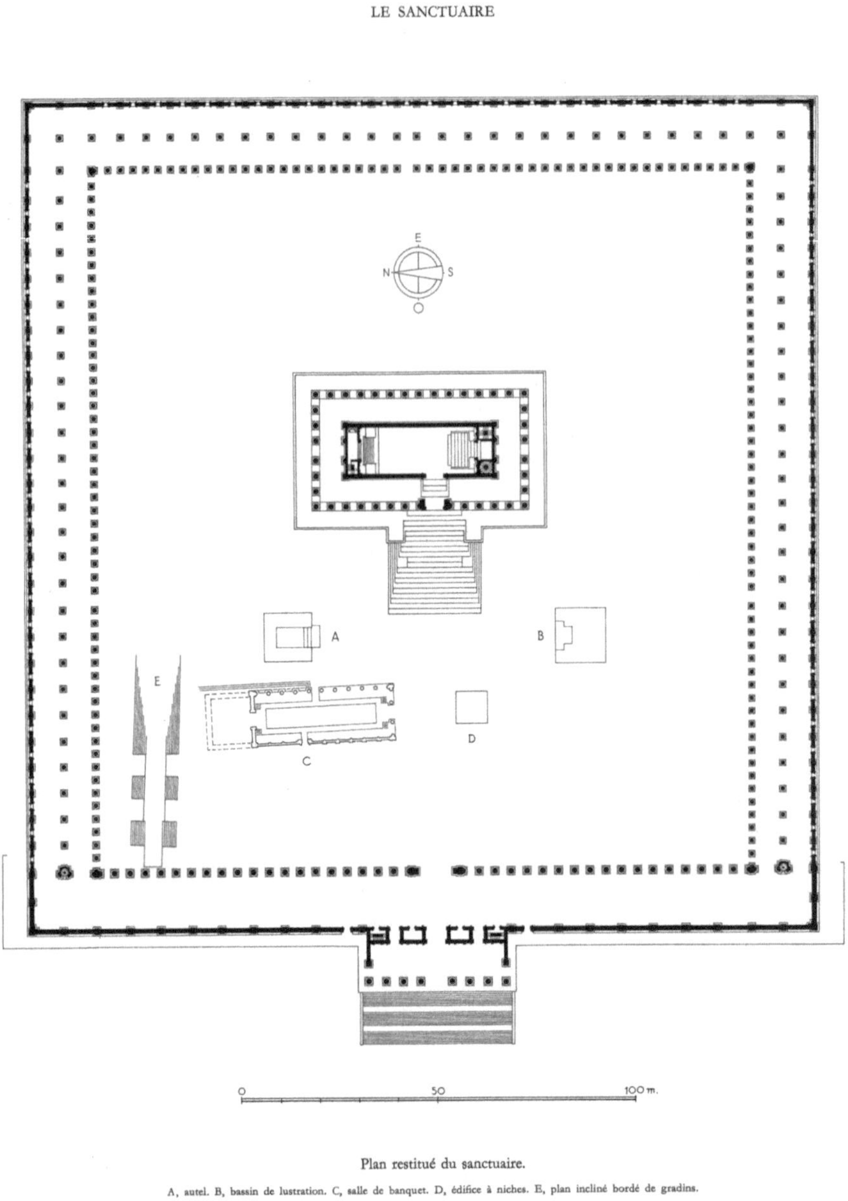

Fig. 2: Plan of the Sanctuary of Bel (Seyrig, Amy and Will 1968, Plan 1)

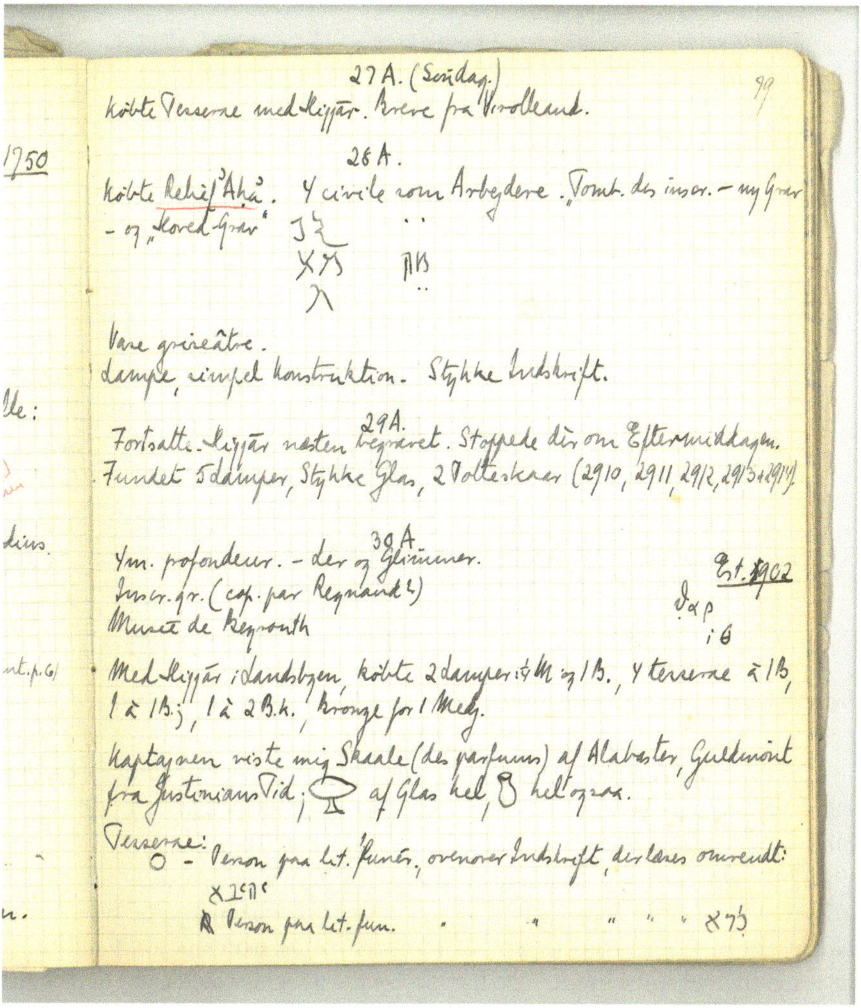

Fig. 3: Page 79 from Harald Ingholt's excavation diary, 1924, showing a list of tesserae that he purchased (Palmyra Portrait Project, Rubina Raja).

mains difficult, if not impossible, to do useful statistics on the frequency over the centuries of the banquets for which the tesserae served as entrance tickets.[24]

24 Seyrig 1940a and Gawlikowski 1990, 2651–2. Also see Kaizer 2002a, 215–216 for a resumé of the scholarship concerned with the interpretation of the use of the tesserae.

Fig. 4: Obverse of tessera showing reclining priest on a kline (photo Rubina Raja).

On the one hand the imagery on the tesserae is highly standardized, showing mostly on the one side (obverse) one or more priests banqueting, and on the other side symbols, gods and offering scenes (reverse). They might carry inscriptions on both sides (obverse and reverse), which give the name of the priest, priests or group of priests issuing the invition for the banquet, the date of the banquet, names of deities as well as for example measures of food and drink to be distributed at the event.[25] On the reverse the tesserae could carry depictions of deities, architectural settings (temple façades, for example), signet seal impressions and a wide range of symbols often combined in enigmatic ways (figs. 5 and 6). So within this fairly standardized iconographic language there was an enormous variety, which indicates that iconography and choice of images mattered to the people who were in charge of having these objects made or who

25 Hvidberg-Hansen and Ploug 1993, 171–181, for tesserae depicting priests and gods, many of which carry inscriptions. Hvidberg-Hansen and Ploug 1993, 189, I.N. 3206 for a tessera most likely displaying a measure. This tesserae also carries a date, namely 460 of the Palmyrene era, equaling 118/119 CE.

ordered them and, therefore, that the iconography might have been important also to the receivers of the tesserae.

Fig. 5: Reverse of tessera showing symbols and deity (photo Rubina Raja).

The production process was one that required each tessera to be produced as a unicum.[26] For each tessera-series two flat moulds were made, each with a relief. In this way a high relief could be produced on each side of the tesserae. The clay was placed between the two moulds and the thickness of the tesserae would depend on how hard the moulds were pressed together. Different and more refined techniques were required for the production of metal, lead and glass tesserae, which are rare in the corpus of the Palmyrene tesserae. Until now no workshops which produced these tesserae have been found in Palmyra.

It is not known in what quantities the single series were made, but the fact that each tesserae was made carefully – each one was pressed into the unique moulds, taken out to dry and be fired before it could be used – shows that consideration was paid in order for the tesserae within each series to look as uni-

26 Hvidberg-Hansen and Ploug 1993, 23.

Fig. 6: Reverse of tessera showing signet seal and deity (photo Rubina Raja).

form as possible. One consideration is that this was done in order to avoid falsifications being made.[27] However, this remains a speculation. It simply might also have been that importance was put on the finish of the tesserae so that they were recognisable as part of a certain series. The examples in lead, metal and glass indicate that this might have been the case. Many series of tesserae carry the imprint of signet rings, which would have connected them closely to one person, indicating that this person's ring would have given the series a concrete stamp of originality.[28]

The tesserae come in numerous shapes. In the collection at the Ny Carlsberg Glyptotek, consisting of 92 tesserae, as many as 18 distinctively different tesserae shapes could be counted.[29] The shape as well as the size and certainly the iconography as well as the inscriptions may all have been parameters that were important to the understanding of these tokens and the way in which they were

27 Hvidberg-Hansen and Ploug 1993, 23.
28 Hvidberg-Hansen and Ploug 1993, 209–210 for examples of signet seal impressions on Palmyrene tesserae from the Ny Carlsberg Glyptotek in Copenhagen.
29 Hvidberg-Hansen and Ploug 1993, 169–210.

used. The tesserae in many ways resembles the funerary portraiture of Palmyra from the Roman period in that they appear extremely standardized at first glance, but turn out to hold a wealth of variety within the range of standardisation when one looks at them in detail.[30] Nothing was left to chance on these small objects.

As well as functioning as entrance tickets to certain events, the tesserae can be viewed as (small) monuments through which communication between group members, invitees and the gods took place. The tesserae do not in themselves express or embody a certain ritual, but they played part in one or more ritual actions revolving around the celebration of a religious banquet. There are several tesserae that carry offering scenes (libations and incense offering for example), indicating that such rituals could have taken place at the banquets (fig. 7).[31] The tesserae were in this respect first and foremost means of communication. They were small monuments attached to a specific event taking place within the religious life of Palmyrene society. However, as much as being a testament to these one-off events where power and control over certain spaces were exercised, they also testify to euergetism in Palmyra. They carry a clear message about who paid for the banquet and sometimes also tells us when the banquet took place. However, as mentioned above, they only seem to have been important before the event in order to gain access, whereas afterward they lost importance to a large extent and were left behind, at least by some of the participants.

Regarding the tesserae as a category of material, it can be concluded that they served as entrance tokens stemming from the Roman period used to gain access to religious banquets or banquets hosted by religious groups which took place in the sanctuaries in Palmyra. The banquets seem to have been organised by priests, most likely by the priests who are almost always depicted reclining on kline on the tesserae. However, the banquets were not necessarily held in honour of the deity to which the sanctuary in which the banquet was hosted was dedicated. This fact speaks to us about the multi-functionality of the sanctuaries in Palmyra, a topic to which we will return below.

---

30 Kropp and Raja (forthcoming) and Raja (forthcoming) for introductions to the corpus of Palmyrene funerary portraits.

31 Hvidberg-Hansen and Ploug 1993, 190 and 193, I.N. 3208 on the reverse depicts two servants pouring wine? Into a crater. Behind both servants small altars can be seen.

Fig. 7: Reverse of tessera showing offering scene (photo Rubina Raja).

3. Religious life and sacred space at Palmyra in the Roman period in light of the tesserae

We lack extensive evidence for the organisation of religion in Roman period Palmyra. The most comprehensive publication remains Ted Kaizer's book from 2002, *The Religious Life of Palmyra.*[32] Kaizer argues that the socio-political model of "the four tribes of the city" was artificially constructed and introduced into Palmyrene society in the Roman period only.[33] Furthermore, in the conclusion to the book, he states that "the combination of this model with the fact that the great temple of Bel was sometimes called 'the house of the gods of the Palmyrenes' has incorrectly led to the application of a modern construct of "civic" vs "tribal" forms of worship to Palmyrene cults and temples, and that this construct ought

32 Kaizer 2002a.
33 Kaizer 2002a, 261.

to be reconsidered."[34] The cultic or religious reality in Palmyra may have been much more complex than expressed in this model, which has been the accepted one for decades. The banqueting tesserae offer a possibility for reconsidering this model, at least in some respects, since they present evidence pertaining to group construction and identity in specific sacred contexts, namely as these served as invitations to single-standing occasions, the sacred banquets. Furthermore the combination of the find spots of the tesserae, mostly from within the parameters of the sanctuaries in the city and the iconography of the tesserae showing priests of various cultic groups tell us about the structure of at least parts of the religious life of Palmyra and not least about the way in which sanctuaries or parts of sanctuaries could be used by a variety of cultic groups at different points in time. This aspect, namely the use of the sanctuary spaces by various cultic groups, also such groups who were not at this given point in time honouring the main deity or deities of the sanctuary in which the banquet took place, is one of central concern to this article. At the core stand questions about definitions of "private" and "public" space in the ancient city as well as about the variety of use of such spaces.

A central issue to take into consideration when discussing the varieties of religious life in Palmyra and the development of cult topography in the city is the languages that were used in the city in the Roman period. Palmyra was a bilingual city: both Palmyrene Aramaic and Greek were used as official languages in inscriptions found across the town.[35] Furthermore we also encounter some Latin inscriptions. In the hinterland a large number of Safaitic inscriptions are found. In general the importance of Safaitic must be taken more serious than it has been earlier and the recent work of MacDonald on the vast amount of Safaitic inscriptions from southern Syria, the Hauran, has shown that Safaitic was a much more prominent language than earlier thought and that we must reconsider the view of this language as the language of nomadic tribes only.[36] Whereas civic inscriptions often were bilingual, written in Palmyrene Aramaic as well as Greek, the inscriptions on the tesserae are almost exclusively written in Palmyrene Aramaic. This might of course have been a matter of lack of space on the tesserae, but it is remarkable that Greek is very rarely found on the tesserae.[37] In the case of the tesserae we may conclude that the local language, Palmyrene Aramaic, was by far the most preferred language, which perhaps is an indication

---

34 Kaizer 2002a, 261.

35 Yon 2002 for a compilation of much of this evidence.

36 MacDonald 1993 and 1998.

37 Hvidberg-Hansen and Ploug 1993, 202 and 205, I.N. 209 shows and describes a tessera with an Egyptian cartouche.

of the nature of the religious events. However, when showing mythological motifs, the tesserae do show Greek motifs, as may be seen in the example from the Ny Carlsberg Glyptotek where Europa is shown on the Bull.[38] Certainly a large number of different Palmyrene deities are depicted on the tesserae, but mythological motives as such remain in a Greco-Roman tradition, which is a general trait for Palmyrene iconography and which is also reflected in the wall paintings of the tombs.

The inscriptions on the tesserae are much more standardized than the iconography. The inscriptions usually give the name or names of male persons (priests) and/or deities.[39] Sometimes a date is given or in rare cases measures for drink and food are inscribed on the tesserae.[40] The inscriptions, however, give no insight into the cultic or religious reasons for the occasions for which the tesserae were made. Were these banquets held in honour of deities or deceased priests, or were they simply celebrations hosted by a variety of groups, which perhaps may be termed as religious associations?[41] Another important question is whether it indeed was possible to easily read the inscriptions on the small tesserae. The legibility of the inscriptions as well as the fact that most of the tesserae did not carry any inscriptions at all leaves open questions about the importance of these inscriptions. Perhaps they were not that important? Perhaps they were even the more important, when they were there? When present, they clearly indicate the identity of the person/s depicted and/or deities and as stated above in some cases even give the date of the banquet as well as measures to be distributed. One interesting tessera of which several examples are known depicts four priests, two on each side.[42] The tessera itself is very plain, only depicting the reclining priests and displaying their names to the left and right of their heads. The interesting thing about this tessera is that the names correspond to the ruling family's names. On the obverse the tessera carries the names Hairan and Odainat, and on the reverse the names Odainat and Wahballat. However, whether this tessera series indeed was produced on demand from the ruling family is impossible to say. Nonetheless it gives an indication of the fact that the inscription, whether difficult to read or not, might

38 Hvidberg-Hansen and Ploug 1993, 186–187, I.N. 3253.

39 Hvidberg-Hansen and Ploug 1993, 177, I.N. 3195; 179–180, I.N. 3198 and I.N. 2770 for examples of tesserae with names of male persons. Hvidberg-Hansen and Ploug 1993, 187–188, I.N. 3263 for an example which carries the inscription "Arsu is great".

40 See above.

41 See Kaizer 2002a, 213–220 for a discussion of the terminology relating to groups, among these possible religious groups, in Palmyra.

42 Hvidberg-Hansen and Ploug 1993, 191 and 193, I.N. 1143.

have been important even if it was hard to read. Combined with the plain iconography on this tessera, this example makes for an interesting case of the complexity of these Palmyrene tokens where both inscriptions and iconography seem to have carried importance.

4. Religious architecture and banqueting rooms in Palmyra

It should be underlined that the notions of public and private are loaded terms, embedded in modern times, which cannot directly be transferred onto ancient society. Nonetheless we work with notions of these terms, both in archaeological and historical research, in the lack of better ones. However, differentiation between various categories of space, including religious space, was a given, also in antiquity. Not everybody had access to all part of a sanctuary at any given point in time.

When looking at the architecture of sanctuaries in the Roman Near East it is clear that so-called public sanctuaries situated in the core of public urban space were not necessarily accessible to everybody at any point in time.[43] Massive, tall walls with gates that could be shut off and locked surrounded these complexes. The general public would not even have been able to look inside most of these complexes if the gates to the temenos were not open. The architecture of these complexes confirms the notion that spatial control stood at the centre of how religious life was structured in many urban societies.[44]

The banqueting tesserae provide another insight into understanding the use of sacred spaces in Palmyra at various points in time and not least the multifunctionality of sacred space. Much more than the interest in what we term private and public, there seems in the case of the Palmyrene tesserae to have been an interest on behalf of the owners of the tesserae in being able to control access to space at certain points in time and thereby asserting power over which groups or individuals could attend various gatherings. Importance was therefore given to the facts that access and participation could be limited and controlled and that sacred space could be appropriated for a period in time. Power is and was in antiquity also achieved through exclusion. By giving access only to a limited number of people, some would naturally have been excluded from taking

43 Raja 2013 and 2009 for case studies relating to the development of sacred spaces, in this case in Gerasa in the Decapolis region.

44 Raja (forthcoming) on the notion of complex sanctuaries.

part in a given event, which in some cases might have made such an event more desirable to attend.

Ritual dining and banqueting rooms are well-known features of religious life in many periods and throughout large areas of the ancient world. This also goes for the Near East in the Roman period in general and for Palmyra in particular.[45] However, in Palmyra we know little about how ritual dining and banqueting was organised.[46] The most recent summary of the state of research on ritual dining, possible associations and banqueting rooms is done by Smith in his recent book *Roman Palmyra. Identity, community, and state formation.*[47] Through his collection of the evidence it also becomes painstakingly clear that any firm evidence about the ways in which public and private dining was organised in Palmyra is lacking.[48] The tesserae remain our best aperçu into this organisation but they still leave many questions open, such as which societal groups were invited to these events and with what frequency these events took place.[49]

In Palmyra we know of four banqueting halls attested through the archaeological evidence, as well as a possible fifth one.[50] The largest one known is the one located in the monumental temenos of the Sanctuary of Bel.[51] It measured more than thirty metres in length, excluding the kitchen annexe, which was lo-

45 Kaizer 2002a, 220 – 234 as well as Smith 2013, 67 – 68 and 109 – 113 for a collection of evidence dealing with ritual dining at Palmyra, including the epigraphic evidence.

46 Both Kaizer and Smith who have collected the evidence do not come to conclusions about the structuring of the ritual dining and the sacred banquets in Palmyra, because the epigraphic evidence does not allow for such conclusions.

47 Smith 2013, 67 – 68 and 109 – 113 presents a solid overview of evidence relating to Palmyra and a comprehensive bibliographic update on the site. He largely follows Kaizer 2002a in his conclusions.

48 Smith 2013, 109 – 116 for a summary of the evidence, both archaeological and epigraphic evidence is collected and Smith concludes that religious dining in Palmyra must have been organized as in many other cities within the Roman empire.

49 Kaizer 2002a, 220 – 229 presents the evidence for banqueting halls in detail and acknowledges that the tesserae hold crucial information, which is however difficult to interpret.

50 Smith 2013, 113 – 114 sums up the evidence, so does Kaizer 2002, 220 – 229. Tarrier 1995, 165 – 166 and Will 1997 remain the basic references for the archaeological evidence of banqueting halls in Palmyra. Al-As'ad, Briquel-Chatonnet and Yon 2005 for the evidence from the sanctuary of Arsu including references to earlier publications.

51 Will, 1997 for an overview of the archaeological evidence related to this banqueting hall. The list of tesserae associated with Bel, which is listed in Ingholt, Seyrig and Starcky 1955, 192 – 193 and quoted by Smith 2013, 113 are not all found in the Sanctuary of Bel. See Seyrig, Amy and Will (1968) and (1975) for publication of excavations at the Sanctuary of Bel. Kaizer 2002a, 67 – 79 for a comprehensive overview of the development of the sanctuary including further references.

cated to the north of it. It seems to have had the capacity to accommodate more than a hundred diners at a time.[52]

Another banqueting hall was situated in the sanctuary of Baalshamin.[53] This banqueting hall, situated immediately north of the cella of Baalshamin, was dedicated to Baalshamin and Durahlun and the dedication of the hall was undertaken together with the dedication of two columns and their architraves.[54] The inscription was placed on a low stone bench (kline) north of the cella of the temple and conveys how members of a group (bny m[rzh']) dedicated "this banqueting hall" to Baalshamin and Durahlun.[55] The bench seems to have been part of a larger construction, but, as Kaizer remarks, smk' holds several meanings including "couch", "banquet" and "banqueting hall".[56]

Two banqueting halls were placed outside temple complexes. One was placed along the main Colonnade between the Arch and the Sanctuary of Bel.[57] The other took the shape of an annexe to the agora.[58] One further banqueting hall is likely to have been located within the precinct of the temple of Arsu where the assemblage of 125 tesserae was found.[59]

It is of course very likely that other banqueting halls existed in Palmyra, but the low number found until now does raise the question how so many, it seems, different groups, honouring deities who have no architecturally defined sanctuaries in Palmyra, would have found space to meet in. Judging from the find spots of the tesserae and the variety of deities depicted on them, it seems clear that the

---

52 Will 1997, 875–877. Tarrier 1995, 165 for an estimation which concludes that only around fifty people would have been able to fit into the banqueting hall. Seyrig 1940a, 240 suggests that a small temple was converted into the banqueting hall at some unknown point in time. Also see Kaizer 2002a, 228 for further references.

53 Collart and Vicari 1969 for the main publication of the sanctuary. See Gawlikowski 1990, 2625–2636 for Baalshamin at Palmyra and Kaizer 2002a, 79–88 for a comprehensive overview of the development of the sanctuary and further references. The temple of Baalshamin is in a bilingual inscription from 132 CE listed as one of the sanctuaries of "the four tribes of the city" (*PAT* 0197).

54 *PAT* 0177. Furthermore Dunant 1971, n.21 and Milik 1972, 120. The inscriptions date to between 59 and 68 CE. The names of the dedicants of the banqueting hall are listed in *PAT* 0178.

55 *PAT* 0177. See Kaizer 2002a, 221–222 for further elaboration on the meaning of this dedication and for further references.

56 Kaizer 2002a, 222 for further discussion of the term and further references.

57 Kaizer 2002a, 228 for this as well as Bounni and Saliby 1965, 124–126.

58 Kaizer 2002a, 228 as well as Seyrig 1940a for the publication of the agora.

59 Al-As'ad, Briquel-Chatonnet and Yon 2005 for the evidence from the sanctuary of Arsu. Earlier publications on the sanctuary, which also constituted one of the four tribal sanctuaries in Palmyra include: Will 1983; Al-As'ad and Teixidor 1985, 286–293 as well as Drijvers 1995.

banqueting halls in the sanctuaries were used by a number of religious groups at various points in time.

The large banqueting hall in the sanctuary of Bel is believed to have hosted "official banquets" of the city and it has furthermore been argued that priority of place was given to the priests of the various Palmyrene deities, assembled under the presidency of the symposiarch of Bel.[60] However, when judging from the variety of the tesserae, this is not completely clear. It seems that gatherings could have been organised in various ways and along different lines. Furthermore the tesserae suggest the variation in the groups could have been large. Most of all the tesserae might reflect a certain level of organisation of worship within the religious life of the city and it seems that several sanctuaries were used by a number of groups who in this way at certain points in time appropriated the space for the cultic activities appropriate for the respective deity. However, first and foremost the tesserae convey a high degree of complexity in the religious life of Palmyra, which is not reflected in the same way in the known epigraphic material or in the architectural layout of the known sanctuaries in Palmyra.

5. Conclusion

The corpus of tesserae shows variety; it also shows how carefully motives were selected in order to convey messages. The banquet scenes with priests lying on a dining bench were by far the most common, dominating the obverse of the tesserae, underlining that the giver/s of the banquet found it important to be represented on these tokens, even when they were not accompanied by an inscription. The inscriptions give us the names of male persons and mostly situated next to the depictions of the reclining priests, it is obvious to conclude that these names should be connected with the priests. The banquet could have been paid for by means donated by the giver or priest, by several priests or perhaps even by the religious group as a whole. The banquet theme, which dominates the reverses, underlines the importance of the sacred meal and tells us about the banquet as an instrument for negotiation between the "public" civic and the "private" religious sphere, in the way that access was regulated. The tesserae were meant as entrance tickets to a banquet that took place in a sanctuary and since there were entrance tickets, there were certainly also people who were not allowed to attend the banquet. In this way the tesserae convey information about control over what we otherwise usually term as "public" spaces, namely

60 Will 1983.

the courtyards of the sanctuaries. This opens a new set of questions to consider, namely to which degree sacred space was "private" or "public" and whether it could range from being more or less private at certain points – sacred space might, so to speak, have been appropriated by certain groups for more exclusive events. The tesserae indicate that this was the case and this allows for speculation about whether sacred space in Palmyra should be interpreted as means or instruments for negotiating the positioning of various groups within the civic sphere. One might speculate that these religious groups were behaving like public civic institutions, using public space to celebrate rituals and banquets, legitimising themselves by letting invited guests take part in their celebrations and thereby gaining acknowledgement on a broader societal scale. Perhaps they were simply playing "by the rules" of Palmyrene societal conventions, which might have differed from what we know from other parts of the Roman Empire. They may have been based on tribal or extended family connections, as can be seen clearly in the genealogy of the Palmyrene funerary portraiture, for example.

The priests, who seem to have been the driving forces as the contractors of the tesserae, can also be viewed as individuals acting in the process of negotiating levels of inclusive- and exclusiveness in religious settings. In these complex processes the tesserae may also have played a role in that they were attached to a specific priest or priests, to the group to which he belonged and to the group of invitees for the specific event, the religious banquet. The tesserae became small media of communication regarding an event that took place at a certain point in time and might have been a one off.

One way to try to gauge these groups, to which the tesserae attest and which appear to have been associational, is to test whether they fulfil the criteria of what might be termed "a model association", including roughly the following parameters:

1. Ritual involved.
2. Hierarchy within the group.
3. Spectators and guests attending.
4. Meeting place (often fixed).

The tesserae give insight into all of these parameters. Often the iconography depicted has to do with rituals, which could have taken place at the event. Altars, offerings (incense), votives, sacrificial animals are all common motives on the tesserae. Through the depiction of one or two priests on the obverse of the tesserae, sometimes with the names of the priests given, a certain hierarchy is also indicated. The priest or priests who invite for the event are singled out as being special in this particular circumstance. The tesserae also indicate that spectators or guests were present, since they served as invitations for these particular occasions. The last parameter, namely, that of indicating a meeting place, is also fulfilled through the tesserae, since they served as invitations for a particular event that must have taken place at a particular place. However, it is interesting to note that none of the tesserae specify a certain location for a banquet and the information about where a specific banquet would take place must have been otherwise communicated.

So the tesserae give insight into parameters that allow us to conclude that these groups behaved in some ways at least as associations as known from other parts of the Roman Empire. In a sense they behaved as private associations, but parallel to this, they behaved as public or semi-public institutions by using public space and inviting guests to some of their events. These groups might have complemented the city's civic life through participating actively in the religious life of the city by using the public sanctuaries as meeting places and as venues for larger banquets. Such events might well have involved more than just their own core members. Furthermore by copying or imitating public patterns, which at Palmyra was tribal or extended family-based, these groups might also have gained legitimisation within the public sphere.

In this way these groups might have been powerful instruments in the construction and development of the city's religious life. What is more, by appropriating for a certain time cultic spaces dedicated to a specific god or gods and using them to honor a different god or gods, they fundamentally if temporarily altered those spaces. Therefore the phenomenon to which the tesserae attest can be viewed as temporary appropriation in a more abstract but no less crucial way.

In the light of the information that the tesserae give about the diversity of religious life in Palmyra, we may reconsider the organisation of religious life in Palmyra in some respects. It seems that apart from being structured both on a civic and tribal level, it also operated on other levels, which may have provoked more societal if not social mixing than the tribal or extended-family structure would have done. It also seems that these groups may have behaved in some ways, at least, as associations, which would point to the fact that Palmyrene society oriented itself more towards a Greco-Roman societal structure, at least in some respects. These groups may have worked as subgroups within the tribal (extended-family) organisation; they might also have operated across the tribes, creating a dynamic religious environment. One pattern would pertain to local tradition; the other would look toward the Greco-Roman world. For understanding and analysing these processes, the banqueting tesserae remain a most crucial category of evidence, one that allows new ways of viewing religious life in Palmyra and the staging of non-civic religion in public spaces.

Works cited

Al-As'ad, K., Briquel-Chatonnet, F. and J.-B. Yon (2005). "The sacred banquets at Palmyra and the function of the tesserae: Reflections on the tokens found in the Arsu temple," in E. Cussini, ed., *A journey to Palmyra. Collected essays to remember Delbert R. Hillers:* 1–10. Leiden.

Al-As'ad, K. and J. Teixidor (1985). "Un culte arabe préislamique à Palmyre d'après une inscription inédite." *CRAI* (1985): 286–292.

Bounni, A. and N. Saliby (1992). "Six nouveaux emplacements fouillés à Palmyre." *AAS* 15.2: 121–138.

Charles-Gaffiot, J., Lavagne, H. and J.-M. Hofman (eds.) (2001). *Moi, Zénobie Reine de Palmyre.* Paris.

Collart, P. and J. Vicari (1969). *Le sanctuaire de Baalshamin à Palmyre i-II, opographie et Architecture.* Rome.

Colledge, M.A.R. (1976). *The Art of Palmyra.* London.

Comte du Mesnil du Buisson, R. (1944). *Tessères et monnaies de Palmyre. Planches.* Paris.

Comte du Mesnil du Buisson, R. (1962). *Tessères et monnaies de Palmyre. Texte.* Paris.

Drijvers, H. J. W. (1995). "Greek and Aramaic in Palmyrene inscriptions," in Geller, M. J., Greenfield, J. C. and M. P. Weitzman, eds., *Studia Aramaica, JSS* Suppl. 4: 31–42. Oxford.

Dunant, C. (1959). "Nouvelles tessères de Palmyre." *Syria* 36: 102–110.

Dunant, C. (1971). *Le sanctuaire de Baalshamin à Palmyre III, Les inscriptions.* Rome.

Gawlikowski, M. (1990). "Les dieux de Palmyre." *ANRW* 2.18.4: 2605–2658.

Hvidberg-Hansen, F.-O. and G. Ploug (1993). *Palmyra Samlingen.* Copenhagen.

Ingholt, H., Seyrig, H. and J. Starcky (1955). *Recueil des tessères de Palmyre.* Paris.

Kaizer, T. (2002a). *The religious life of Palmyra. A study of the social patterns of worship in the Roman period.*Stuttgart.

Kaizer, T. (2002b). "The symposium of the *konetoi* in an inscription set up in honour of Odaenathus at Palmyra." *Studi epigrafici e linguistici sul Vicino Oriente antico* 19: 149–156.

Kropp, A., Raja, R. (forthcoming 2014). "The Palmyra Portrait Project." *Syria. Revue d'art oriental et d'árchéologie.*

MacDonald, M. C. A. (1993). "Nomads and the Hawran in the late Hellenistic and Roman periods. A reassessment of the epigraphic evidence." *Syria* 70: 303–413.

MacDonald, M. C. A. (1998). "Some reflections on epigraphy and ethnicity in the Roman Near East," in *Identities in the Eastern Mediterranean in Antiquity, Mediterranean Archaeology* 11: 177–190.

Milik, J. T. (1972). *Dédicaces faites par des dieux (Palmyre, Hatra, Tyr) et des thiases sémitiques à l'époque romaine. Recherches d'épigraphie proche-orientale I.* Paris.

Millar, F. (1993). *The Roman Near East, 31 B.C. – A.D. 337.* Cambridge (Mass.).

Raja, R. (forthcoming). "Complex sanctuaries, " Raja, R. and R. Rüpke, *A Companion to the Archaeology of Religion.*London.

Raja, R. (forthcoming 2014). "Palmyrene funerary portraits in context. Portrait habit between local traditions and imperial trends." *Acta Hyperborea.*

Raja, R. (2013). "Changing spaces and shifting attitudes. Revisiting the Sanctuary of Zeus in Gerasa," in Kaizer, T., Leone, A., Thomas, E. and R. Witcher (eds.), *Cities and gods. Religious space in transition:* 31–46. Leuven.

Raja, R. (2009). "The Sanctuary of Artemis in Gerasa. In From Artemis to Diana. The Goddess of Man and Beast." *Acta Hyperborea 12:* 383–401. Copenhagen.

Raja, R., Sørensen, A.H. and J.-B. Yon (forthcoming). *The excavation diaries of Harald Ingholt.* Copenhagen.

Sartre, M. and Sartre-Fauriat, A. (2008). Palmyre. *La cité des caravanes.* Paris.

Schmidt-Colinet, A. (2005). *Palmyra: Kulturbegegnung im Grenzbereich.* Mainz am Rhein.

Schnädelbach, K. (2010). *Topographia Palmyrena.* Damascus.

Seyrig, H. (1940a). "Rapport sommaire sur les fouilles de l'agora de Palmyre." *CRAIBL* 84: 237–249.

Seyrig, H. (1940b). "Les tessères palmyréniennes et le banquet ritual," in *Mémorial Lagrange*, 51–58.

Seyrig, H., Amy, R. and Will, E. (1968). *Le temple de Bel à Palmyre. Album.* Paris.

Seyrig, H., Amy, R. and Will, E. (1975). *Le temple de Bel à Palmyre. Texte et planches.* Paris.

Smith, A. M. (2013). *Roman Palmyra. Identity, community, and state formation.* Oxford.

Spoer, H. H. (1905). "Palmyrene tesserae." *JOAS* 26: 113–116.

Starcky, J. and M. Gawlikowski (1985). *Palmyre. Édition revue et augmentée des nouvelles découvertes.* Paris.

Tarrier, D. (1995). "Banquets rituels en Palmyrène et en Nabatène." *Aram* 7: 165–182.

Will, E. (1997). "Les salles de banquet de Palmyre et d'aures lieux." *Topoi* 7: 873–887.

Will, E. (1992). *Les Palmyréniens: La Venise des sables (Ier siècle avant – IIIène siècle après J.-C.).* Paris.

Will, E. (1983). "Le développement urbain de Palmyra: Témoinages épigraphiques ancient et nouveaux." *Syria* 60: 69–81.

Yon, J.-B. (2002). *Les notables de Palmyre.* Beirut.

Natalie B. Dohrmann

9. Can "Law" Be Private? The Mixed Message of Rabbinic Oral Law[1]

> The only phenomenon with which writing has always been concomitant is the creation of cities and empires, that is, the integration of large numbers of individuals into a political system.
>
> Claude Levi-Strauss. 1955

> What is the difference between us and the gentiles? Those bring forth their books and these bring forth their books, those bring forth their documents and these produce their documents. (yPeah 2.6, 17a)

Abstract: A great deal of ink has been spilled on the question of early rabbinic literary culture and the rabbinic dedication to the development of an explicitly oral legal tradition. In this essay I will argue that given that the manifest content of early rabbinic discourse is law, it is productive to look to the very public practices of communication inscribed, literally and figuratively, in the Roman legal culture of the east. Within this context, the rabbinic legal project makes sense as a form of provincial shadowing of a dominant Roman legal culture. This paper will explore the paradoxical rabbinic deployment of the most public of Roman genres, law, in a manner explicitly coded as private. How does one make sense of the public aspirations of rabbinic law with its choice to remain unwritten and therefore largely invisible in the imperial landscape of the rabbinic city?

1. Introduction

A robust scholarly discussion swirls around the rabbinic development of an oral ideology. To date, when the oral component of rabbinic oral law has been studied and set in socio-historical context, explanatory paradigms have been, broadly speaking, two: polemical and (Greco-) philosophical—either as an ideology that emerged as a way to control access to a contested but shared scriptural tradition, and/or drawing from the master-disciple modalities of philosophical schools and Greek rhetorical paideia. In this essay I will argue that while illumi-

1 I am grateful to the many people who read drafts of this paper and engaged me in useful conversation, debate, and corrective: Elsie Stern, Seth Schwartz, Ra'anan Boustan, Annette Yoshiko Reed, Ishay Rosen-Zvi, Talya Fishman, Cliff Ando, Jörg Rüpke, and the participants in the conference from which this paper sprung (Erfurt, 2013).

nating, these positions have not sufficiently taken into account the culture of legal writing in the Roman east, and that so doing will add a modest but important facet to our understanding of emergent rabbinic culture.

The rabbinic legal project makes sense as a form of provincial shadowing of a dominant Roman legal culture.[2] Given that the manifest content of early rabbinic discourse is law, it seems not unreasonable to look to the very public practices of communication inscribed, literally and figuratively, in the Roman legal culture of the east. This paper will raise the problem of the paradoxical rabbinic deployment of the most public and self-consciously inscribed of Roman genres, law, in a manner at once coded as private. How does one make sense of the public aspirations of rabbinic law with its choice to remain formally unwritten and therefore largely invisible in the imperial landscape?

As a way to frame the problem as a problem, I want to home in on the imbrication of Roman imperial law and ideology with its modes of communication. The message of imperial rule is folded in good measure with its medium—writing practices, media, circulation, public reading, storage, citation, and publication. This written culture was a visible, ubiquitous aspect of the Roman urban space and of the citizen's sense of his connection to the state. Eschewing writing is itself then a form of engagement with this public economy of power. The rabbinic development of a new Jewish religious discourse in a legal mode exemplifies the process by which the empire's normative order insinuated itself among a certain subject (and stubbornly resistant) population. Why, then, having absorbed the empire's ambient legalism, do the rabbis reject its medium, and what might that tell us about the public and the private in one provincial religious community.

The empire defined, populated, and furnished the "public" for the increasingly urban rabbi.[3] Not insignificant was the publication of the law, and it is in this sense of public/ation that I will approach the topic at hand. Through the medium of law, the rabbi insinuates his self into a public space in a most unlikely mode, complicating easy ideas of provincial participation in the Roman polity. This case below, ideally, will contribute to the accumulated knowledge of how a polyethnic empire might be imagined as multiply Roman; how Romanization is a major factor for even the most inward-looking populations; and how state power may impact cultural modalities and media at the margins.

2 Dohrmann 2013; Hezser 1998.

3 Whittaker 1997; Hanson 1997; Lapin 2012: 67–69.

2. Some background

When the dust settles after the two major revolts against Rome in 66 and 132 CE, we witness the rise of the so-called "rabbinic movement"—a loose collective of learned promulgators of the Jewish law, Torah experts. The nature of early rabbinic (*tannaitic*, 2nd–3rd c) "literature" is more than a little difficult to map onto the contours of the eastern Roman empire.[4] For a small provincial population, the earliest generations of rabbis (the *tannaim*) are responsible for a rather large corpus of preserved materials—the Mishnah and Tosefta, substantial compendia of legal dicta and debate, as well as a series of lemmatic commentaries on the four books of the Pentateuch containing legal material, known as the halakhic (legal) midrashim. Tannaitic material is not authored (received tradition attributes the Mishnah's redaction to the rabbinic Patriarch, Rabbi Judah ha-Nasi, 2–3rd c.). It is preserved in mishnaic Hebrew, which was neither the Greek of the empire nor the Aramaic spoken by Jews. With rare exception, the Mishnah itself is not explicit about its transmission and publication,[5] though there is broad scholarly consensus that it was only committed to writing in any sort of official manner well after the tannaitic era.[6] It was stored, managed, and promulgated orally, any sporadic reliance on notes remaining partial and informal.[7] There is evidence that this was the case with the commentarial corpus as well.

3. Rabbinic project as legal project

The Mishnah, the most significant tannaitic work, is an extensive corpus covering a wide range of civil, criminal, and ritual law. Only one of its sixty-three tractates is not law, and its legal voice can be seen in these entirely unremarkable passages:

> An object found by a man's son or daughter who are minors, or by his Canaanite slave or maidservant, or by his wife, belongs to himself. An object found by his son or daughter who are majors, or by his Hebrew slave or maidservant, or by his wife whom he has divorced,

4 On the economic and social stability of Palestine through the 3rd c. "crisis", see Bowersock 1998: 35; Schwartz 2007: 78–79; Goodman 1992: 127–39; Appelbaum 2011. Cf Ando 2012: 224–29.
5 mAvot 1.1. Jaffee 2000; 2001: ch. 4; Lieberman 1950: 83–99.
6 Rosental 1987.
7 Jaffee 2001: 69. Contra Sussman 2005.

> although he has not paid [her according to] her marriage-contract, belongs to the finder. (mBM1.5)
>
> Some finds belong to the finder; others must be announced. The following articles belong to the finder: if one finds scattered fruit, scattered money, small sheaves in a public thoroughfare, round cakes of pressed figs, a baker's loaves, strings of fishes, pieces of meat, fleeces of wool which have been brought from the country, bundles of flax and stripes of purple-colored wool; all these belong to the finder. This is the view of R. Meir. R. Judah says: whatsoever has in it something unusual must be announced, as, for instance, if one finds a round [of figs] containing a potsherd, or a loaf containing money. R. Simeon b. Eleazar says: new merchandise need not be announced. (mBM 2.1)

This is just a sample of tannaitic legal efflorescence and ambition, one that emerges from a group without prestige or influence outside of small local circles, and to whom most Jews did not appeal for legal guidance or adjudication.[8] The early sage's authority had no institutional or state backing; it grounds itself in the learning and piety of the individual, and is checked by the wisdom and ethics of the collective.[9] Scripture, citationally speaking, is a bit player in the Mishnah; Moses and God by this measure are entirely off stage.[10] Outside of Scripture, books or texts are not brought to bear.[11]

For the tannaim, the word Torah does not signal solely a circumscribed written corpus, but names the work of doing God's law for the Jews—inhabiting it, applying it, obeying it, studying it, expounding it. The core of the enterprise was legal, and while this statement may seem obvious, it should by rights be jarring. There is nothing inevitable or natural about the translation of Torah into law (*halakhah*). While Torah had always been a central Jewish religious idea, and God's law had been culturally defining, this grand translation of religious knowing into legal expertise; worship into legal study,[12] is unprecedented.[13] Neither other Jewish groups nor early Christians, who share a Torah tradition, develop in this direction. Yet the rabbis' cultural swerve has been understudied, in large measure because of prejudices, both internal and external, that ascribe to Judaism an inherently legal orientation. The result being that somehow, rabbinic Judaism—in its macro-structure, in its legalism—has managed to be seen as coterminous with what is "Jewish," continuous with past traditions, and essen-

8 Lapin 2010; S. J. D. Cohen 1992.

9 mKid 1.11; mEduy 5.7. Cf. Rüpke 1996.

10 Neusner 1982: 139–47. Cf. S. J. D. Cohen, 2007: 123–25.

11 One exception being Megillat Ta'anit (mTa'an 2.8); on the LXX, cf. Simon-Shohan 2007.

12 mAvot 3 passim.

13 Neusnser 1984; S. J. D. Cohen 2007: 138–40; Shemesh 2009: 3–7, and bibliography there; Halivni 1986.

tial. Noting the innovation in this adoption of a legal idiom forces one to take the claims embedded in such a choice seriously.

I have contended elsewhere that this seismic formal shift reflects the Roman culture of law and expansion of legal expertise so useful for success in and under Rome.[14] Roman legality made categorical and theological sense to the rabbis, echoing as it did already indigenous ideas of Torah. However the pre-rabbinic Jewish framing of Torah as law is far different from its formation in the rabbinic ambit. In the rabbinic theological imaginary, the rabbis function in relation to their god as do the legal experts in the inner circle of the deified *princeps* who translated and mediate his will. The rise of the Roman jurist as a new mode of authority and avenue for professional advancement finds resonance in the rabbis as Jewish sub-elite on the make, also looking for ways to rise in prominence, and to increase access to their own ultimate lawgiver.[15] The emperor, accessible, even at a distance, by the common legal petitioner, finds a parallel in a rabbinic privileging law as language with which one best communicates with a distant but omnipresent God.

Accompanying the rabbinic elevation of legal discourse and expertise is a devaluation of other models of religious writing and other types of holy man and religious elite.[16] At issue is not the existence of religious law and legal experts, which we can presume in all eras. Rather, it is the transformation of religious thought and discourse; the rabbis make legalism conceptually coterminous with Judaism. In committing to law, the rabbis are defining themselves and building their Judaism on and through a matrix of elements collected from and filtered through the Roman world.[17] Granting the homology between rabbinic law and Rome's nomic sensibility, it is worth underscoring the manifest disanalogies. As legal system, halakhah is of course severely truncated—a sovereign, jurisdiction, courts, enforcement, even subjects, are ghost limbs; dominion is only a fantasy.[18]

---

14 Dohrmann 2013.

15 Hezser 2007; Cf. Appelbaum 2010: 217–22.

16 The rabbinic teacher not only displaces father, prophet, priest, even healer, he becomes a walking talking Torah—his words and actions a realized and ongoing revelation. Jaffee 2001: 155.

17 "Jurists, legislators, and judges needed, in other words, to acknowledge the fact of contingent divergence from Roman practice by nominal Roman citizens at some primary level of analysis in such a way that permitted the redescription and reorientation of that practice over time into alignment with Roman norms" (Ando 2011: 21). The ideas in this section summarize a longer essay on the theme, Dohrmann 2013. Cf. Woolf 2000: 24 n. 2. Schwartz 2010: 399; Lapin 2013.

18 Lapin 2012: 20–24; Schwartz 2004; Jacobs, 1995.

4. The legible *leges*, or, putting the public in publication

Rome by contrast had full use of all her legal limbs. My interest in this essay is on the ubiquity of writing in this system. If one were do a heat sensitive mapping of writing in the largely pre-literate Roman world, law would constitute a rather glaring hot spot. Laws were public domain, and were communicated variously (what good is a law that no one knows?), from posted edicts to traveling courts. Ando writes that "even a skeptical reading of extant (legal) texts reveals abundant evidence of authors' desire to disseminate and recipients' desire to record official publications of every kind."[19] He goes on: "The government at Rome exploited every opportunity to send documents to the provinces... the sheer abundance of Roman texts is striking... Above all, the government at Rome always paraded its wish that its words should come to the attention of all its subjects."[20] Writing, Ando shows, was far more than merely a medium—but was essential to Roman thinking about imperial administration, to a ventriloquism of the center to periphery, and to the accountability of subjects and rulers alike.

What is more, the connection between law and writing was self-conscious, and the legal record is rife with awareness regarding medium, be it stone, metal, wax tablet, papyrus, wooden board.[21] Legibility meant that these artifacts were visible, often "eye level" throughout the urban space. Ulpian signals both the ways that the public space was overwritten by the law, and the ways the law designated the creation of a textualized public landscape.

> By "public notice" we mean one written in clear letters, posted in such a way that it may be read properly from the ground level, in front of an inn, for example... not in a hidden place, but in the open.[22]

It did not matter that the bulk of the law's intended audience could not read. Its physical publication in words served its authority nonetheless.[23] Legal documents of empire are as aware of the power of their own inscription as were the rabbis. Given the suggestive legal homologies between the cultures, the rabbis' ideological amputation of writing from law has special significance.

---

19 Ando 2000: 109.

20 Ando 2011; 2000: 81.

21 E.g., Meyer 2004; 2007; Altman 2003.

22 Ulpian, *Dig.* 14.3.3, from Ando 2000: 98.

23 Corcoran 2004: 65, 56–73.

5. Tannaitic orality

In Jewish Palestine of the Hellenistic and early Roman eras, the extensive corpus of **non-rabbinic** Jewish, literature is marked by a wide variety of literary forms and genres in a range of languages—Hebrew, Greek, and Aramaic. This diverse library is predominantly narrative in structure and thought process, and most of it can be described loosely as parabiblical. The idea of the author is vibrant, even if most "authors" are hoary pseudepigraphical I's.[24] We have in addition a range of non- or more weakly narrative materials drawn from liturgical, oracular, and sapiential forms, a smattering of law, and, in the diaspora, philosophy. An investment in revealed books qua books is increasingly central to the evolving notions of prophecy, epistemology, and the history of revelation. A scribal strain studs the primordial and national epic with a series of mythic texts. In this horizon of revealed writings, the written Torah revealed at Sinai, becomes just one, if first, among many divine texts.[25]

In stark contrast, for the tannaim, book production and publication, both mythic and actual, screeches to a halt. Moreover, Second Temple literature itself finds no place in emergent rabbinic Judaism—the sole exception being the works comprising the newly/increasingly canonized scripture, and predominant among its books, the Torah, or Pentateuch.[26] These sage scribes are not operating in the same discursive space as had Second Temple Jews, literarily or conceptually; they do not compose any extended narrative[27]; they do law, and with a novel totalizing focus and singular intensity. What is more, they develop their new religious discourse in an emphatically oral mode.[28]

Martin Jaffee writes that regardless of the uses of writing in practice, "no sage in the entire corpus of rabbinic literature was ever portrayed consulting a book in order to verify his rendition of a teaching of early masters of the tradi-

---

24 Schneidewind 2004: 7–9.

25 The apocalyptic and late prophetic traditions, esp. Jubilees and the Enoch traditions, are rife with books and writing. In addition, written documents figure prominently in texts as diverse as Deuteronomy, Esther, Aristeas, 1 Maccabees, and the Testaments of the 12 Patriarchs. See, i.e., Reed 2011; 2014; Najman 2003: 117–26; Himmelfarb 1993: 101–2.

26 mSan 10.1: Among "those who have no portion in the world to come: ...one who reads in the outside books (*ba-sefarim ha-ḥitsonim*)."

27 Dohrmann 1999. Contra Meir 1994; Fraenkel 2005; Rubenstein 2010; Wimpfheimer 2011; Simon 2012. The literary scholar must be content analyze as "narrative," literary snippets of a few lines at most. This cannot be seamlessly compared to epic, novel, apocalyptic, or historiographic forms widely known from the non-rabbinic Jewish and Greek and Latin literary ambit.

28 Jaffee 2001: 97–99; Alexander 2006); Yuval 2011: 237–60, nn. 4 and 9; Heinemann 1974; Fraade 2012.

tion."[29] Authority moves from masters through disciples by means of mouth and ear (both tropes heavily valorized in the corpus), repetition is how they both disseminate and archive the law, they apply the law in person, and adjust it collectively.[30] In addition to naming the first five books of the Hebrew Bible, in early rabbinic Judaism the word "Torah" comes to indicate the full world of specialized knowledge and expertise, and even behavior, derived and generated by and in the triangular space marked out between the sage, Scripture, and God. Tannaitic (oral) literature is then a record and performance of this Torah in its fullness.

The centrality of an oral medium leaves traces in frequent concerns about one of its main drawbacks, its fragility: "Just as one must be careful not to lose his money, so must he be careful not to lose his learning... the words of Torah are as difficult to acquire as gold and as easy to destroy as a glass vessel" (SifreDt §48[31]). The solution to this anxiety over forgetting is never inscription or other aides-mémoire, but increased diligence, and "the raising of many disciples" (mAvot 1.1). Clearly for the tannaim the benefits of orality outweigh its risks.

While early literature communicates its oral predilection unsystematically, in the amoraic era, 4–6th c. and beyond, these seeds develop into a mature idea that two Torahs were revealed to Moses at Mount Sinai, one in writing (the Pentateuch), and the other oral—the rabbis not only inherit and control the latter, in fact, anything a guild member says is itself Torah, direct from God.[32] Written Torah (*torah she bi-ktav*) is then merely a partial revelation, and cannot be properly understood without its *symbolon*—the oral Torah (*torah she-be-ʿal-peh*). It goes perhaps without saying in such a set up that oral Torah functions as prime minister to written Torah's queen of England. "Matters derived from [what is taught] by mouth are more precious than those derived from Scripture" (yPeah 2:6, 17a). The question, often raised and rarely answered, is why the rabbis embrace orality—not as the transparent medium we know to have been widely employed by literate elites in the ancient world, but as a conscious, and increasingly theorized ideology.

---

29 Jaffee 1999: 10. E.g., mTaʿan 4.4 and passim. Hezser 2007: 158–59.

30 Fraade 2008.

31 Cf. mOhal 16.1; mEduy 1.5–6. Naeh 2005.

32 ExR 47.1. Jaffee 2001: 63–85, 142–43; Yuval 2011; Schäfer 1978. On the apparent demotion of the scribe in rabbinic materials: mSot 9.15; mGit 3.1; mBM 5.11.

6. Whence oral ideology?

Oral instruction and technes of memorization were of course the koine of the realm. Rabbinic orality is distinguished not by the fact of rabbinic oral praxes, but by the rabbis' explicit thematization of what we could presume to be standard operating procedure.[33] A related, though not identical, distrust of writing can be found expressed by pagan philosophers and Christian theologians from Plato's well-known screed against writing in the Phaedrus (276a) to Paul, for whom the letter kills but the spirit gives life, and whose texts are inscribed on the heart.[34] It is in these two contexts, religion and philosophy, that most discussions of rabbinic transmission focus.[35] Indeed, regnant scholarly explanations for oral ideology may be folded into a fairly short list.

i. Conservatism and canon formation. Oral Torah is a way to distinguish rabbinic teachings from the relatively newly demarcated boundaries of their written canon and the authoritative sanctity of the Pentateuch, and at the same time establish the rabbis themselves as its sole authorized interpreter.[36]
ii. Rabbi as sage. Pivoting on a reading of Torah as wisdom, rabbinic oral praxes are read as an embrace of the master-disciple models of philosophical academies. This approach understands the rabbis as a form of school. The Mishnah thus reflects the manner that Roman elites were taught to reason, declaim and persuade orally, especially in preparation for public life including the courtroom.
iii. Christian Polemic.[37] Not unconnected to reason (i) Oral Torah here is a boundary marker— invented to counter Christianity's gospel, claims to being the new Israel, and its relatively expansive book culture.[38] Sinaitic oral Torah wrests Scripture from Christians, and attests the primacy of the Jewish cov-

---

33 Schäfer 1978: 193–95. See *Oral Tradition* 14.1 (1999), and articles there for an excellent overview of the status quaestionis. Heszer 2001.

34 Loveday 1990: 221–47; Maxwell 2006; Hezser 2001: 94–101; Gamble 1995: 31 and n. 106. Interestingly, Christian and pagan logocentrism does not translate to a culture without books. It is ironic perhaps that the rabbis—the most maligned book-olators and accused slaves to the letter —produced perhaps the least bookish culture of any literate elite.

35 Work remains to be done comparing rabbinic writing culture to that of writing in Roman religion, on which see Beard 1991: 54–56 for a suggestive link between calendars, polities, bureaucracy, and religious writing; Scheid 1994; North 1998; Rüpke 2004; and Scheid 2006.

36 Sussman 2005; mYad, i.e., 4.5; Naeh 2008; Veltri 1990.

37 E.g., Boyarin 2004; Yuval 2011.

38 Gamble 1995; Haines-Eitzen 2000: esp chaps. 1, 4.

enantal bond with God, thus trumping Christian claims to a new and superior covenant.[39]

Because proof for direct influence is so elusive, each theory of the reason for rabbinic orality is built circumstantially. The rabbis themselves never tell us why they "go oral," and their literature is achingly thin on contextual cues.

I will address the second and third categories first. The vein of inquiry that has produced (ii) has yielded much fruit. Jaffee has built an argument for the rhetorical-performative ends of this process of study.[40] While this has contributed greatly to the formal analysis of individual mishnayot, it remains a stretch to equate the declamatory eloquence and public aims of the ambitious 2nd c. rhetor with the crabbed specialized shorthand of rabbinic legal give and take. It is unclear why the rabbis would invest ideologically in a training regime so at odds with their own social concerns.[41]

There is some precedent to thinking of similar collectives of Jewish Torah experts as akin to Greek philosophical schools.[42] Like a philosopher, the rabbinic sage is disciplined and masters his passion, he strives to embody ideas in word and deed. There are in addition obvious parallels between the place of orality in rabbinic, pagan, and Christian chain of teachers/apostolic traditions.[43] In the end, however, differences remain: for one, rabbis don't in fact do philosophy, either formally or conceptually. [44] The Mishnah is only philosophy to the extent that we can categorize the Plato's *Republic* as law.

Anti-Christian polemic (iii) is difficult at best to pinpoint in late antique and early medieval rabbinic sources but a rare few deictics appear in the obfuscating corpus[45]:

> R. Haggai in the name of R. Samuel bar Nahman: Some teachings were revealed orally and some teachings were revealed in writing. We do not know which of them is more beloved, except from that which is written, ***For in accordance with* (*'al pi→'al peh* = by the mouth of, orally) *these things I make a covenant with you and with Israel*** (Ex 34.27), which is to say that those that are transmitted orally are more beloved. (yMeg 4.1, 74d, 4–5th c.)

39 "Orality is the language by whose means there was created the rabbinic answer to soteriology." Yuval 2011: 248.

40 Jaffee 2001: 130–40; Brodsky forthcoming.

41 Hezser 2001: 106.

42 Josephus, *Ant.* 13.171; 15.371; 18.11; 20.199; *War* 8.

43 Alexander 2007; Schofer 2005: 45–46; Tropper 2004.

44 Jaffee 1991: 20; Boyarin 2004: 77–86; Mason 1996: 38 n. 45; see also articles by Seland and Richardson there. A. D. Nock, 1933. Lapin 2012: 92–93, cf. Crouzel 1970; Swartz 2013.

45 See also Schäfer 1978: 196–97; Simon 1996: 189–190.

While Christians are not named, this passage connects oral teachings and the true covenanters. Yuval argues that the oral law, Mishnah, developed in parallel with Christian gospels—both extra-scriptural corpuses that serve to distinguished each from their Bible-reading neighbors, and claim sole possession of the divine promise.[46]

The prominence of "Jews" in Christian polemical literature as the largely rhetorical figure marking heretical boundaries—compounded by the last 2000 years of Jewish-Christian entanglement—has prejudiced a scholarship that wants to find a reciprocal dichotomous self-fashioning coming from the early rabbis.[47] The evidence of such however is absent. Any argument about anti-Christian positions of any sort in the early material must be content to argue from anachronism or silence.[48] The preserved material gives us no reason to believe that early rabbinic identity was hardened on a "battlefield between the two competing religions"[49] when there is scant reference to anything obviously Christian in Palestinian sources before the empire shifts in the 4th c.,[50] and even then creative exegesis is often required. Current analyses of the mid first millennium too easily elide the early centuries into a late antique narrative.[51]

It somehow is still to be stated that the rabbis are not theologians, philosophers, or rhetors, they are not seeking first principles, the nature of god or the good, nor are they trying to teach, preach, lead or inspire the masses—they are expounding, analyzing, promulgating, and adjudicating a **law** before fellow experts. It cannot be often enough stressed that the tannaim do not inherit rabbinic Judaism; they invent it. Neither are they proto-talmudists—they are provincials of the sun-drenched landscape of the Roman east.

The main paradigm (i) is one shared, with variants, by scholars and practitioners of Judaism alike—and sees the oral as a protective barrier around the revealed scripture. The oral becomes not merely a religious practice but theological

46 Yuval 2011: 243.

47 Fredriksen 2007; see also Nirenberg 2013: 87–134.

48 Goodman 2007a: 124.

49 Yuval 2011: 248.

50 Schäfer 2007 makes the case that a Christian empire and its anti-Jewish legislation catalyzed Jewish learning about Christianity, hardened a response to it, and forced its suppression. This suppressed negativity was expressed more safely in Babylonian sources (the Bavli), where the marginal and persecuted place of Christians under the Zoroastrian regime would have emboldened the stronger anti-Christian voices (pp. 115–22). This logic implicitly confirms my reading that the fact that 2nd – and early 3rd – century Christians do not appear in tannaitic sources, despite the fact they are similarly marginalized and persecuted, is evidence that they are not a significant blip on the early rabbinic radar. Stemberger 2010; Yuval 2006: 16–17.

51 Jaffee 2001: 146.

dogma in which writing is the reserve of the Bible. This is a strategy that serves to delegitimize rival scriptures and rival exegetes. This model is commonly argued or presumed and requires no elaboration here.[52]

In a marketplace of competitive religious authority a new religious group will be expected to assert its claims over members and adversaries. However what these theories of orality do not account for is the *confluence of legal content and oral form*. There are many ways to delegitimize rivals—oral ideology is not inevitable. Additionally the fact that legalism is also a creation of rabbinic religiousity is undertreated in discussions of form. So while orality asserts that the rabbis' Bible is the only divinely authorized holy document, there is still to be accounted for the positive expansion of constructive legal thought occuring concurrently.

In the end, these models, as with so many others brought to the analysis of the rabbinic world, do not take seriously the implicit claims made by the system *as a legal system*, thereby divorcing the Mishnah from the legal work of torts, criminal, and civil law in key ways. *None sufficiently reckons with the cultural apparatus that accompanies this rabbinic choice of law as the predominant religious language.*

I propose then a new paradigm (iv)—Roman legal culture. A search for the genealogy of oral ideology would benefit from juxtaposition with Roman legal media. My model is additive—and is not meant to displace the paradigm that sees orality as the primary gesture of audacious modesty asserting the primacy of rabbinic Torah in all its iterations. To the extent that rabbinic religious discourse is legal discourse, and religious engagement is about the law, one should expect to figure external threats primarily *not* as doctrinal[53] but as *jurisdictional* —concerning questions of sovereignty. Law after all is a discourse about power. Following the cultural logic of the rabbis own priorities (and not those imposed by a back projected Jewish-Christian encounter on the field of "religion"), dangers should not be first expected to be those posed by apocryphal books, rival sermons, or even false messiahs, and heretics—despite their distaste to the rabbis—but posted imperial edicts.

My approach has been inspired by insights garnered from polysystem theory. Tannaitic law is what Even-Zohar would call a "polysystem," itself a component of a larger polysystem—"that of 'culture' to which it is, semiotically speaking, both subjugated and iso-morphic."[54] Polysystem theory analyzes literature as

52 Sussman 2005.

53 Hirshman 2000; Schremer 2012.

54 Even-Zohar 1978; 1979: 290.

representing a collection of systems, each of which is a web-of-relations that gains its value through respective oppositions.[55] This approach discourages a static model with a single center and its periphery in favor of dynamic multiple centers, while scanning the historical horizon for loci of ideological domination.[56] An awareness of power resists in turn overreliance on a literature’s self-articulated orientation.[57] It takes seriously culture’s dominating centers[58] (e.g., imperial law), and, significantly, permits us to deprivilege the influence of comparably marginal systems—Christianity, philosophical schools, and even scripture, for example—as the guiding paradigms for analysis, without discounting them.

7. Rabbis and written Romans

The regnant theories of rabbinic orality listed above attempt variously to naturalize the phenomenon; for each, orality as they frame it, looks like something we already know (the rabbis are *like* rhetors, the oral law functions *like* the gospels). By situating orality in the context of Roman legal circulation, we must confront a discordant paradigm. How dissonant is the severing of law from writing, not only with Roman practices, but with Jewish ones?

The non-rabbinic Jewish documentary evidence is slim, but suggestive finds exist, most famously the Babatha archives, which are consistent with legal practices in Egypt and elsewhere, combining an expected admixture of local and imperial elements.[59] Similarly, Josephus is a typical first-century elite in his awareness of, reading, and transcribing law that he thinks will serve his purpose, and Rajak charts in detail the ways he manipulates this self-selected and copied legal anthology to attempt to better Jews’ legal position.[60]

How did the rabbis think they fit into this world of ever encroaching imperial law, even as they were building a sprawling legal cosmos of their own? It is clear that on the whole, rabbinic laws simply ignore Roman law, implicitly allowing it

---

55 Even-Zohar 1979: 291.

56 Lotman 1976; Even-Zohar 1979: 293–94, 295, 303–304.

57 Even-Zohar 1979: 300–303.

58 Even-Zohar 1979: 296.

59 Bagnall 2011: 113–16.

60 Rajak 1984; Ando 2000: 85–87. Paul Kosmin (in a workshop at the University of Pennsylvania on Feb. 2, 2014) suggests that Josephus’s legal anthologizing may in fact adapt the inscriptional practice of creating an archive wall of all laws relevant to a local polity such as the one in such as on the north *parados* in the theater of Aphrodisias.

no jurisdiction. But there is evidence of anxiety about the draw exerted by the competition. Tannatic sources forbid recourse to gentile courts, even if they adjudicate according to rabbinic law.[61] That said, they did not live in a remote desert compound. The rabbis were a mobile collective, and an increasingly urban movement, even as the cities of Palestine were Romanized.[62] While inscriptional evidence in the area is slight, there is little reason to imagine a legal landscape different from other provincial cities and towns.

> [The words of the *Shema'*] should not be in your eyes like some antiquated edict to which no one pays any attention, but like a new edict (*ke-diatagma*) which everyone runs to read. (SifreDt §33)

The rabbis' central credal daily prayer (the *Shema'*) proclaiming the unity and dominion of God, here receives less respect than the posting of an imperial edict in the town square (note also the awareness of the visible vestiges of older laws still posted and marking the public space). Tropper following Lieberman has recently trolled this and similar passages for Roman legal terms proving that the rabbis were cognizant of Roman imperial processes and protocols for the promulgation of edicts even as they fought their allure[63]; but stepping back, this hardly seems necessary. Proving that a well-to-do resident of the bustling 3rd-c. Galilee knew something about Roman law is a bit like proving that a 21st-c. American had access to television.[64] This is not to imply that they knew legal detail, as indeed even Roman judges often did not,[65] but like other provincials, they were surrounded by a dominant culture that defined itself in and through its idea of justice. Rabbis were cognizant of archives,[66] the workings of the Roman court,[67] and while I do not know of preserved petitions from or rescripts addressed to a known rabbi, we have the letters of Babatha from early second-cen-

---

61 Mek *Nezikin* 1. Lapin, 2012: 98–111; Mek *Kaspa* (on Dt. 16.19) Hezser 1997: 476–77, and notes there.

62 Lapin 2000; Klein 1929: pt. 1. (Miller 2007). Isaacs 1990; Sperber 1998; Schwartz 2001a: 154–55; Fonrobert 2004; cf. Hezser 1997: 157–64; but 2011; Levenson 2013.

63 Tropper 2005; Lieberman 1944. The sources here are all late, but confirm what we know of the wide visibility and popularity of Roman courts from papyrological evidence and rescripts from the late second and early 3rd-century East.

64 Ando 2000: 364–65 and passim.

65 Bryen 2012: 771–811; Meyer 2004: 3.

66 mKid 4.5; tMK 1.12; tBB 8.3; cf. mEduy 1.5–6. Hezser 2001: 150–60. Cf. The Sepphoran archives appear to have been centrally located. Ando 2000: 80–96, 187. Cotton and Yardeni 1997: no. 64. If archives were housed in temples, this may have added to the gentile/imperial taint of writing.

67 yBer 2.5c. Lieberman 1944: 86–88, 207–8.

tury Arabia, which along with the sheer volume of petitionary evidence proves there was pervasive opportunity for legal access and address in the legal life of the regular provincial.[68] Ando says that domestically held copies of legal documents provide evidence of the provincials' "faith in the rationality of imperial administration."[69]

Rabbinic law by contrast evidences a distinct lack of faith in that rationality. Tannaitic law shows few direct incursions of Roman legal forms, and aggadic literature regularly ridicules the emperor, and bemoans the corruption of non-rabbinic courts. Use of Hebrew, moreover, did not merely signify an embrace of the holy tongue, but a clear rejection of Greek, the language of the "kingdom."[70]

Disdain for Roman laws/courts was as much prescriptive as descriptive. Hear the rabbis project their anxiety into the mouth of an imagined doubting Jew:

> Lest you should say: **They have statutes and we have no statutes,** Scripture says *You shall keep my ordinances, and my commandments/statutes you shall observe, to walk in them. I am the Lord your God* (Lev 18:4). Still, there is hope for the evil inclination to deliberate on it and say: **Theirs are nicer than ours**, [therefore] Scripture says, *You shall observe and do [my ordinances], for it is your wisdom and your understanding [in the eyes of the nations, who, when they hear all these statutes will say... "What great nation has such statues and ordinances such as this entire law (torah)?"]* (Dt 4:6–8) (Sifra *Aḥare Mot* 9.13.11)[71]

Roman law is an attractive nuisance (it is nicer than ours), but worse, without sanction, is rabbinic law even law at all?

I have been suggesting that oral ideology be seen as a rabbinic recusal from Roman legal life and the normative order proffered by the Empire. In building what must be a circumstantial case, I have looked at the rabbinic reception of biblical depictions of legal writing. For biblicists interested in the question of when the bible became a book, and why the idea of God became linked to writing at all, Deuteronomy is a vital source. Writing is rarely depicted in the bible, but in the Deuteronomic corpus there is a relative explosion of depictions of texts, beginning from the discovery of the scroll of the lost law in 2 Kgs 22, threading through the repeated hexateuchal tellings of the revelation, writing, and posting, reading, sealing, and deposit of the covenant before gathered Isra-

---

68 Cf. P.Babatha 13; Cotton 1993: 94–108; Bowerock 1994: 336–44. For Egyptian petitions, Bryen 2012. On the denigration of scribes: mSot 9.15; Bar-Ilan 1989: 21–38; Jaffee 2001: 92–99; Goodman 1994.

69 Ando 2000: 79; contra Isaacs 1998: 329.

70 tSot 15.8; mSot 9.14; SifreDt §34; Sifra *Aḥare Mot*, 9.13.11; Lieberman 1950b: 100–115. On Greek usage in documents, Bagnall 2011: 95–116 Cotton 2013: 209–21; Hezser 2001: 150–60.

71 Berkowitz 2012: 77–111.

el.[72] Van der Toorn theorizes that the physically written Torah was created to serve as a substitute icon for a nation whose local altars had been outlawed by the Deuteronomic reforms of the 7th c BCE.[73]

Deuteronomic legal performances share several elements with what we know of Roman legal communication, and these would have been apparent to a rabbinic reader. There is a divine lawgiver (God/King) a comparison of which the rabbis are keenly aware.[74] Once revealed, the law is written (Ex 24:4, 7, 12; Dt. 4:13; 5:22), displayed before the people, the manner of its display is written into the law itself. The law is both on a scroll (Ex 24; Dt 29) and inscribed on a plaster covered stele or stone (Ex 24:12; Dt 9:9; 27:8; Josh 4, 8). It is copied and promulgated through the territory (Josh 8:12). The posted laws is then read before the people (Ex 24:7–8; Dt 29:20–21; Josh 8:35; cf. Neh 8:5), who are meant to accede to its commands—the details received aurally, the conceptual whole communicated symbolically through the ritual performances surrounding writing. There is also instruction for its storage, in this case in the tabernacle (Dt. 10:1–5; 31:24–26; Ex 25:21), and later, the Temple (2 Kgs 22:8, 10). The law, like Roman laws, includes rules for its own publication and deposit.

The tannaim devote a lengthy commentary to the book of Deuteronomy (SifreDt). It is striking that in their granular engagement with this text—along with Genesis, the most copied and important of the books in the Pentateuch for Second Temple Jews[75]—the key scenes of writing and deposit of the law are consistently and flagrantly ignored. Two brief examples will have to suffice. Deuteronomy 27 describes God's command for the posting of the laws, and their ceremonial covenantal acceptance by the nation.

> On the day that you cross over the Jordan into the land that the Lord your God is giving you, you shall set up large stones and cover them with plaster. You shall write on them all the words of this law... you shall write on the stones all the words of this law very clearly. (vv. 2–3, 8)

As with all other such dramatic mentions of the book or writing of the law, this passage is omitted from the midrash's lemmatic sequence. When the verses do appear elsewhere it is as prooftexts used (out of context) to determine the mate-

---

72 Schneidewind 2004: 106–17; 119–41.

73 van der Toorn 1997: 229–48.

74 SifreDt §343; Appelbaum 2010: 217–22.

75 33 scrolls of Deuteronomy were found at Qumran, second only to Psalms (39) in numbers of copies, and outstripping Genesis (24) and Exodus (18), Leviticus (17) and Numbers (11) buy a wide margin. See also Reeves 2010: 139–52.

rial required for making the brief ritual texts (biblical verses from the *Shema*') encased in mezuzot and phylacteries (SifreDt §36, to Dt 6:9). Beyond these ritual items, the exegete skips depictions of writing entirely or transforms them into scenes of emphatically oral communication (SifreDt §306).

The second example: Dt 25:17 reads: "**Remember** what Amalek did to you on your journey out of Egypt," alluding to Ex 17, where, following a military victory over the Amalekites, God commands Moses to "**write** [of God's obliteration of Amalek] as a reminder **in a book**, and recite it in the hearing of Joshua" (Ex 17:14). In SifreDt §296 the command to write in a book has been altered:

> ***Remember*—with an utterance of your mouth** (*ba-peh*). *You shall not forget*—in your heart (*ba-lev*). As it is said, *Your people have heard, they tremble* (Ex 15:14).

Here again, scenes of legal writing are either ignored or recast as oral—the book is displaced by the heart, the locus of memory. This strange black-out of passages dealing with the publication and deposit of the law is, I suggest, a tell. Here at the very core of the soteriological epic is a narrative that binds the sanctity and power of the law into performances of writing and transmission. The rabbis could have located an internal "Jewish" model for writing the law in these prooftexts—a strategy that they commonly employ to domesticate other Roman or Hellenistic practices—yet here they choose overwhelmingly to efface them. In SifreDt writtenness is surgically excised from authorizing penumbra of Sinai at key Scriptural junctions. This trend only accelerates in the later material where we find even the two tablets paradoxically *inscribed* with the *oral* law! (ExR 45.1[76]).[77]

In the few places where rabbinic materials do not duck or elide biblical depictions of the inscription/publication of the Torah, the passages are consistently run through with concerns over imperial jurisdiction. One tannaitic pericope says that just as the Roman edict is not binding from its conception, but only from its public posting, so too one is not liable to punishment for transgressing Torah law at Sinai, but rather from its public presentation from the Tent of Meeting. Note the disanalogy in this parable: while the edict (*diatagma*) is described as written/sealed, Torah law is re-published only orally from the Tent of Meeting (tSot 1.10). The adjacent passage makes the stakes of the medium explicit. The oral publication of the law from the Tent of Meeting (*kol ha-dibur*) causes gentiles to flee in fright (tSot1.11) so that only Israel hears its content and only Israel is

---

76 Cf. yMeg 4.1, 74d, on Dt 9.10.

77 An identical set of aporiae mark the Mekiltan corpus (on Exodus), and can be traced through nearly the entire tannaitic library.

liable to follow it, knitting a notion of orality to a notion of legal-national exclusivity.

In the few other places where strong biblical images of God's law inscribed on stone are not entirely sublimated, an anxiety of an imperial sort hovers. The inscription of the Torah onto stone pillars by Joshua is tied to images that underscore an inability (or refusal) to nativize the medium. The laws on the stelae lead the rabbis to conjure images of paranoia about Roman contagion and threat—*notarii* copying down Torah for deposit in their own archives (tSot 8); gentiles upsetting Jewish military success by quoting these archived laws against Israel (GenR 74.15); or rabbis asserting that the law on the stelae was only a small part of the full Torah corpus—censoring from it all laws that do not touch on international law[78]—clearly a strong deviation from the biblical plain sense.

The public writing of law is not a neutral or transparent mode of communication for the rabbis. It was a distinctly Roman form whose uses, seductions, and dangers were clearly understood. Despite a powerful biblical tradition of the public inscription of the God's laws, for the early rabbis, by contrast, law communicated in plaster or stone was treated as adulterated. The biblical tradition had to be effaced, over-written—orally.

8. "Not in a hidden place, but in the open"

Tannaitic law moves lightly through the 2nd and 3rd centuries—rabbis are all but invisible in the material remains of this period.[79] By contrast, in this same era, Rome formed and filled the public space of the "Jewish" city, figuratively and literally from the early 2nd c. Art, city planning, architecture, and numismatics all attest to this physical transformation. Rabbinic accommodation to pagan realia such as idols and bath houses, for example, show us that they are processing and domesticating this reality.[80] Jewish items in the material record, such as ritual baths and the rare synagogue, or inscribed symbols such as menorahs, are not identifiably rabbinic—and in the case of synagogues and temple iconography, are probably explicitly *non*-rabbinic. It is may be significant to our topic that the extant "rabbis" of the epigraphical sources do not represent the rabbis of the literary sources,[81] which, following MacMullen and Woolf, might have

---

78 Lieberman 1950: 200–202 and parallels cited there.

79 Weiss 1998: 219–46; Goodman 2007: 501. While Jews show up in imperial legislation in the 3rd century, "rabbis" do not.

80 Schwartz 2001b; Halbertal 1998; Neis 2012; Klein 2012; Fonrobert 2009: 5–21.

81 Lapin 2011; 1999; Hezser 2001: 357–97; Negev 1971.

been expected of a differently ambitious provincial elite.[82] Orality likewise leaves no marks. To what extent is invisibility its aim?

Orality can be deployed to control access and demarcate a private space. When we remember that the tannaim worked in Hebrew, this space becomes even harder to access, for Romans and non-rabbinic Jews (and Christians) alike.[83] Indeed, access to the rabbinic nomos is as difficult to obtain as participation in the Roman one is impossible to evade. But to posit esotericism as the driver of oral ideology raises as many questions as it answers.[84] Jewish authors had at their disposal a wide range of options for the creation of a secret or closed religious world, yet by most metrics, the rabbis adopt an emphatic exotericism. Rabbinic texts doggedly de-authorize direct divine-to-human revelation, deny that knowledge can be found in hidden books, and avoid the symbolic and eschatological vocabulary of apocalyptic. Rare mentions of mystical knowledge exist, but deviate from a dominant paradigm that discourages metaphysical speculation.[85] The rabbis believe in a messiah and a world-to-come, but tannaitic references to each are lax and formulaic. Rabbinic rituals don't require secret admission. And even rabbinic biblical exegesis, while it borrows many of its habits from mantic and dream interpretation, does not sell itself as unlocking any scriptural or cosmic mysteries (in contrast to the Qumran *pesharim*).[86] The halakhah itself is anti-sectarian.[87]

Palestinian rabbis function in a democratic mode, demanding only adherence to the sanctity and primacy of Torah. They are a meritocracy—Torah-learning and male Jewishness, which need not be genetic, are the only requirements for "admittance" to their loose and shifting network, and they tout the simple origins of some of their most prominent exemplars.[88] They eschew bloodline and deny special knowledge of "sacred" law to the priesthood. Sacred law is not generically distinguished from other branches of law.[89] Most importantly, de-

82 MacMullen 1982; Woolf 1996; Naveh 1979: 27–30.

83 Cf. mMeg 2.1; mSot 7.1 on synagogue readings in other vernaculars. The confabulation of oral transmission and exclusion is made explicit in some later materials, but the obviously anti-Christian vein—as in 9th c. Pesikta Rabbati 5 text that equates oral Torah and a god's mysteries—is alien to the tannaitic strata. Cf. Tanḥuma, *Ki-tisa* 34:27. On *mistorin*, see Yuval 2011: 248–51.

84 Yuval 2011: 245.

85 i.e., mḤag 2.1; GenR 1.10; tḤul 2.22, 24; mSan 10.1. Cf. Hezser 2001: 209–26.

86 Fishbane 1977; Finkel 1963/64.

87 Cohen 1984.

88 Schremer 2012: 249–75.

89 mAvot 1.1; mYoma passim; Swartz 2013. Contrast Scheid 1990; 2006.

spite their disdain for the unlearned Jew, tannaitic law everywhere signals that corporate Israel is the community under its (imagined) jurisdiction.

Note that **both** the oral and the written can be tools of secrecy, and so orality on its own is not an indicator of exclusion. While later rabbinic texts link writing with the fear of too-easy access, in early Jewish sources writing is as often associated with "obscurantism" and elitism[90]—scrolls unfurled and performed from a dais before the illiterate, books sealed for the end of days, oracles interpreted by priests, texts flying through the air, or penned by God himself, not to mention the use of writing in many branches of magic.[91]

Esotericism, in sum, can be heuristically useful, pointing to literary markers of self-alienation, its inaccessibility, its use of Hebrew, and its resistance to the state.[92] But it is a limited idea if it does not take into account *the inherently public claims of its content*. If the rabbis intended to create a closed, private world, they did so in a very odd manner. Tannaitic law qua law communicates permeability and openness. The following late passage captures a revealing schizophrenia at the heart of the project:

> It happened that the government sent two soldiers (*istratiotot*) to learn Torah from Rabban Gamaliel. And they learned from him Bible and mishnah and talmud and laws (*halakhot*) and homilies (*agadot*). At the end they said to him, "All your Torah is fine and praiseworthy except for the following two things." [...] **Nevertheless**, by the time they reached the Ladder of Tyre, **they forgot everything they had learned.** (yBK 4.3 [4] 4b)

The law here is not hidden from the government's gaze, but is easily communicable to regular Roman keepers of the peace, and is even admired by them. In the end, though, the desire to be admired[93] is trumped by the desire to disengage. Forgetting—the great bane of the rabbi, for whom loss of memory is a loss of God's covenant—befalls the Roman (whether by human nature or divine intervention is unclear). This passage is a wishful inversion of their own confrontation with an imperial law they can neither admire nor forget.

---

90 Beard 1991: 57.

91 M. Bar-Ilan 1989: 35.

92 Cf. McInerney 2004; Frankfurter 2008: 221.

93 Cf. Sifra *Aḥare Mot* 9.13.11; m'AZ 3.4.

9. Mixed messages: Public language/private medium

In the legal realm, “the search for positive rabbinic engagement with the idea that the Roman state had legitimate authority as a maker or executor of law has yielded little.”[94] So writes Seth Schwartz in his social history of rabbinic disaffection from Roman and classical norms. This estrangement is clearly complicated.[95] The totalizing legal horizon of the Mishnah refuses to acknowledge Roman law, even while it is impossible that the rabbis were not fully aware of the demands of licit life in the eastern provinces. The rabbis knew the law of the land and how it operated, and moreover, it is apparent that they (and their non-rabbinic coreligionists) followed it. Moreover, rabbinic theology draws on Roman imperial logics of self, justice, power, communication, and order—the raw materials from which it constructs a resistant counter nomos.

As the deep grammar of rabbinic religious thought, we are forced to play out law’s logic. Law was an ambitious discursive cooptation for a small group of marginal, powerless, religious academics. Legal systems by nature think in terms of sovereignty— tannaitic jurisdictional purview encompasses everything from bedroom, to courtyard, market, court, field, nation and even diaspora. Comparison of oral Torah with other literary praxes (exegesis, philosophy, etc.) overlooks the full signifying complex bound to the choice of legalism. Orality may not in the end be a way to make Jewish Scripture the private domain of the rabbi, but rather may be a more ambitious making-private of the most public sort of claims of law, as well as a digesting and inverting the essentially public modality of its communication. Let us return here to SifreDt §33:

> [The words of the *Shema‘*] should not be in your eyes like some antiquated edict to which no one pays any attention, but like a new edict which everyone runs to read.

The *Shema‘* is built from three passages from Numbers and Deuteronomy, the prayer’s own words command that God’s law be posted on one’s door posts, arm, and head (Dt 6:8–9). The midrash then is setting the posted word of the emperor against the posted word of God, doubly ironic in that the prayer is the assertion of god’s unitary dominion. To what extent is the *Shema‘* ever in any rabbi’s “eyes” (that is: read)? It was and remains for the rabbis their most

---

94 Schwartz 2010: 128.

95 Schwartz’s characterization of the Mishnah as “utterly un-Western,” for example, is overstated. Ibid., 114.

universally memorized and recited mantra.[96] Moreover, its written materiality is bound inside sealed amulets on doorpost, arm and head. The writing is invisible.[97]

> Precious are Israel, for **Scripture has surrounded them with commandments:** phylacteries on their heads, phylacteries on their arms, mezuzahs on their doors, ritual fringes on their garments... When David went to the bathhouse and saw himself naked, he said, "Woe is me, I am naked of commandments," but then he saw his mark of circumcision. (SifreDt §36[98]).

In this passage the rabbis move through the Roman city (David is in a bath house!) surrounded by law—*rabbinic* law. Public law, made private through a series of erasures, is transported back into the public on (and in) the rabbinic body. Orality and memorization function to render invisible, but also ubiquitous. By nature of the legal ambitions of the tannaim and the scope of the Mishnah, the law finds a way to overwrite the Roman urban/nomic space in countless micro and macro forms. It is a sort of utopia that functions in the here and now, like a halakhic lens that interposes Mishnah between the rabbi and the posted edicts and rescripts that surround them.

The oral Torah defers to the written Torah but colonizes it audaciously—in a like manner oral law defers to Roman (written) law while deftly "maneuvering around existing structures of control."[99] Controlling access to Roman law is at least as vital to tannaitic survival and success as controlling the meaning of Scripture. Romans have over built the Jewish landscape and the rabbis do it right back. Less esoteric than it is utopian—rabbis inhabit and regulate a parallel city, their private public. My essay suggests that from the perspective of law's logic, a critical structural counterpart to oral law (*torah she-be-'al peh*) is (written) Roman law. Oral Torah makes rabbis the intermediary between scripture and the Jews, this much is obvious, but *it also allows rabbinic law to set itself between the state and the Jew.* Law becomes the proving ground for Jewishness, facing off against Roman law – the dominant marker of civic membership in the

---

96 The prayer's anthology of passages from Deuteronomy and Numbers is saturated with directions for its own oral transmission: (Dt 6:4, "hear"; Dt 6:7: "repeat them" and "speak of them"; Dt.11:18 "Put these words on your heart"; Dt.11:19 "teach them to your children to speak of them"; Num 15:38 "Speak"; Num 15:40 "remember and do all my commandment" It reads like a condensed proto-manifesto to rabbinic oral ideology. Cf. Stern 2012.

97 SifreDt §36; Bar-Ilan 1989: 25.

98 Cf. yBer 4.2 4c. Yinon/Rosen Zvi 2010.

99 Fonrobert 2005: 29.

Roman polity. Orality permits this confrontation to be done in plain sight of the state.

Bringing Roman legal culture more squarely into the rabbinic constellation as a driver and comparison clarifies certain persistent problems. Oral Torah draws its meaning from a network of associated systems, both from within Jewish tradition and from without. Adding Roman legal writing to the conversation both better integrates the rabbis into the imperial history of the Roman east, and serves to narrate their own self-severing from it. The push-me-pull-you force of this comparison can contribute to our understanding of Romanization and the processes of imperialism. The rabbis have imbibed an argot of and logic from Roman rule, and used it to articulate a distinctive counter-imperial world. The reading of oral Torah sets Jews on a continuum with others under Rome who variously leverage the writtenness of the law, an unintended consequence of law's written domain—and represents another example of the legal ingenuity of the marginal before the law.

Works Cited

Rabbinic sources

Mishnah (m +tractate abbreviation)
Tosefta (t +tractate abbreviation)
Jerusalem Talmud (y +tractate abbreviation)
Babylonian Talmud (b +tractate abbreviation)
Sifre Deuteronomy (SifreDt)
Mekilta de Rabbi Ishmael (Mek)
Sifra
Genesis Rabbah (GenR)
Exodus Rabbah (ExR)
Tanḥuma
Pesikta Rabbati

Secondary sources

Alexander, E. S. (2006). *Transmitting Mishnah. The shaping influence of oral tradition.* Cambridge.

Alexander, P. S. (2007). "Jewish believers in early rabbinic literature (2nd to 5th centuries)," in O. Skarsaune and R. Hvalvik eds., *Jewish believers in Jesus. The early centuries:* 659–70. Peabody.

Altman, R. I. (2003). "The size of the law: document dimensions and their significance in the imperial administration," in L. J. Hall, ed., *Confrontation in late antiquity. Imperial presentation and regional adaptation:* 11–28. Cambridge.

Ando, C. (2000). *Imperial ideology and provincial loyalty in the Roman empire.* Berkeley.

Ando, C. (2011). *Law, language, and empire in the Roman tradition.* Philadelphia.

Ando, C. (2012). *Imperial Rome AD 193 to 284.* Edinburgh.

Appelbaum, A. (2010). *The rabbis' king parables. Midrash from the third-century Roman empire.* Piscataway.

Appelbaum, A. (2011). "The rabbis and Palmyra." *Jewish Quarterly Review* 101: 527–44.

Bagnall, R. S. (2011). *Everyday writing in the Graeco-Roman east.* Berkeley.

Bar-Ilan, M. (1989). "Writing in ancient Israel and early Judaism: scribes and books in the late second commonwealth and rabbinic period," in M. J. Muler and H. Sysling, eds., *Mikra:* 21–38. Philadelphia.

Beard, M. (1991). "Writing and religion. Ancient literacy and the function of the written word in Roman religion," in J. H. Humphrey ed., *Literacy in the Roman world:* 35–58. Ann Arbor.

Berkowitz, B. (2012). *Defining Jewish difference from antiquity to the present.* Cambridge.

Bowersock, G. W. (1994). "The Babatha papyri, Masada, and Rome." *Journal of Roman Archaeology* 4: 336–44.

Bowersock, G. W. (1998). "The Greek Moses: confusion of ethnic and cultural components in later Roman and early Byzantine Palestine," in H. Lapin, ed., *Religious and ethnic communities in later Roman Palestine:* 31–48. Bethesda.

Boyarin, D. (2004). *Borderlines. The partition of Judaeo-Christianity.* Philadelphia.

Brodsky, D. "From disagreement to talmudic discourse: *progymnasmata* and the evolution of a rabbinic genre" (in draft).

Bryen, A. Z. (2012). "Judging empire: courts and culture in Rome's eastern provinces." *Law and History Review* 30: 775–76.

Bryen, A. Z. (2013). *Violence in Roman Egypt.* Philadelphia.

Cohen, S. J. D. (1992). "The place of the rabbi in Jewish society of the second century," in L. I. Levine, ed., *The Galilee in late antiquity:* 157–73. New York.

Cohen, S. J. D. (2007). "Judaean legal traditions and the *halakhah* of the Mishnah," in C. E. Fonrobert and M. S. Jaffee, eds., *The Cambridge companion to the Talmud and rabbinic literature:* 121–43. Cambridge.

Cohen, S. J.D. (1984). "The significance of Yavneh: Pharisees, rabbis, and the end of Jewish sectarianism." *Hebrew Union College Annual* 55: 27–54.

Connelly, S. (2010). *Lives behind the laws. The world of the* Codex Hermogenianus. Bloomington.

Corcoran, S. (2004). "The publication of the law in the era of the tetrarchs—Diocletian, Galerius, Gregorius, Hermogenian," in A. Demandt, et al., eds., *Diokletian und die Tetrarchie: Aspekte einer Zeitenwende:* 56–73. Berlin.

Cotton, H. and A. Yardeni (1997). "Aramaic, Hebrew and Greek documentary texts from Naḥal Ḥever and other sites." *DJD.* Oxford.

Cotton, H. M. (1993). "The Guardianship of Jesus, son of Babatha. Roman and local law in the province of Arabia." *JRS:* 94–108.

Cotton, H. M. (2013). "Change and continuity in late legal papyri from Palaestina Tertia. *Nomos Hellênikos* and *Ethos Rômaikon*," in N. B. Dohrmann and A. Y. Reed, eds., *Jews,*

Christians and the Roman empire. The poetics of power in late antiquity: 209 – 21. Philadelphia.
Crouzel, H. (1970). "L'école d'origène a Césarée." *Bullétin de Litérature Ecclésiastique* 71: 15 – 27.
Dohrmann, N. B. (1999). "Law and narrative in the *Mekilta de-Rabbi Ishmael.* The problem of midrashic coherence." Diss. University of Chicago.
Dohrmann, N. B. (2002). "Analogy, empire, and political conflict." *Journal of Jewish Studies* 53: 273 – 97.
Dohrmann, N. B. (2003). "The boundaries of the law and the problem of jurisdiction in an early Palestinian midrash," in C. Hezser, ed., *Rabbinic law in its Roman and near eastern context:* 83 – 103. Tübingen.
Dohrmann, N. B. (2008). "Manumission and transformation in Jewish and Roman Law," in N. B. Dohrmann and D. Stern, eds., *Jewish biblical interpretation and cultural exchange:* 51 – 65. Philadelphia.
Dohrmann, N. B. (2013). "Law and imperial idioms: rabbinic legalism in a Roman world," in N. B. Dohrmann and A. Y. Reed, eds., *Jews, Christians and the Roman empire:* 63 – 78. Philadelphia.
Even-Zohar, I. (1979). "Polysystem Theory." *Poetics Today* 1.1/2: 287 – 310.
Finkel, A. (1963/64). "The *pesher* of dreams and scriptures." *Revue de Qumran* 4: 364 – 70.
Fishbane, M. (1977). "The Qumran *pesher* and traits of ancient hermeneutics." *World Congress of Jewish Studies* 6.1: 97 – 114.
Fishman, T. (2011). *Becoming the people of the Talmud. Oral torah as written tradition in medieval Jewish cultures.* Philadelphia.
Fonrobert, C. E. (2001). "The *Didascalia Apostolorum:* a Mishnah for the disciples of Jesus." *JECS* 9: 483 – 509
Fonrobert, C. E. (2004). "From separatism to urbanism: the Dead Sea Scrolls and the origins of the rabbinic *Eruv.*" *Dead Sea Discoveries* 11: 43 – 71.
Fonrobert, C. E. (2005). "The Political Symbolism of the *Eruv.*" *Jewish Social Studies* 11: 9 – 35.
Fonrobert, C. E. (2009). "Une cartographie symbolique: L'*eruv* en diaspora." *Les cahiers du Judaïsm* 25: 5 – 21.
Fraade, S. D. (2008). "Hearing and seeing at Sinai: interpretive trajectories," in G. J. Brooke, *et al.*, eds., *The significance of Sinai. Traditions about Sinai and divine revelation in Judaism and Christianity:* 247 – 68. Leiden.
Fraade, S. D. (2012). "Concepts of scripture in rabbinic Judaism: oral and written Torah," in B. D. Sommer, ed., *Jewish concepts of scripture:* 31 – 46. New York.
Fraenkel, Y. (2005). "The aggada in the Mishnah" (Hebrew). *Meḥkere Talmud* 3: 655 – 83.
Frankfurter, D. (2008). *Archiv für Religionsgeschichte* 10: preface to part II.
Fredriken, P. (2007). "What parting of the ways? Jews, gentiles, and the ancient Mediterranean city," in A. Becker and A. Y. Reed, eds., *The ways that never parted. Jews and Christians in late antiquity and the early middle ages:* 35 – 63. Minneapolis.
Gamble, H. Y. (1995). *Books and readers in the early church.* New Haven.
Goodman, M. (1992). "The Roman state and the Jewish patriarch in the third century," in L. I Levine, ed., *The Galilee in late antiquity:* 127 – 39. New York.
Goodman, M. (1994). "Texts, scribes, and power in Roman Judaea," in A. K. Bowman and G. Woolf, eds., *Literacy and power in the ancient world:* 99 – 108. Cambridge.
Goodman, M. (2007). *Rome and Jerusalem. The clash of ancient civilizations.* London.

Goodman, M. (2007a) "Thinking about the early separation of Judaism and Christianity in pictures," in A. Becker and A. Y. Reed, eds., *The ways that never parted. Jews and Christians in late antiquity and the early middle ages:* 119–30. Minneapolis.

Haines-Eitzen, K. (2000). *Guardians of letters: Literacy, power, and the transmitters of early Christian literature.* Oxford.

Halbertal, M. (1997). *People of the book. Canon, meaning, and authority.* Cambridge, Mass.

Halbertal, M. (1998). "Coexisting with the enemy: Jews and pagans in the Mishnah," in G. N. Stanton and G. Stroumsa, eds., *Tolerance and intolerance in early Judaism and Christianity:* 159–72. Cambridge.

Halivni, D. W. (1986). *Midrash, mishnah, and gemara. The Jewish predilection for justified law.* Cambridge, Mass.

Hanson, W. S. (1997). "Forces of change and methods of control," In D. J. Mattingly, ed., *Dialogues in Roman imperialism. Power, discourse, and discrepant experience in the Roman empire:* 67–80. JRA Supplementary Series 23.

Hayes, C. E. (2000). "*Halakhah le-Moshe-mi-Sinai* in rabbinic sources: a methodological case study," in S. J. D. Cohen, ed., *The synoptic problem in rabbinic literature:* 61–117. Providence.

Heinemann, J. (1974). *Aggadah and its development.* (Hebrew). Jerusalem.

Hezser, C. (1997). *The social structure of the rabbinic movement in Roman Palestine.* Tübingen.

Hezser, C. (1998). "'Privat' und 'öffentlich' im Talmud Yerushalmi und in der griechisch-römischen Antike," in *P.* Schäfer, *ed., The Talmud Yerushalmi and Graeco-Roman culture, vol. 1:* 423–579. Tübingen.

Hezser, C. (2001). *Jewish literacy in Roman Palestine.* Tübingen.

Hezser, C. (2007). "Roman law and rabbinic legal composition," in C. E. Fonrobert and M. S. Jaffee, eds., *The Cambridge companion to the Talmud and rabbinic literature:* 144–64. Cambridge.

Hezser, C. (2011). *Jewish travel in antiquity.* Tübingen.

Himmelfarb, M. (1993). *Ascent to heaven in Jewish and Christian apocalypses.* New York.

Hirshman, M. (2000). "Rabbinic universalism in the second and third centuries." *Harvard Theological Review* 93: 101–15.

Honoré, T. (2nd ed. 1994). *Emperors and lawyers.* Oxford.

Isaacs, B. (1990). *The Limits of Empire.* Oxford.

Jacobs, M. (1995). *Die Institution des jüdischen Patriarchen: eine quellen- und traditionskritische Studie zur Geschichte des Juden in der Spätantike.* Tübingen.

Jaffee, M. S. (1999). "Oral tradition in the writings of rabbinic oral torah: on theorizing rabbinic orality." *Oral Tradition* 14: 3–32.

Jaffee, M. S. (2000). "The oral-cultural context of the Talmud Yerushalmi: Greco-Roman rhetorical paideia, discipleship, and the concept of oral torah," in Y. Elman and I. Gershoni, eds., *Transmitting Jewish traditions: orality, textuality, and cultural diffusion:* 27–73. New Haven.

Jaffee, M. S. (2001). *Torah in the mouth: writing and oral tradition in Palestinian Judaism 200 BCE–400 CE.* Oxford.

Klein, G. (2012). "Torah in *triclinia:* the rabbinic banquet and the significance of architecture." *Jewish Quarterly Review* 102: 325–70.

Klein, S., ed. (1929). *Sefer ha-yishuv:* pt. 1. Jerusalem.

Lapin, H. (1999). “Palestinian inscriptions and Jewish ethnicity in late antiquity,” in E. M. Meyers, ed. *Galilee through the centuries. Confluence of cultures:* 239–68. Winona Lake.

Lapin, H. (2000). “Rabbis and cities. Some aspects of the rabbinic movement in its Graeco-Roman environment,” in P. Schäfer and C. Hezser, eds., *The Talmud Yerushalmi and Graeco-Roman culture*, vol. 2: 51–80. Tübingen.

Lapin, H. (2010). “The rabbinic class revisited: rabbis as judges in later Roman Palestine,” in Z. Weiss, et al. eds., *“Follow the wise”. Studies in Jewish history and culture in honor of Lee I. Levine:* 255–73. Winona Lake.

Lapin, H. (2011). “Epigraphical Rabbis: a reconsideration.” *Jewish Quarterly Review* 101: 311–46.

Lapin, H. (2012). *Rabbis as Romans. The rabbinic movement in Palestine,* 100–400 CE. Oxford.

Lapin, H. (2013). “Law of Moses and the Jews: rabbis, ethnic marking, and Romanization,” in N. B. Dohrmann and A. Y. Reed, eds., *Jews, Christians and the Roman empire: 79–97.* Philadelphia.

Levenson, J. (2013). “There is no-place like home: rabbinic responses to the Christianization of Palestine,” in N. B. Dohrmann and A. Y. Reed, eds., *Jews, Christians and the Roman empire:* 99–120. Philadelphia.

Lieberman, E. S. (1987). “The history of the text and problems of redaction in the study of the Babylonian Talmud” (Hebrew). *Tarbiz* 57:1–36.

Lieberman, S. (1944). “Roman legal institutions in early rabbinics and in the *Acta Martyrum*,” *Jewish Quarterly Review* 35: 1–57.

Lieberman, S. (1950). *Hellenism in Jewish Palestine.* New York.

Lotman, J. (1976). “Un modèle dynamique du système sémiotique,” in Lotman and B. A. Ouspenski, eds., *Travaux sur les systèmes de signes. Ecole de Tartu:* 77–93. Paris.

Loveday, A. (1990). “The living voice: skepticism towards the written word in early Christian and in Graeco-Roman texts.” *JSOT* 87: 221–47

MacMullen, R. (1982). “The epigraphic habit in the Roman empire.” *American Journal of Philology* 103: 233–246.

Mason, S. N. (1996). “*Philosophiai.* Graeco-Roman, Judean and Christian,” in J. S. Kloppenborg and S. G. Wilson, eds., *Voluntary associations in the Graeco-Roman world:* 31–58. London.

Maxwell. J. L. (2006). *Christianization and communication in late antiquity. John Chrysostom and his congregation in Antioch.* Cambridge.

McInerney, J. (2004). “‘Do you see what I see?’: Plutarch and Pausanias at Delphi,” in L. de Blois, ed., *The statesman in Plutarch’s works:* 43–55. Leiden.

Meir, O. (1994). “Hashpa‘at ma‘ase ha-‘arikha ‘al hashkafat ha-‘olam shel sipure ha-’agada.” *Tura* 3: 67–84.

Meyer, E. A. (2004). *Legitimacy and law in the Roman world.* Tabulae *in Roman belief and practice.* Cambridge.

Meyer, E. A. (2007). “Roman tabulae, Egyptian Christians, and the adoption of the codex.” *Chiron* 37: 295–347.

Millar, F. (1986). “A new approach to the Roman jurists.” *JRS* 76: 272–80.

Miller, S. S. (2007). *Sages and commoners in late antique Erez Israel. A philological inquiry into local traditions in Talmud Yerushalmi.* Tübingen.

Naeh, S. (2008). "The script of the Torah in rabbinic thought, (a)" (Hebrew). *Leshonenu* 70: 125–41.
Najman, H. (2003). *Seconding Sinai. The development of mosaic discourse in second temple Judaism.* Leiden.
Naveh, J. (1979). "Grafitti and dedications," *BASOR* 235: 27–30.
Negev, A. (1971). "Inscriptions hébraique, greques et latins de Césarée Maritime." *Revue Biblique* 78: 247–63.
Neis, R. (2012). "Eyeing idols: rabbinic viewing practices in late antiquity." *Jewish Quarterly Review* 102: 533–60.
Neusner, J. (1982). *Formative Judaism. Religious historical and literary studies.* Chico.
Neusner, J. (1984). *From Mishnah to Scripture. The problem of the unattributed saying with special reference to the division of Purities.* Chico.
Nirenberg, D. (2013). *Anti-Judaism. The western tradition.* New York.
Nock, A. D. (1933). *Conversion.* London.
North, J. (1998). "The books of the *pontifices*," in C. Moatti, ed., *La mémoire perdue. Recherches sur l'administration romaine*, CÉFR 243: 45–63. Rome.
Novick, T. (2013). "Liturgy and law." *Jewish Quarterly Review* 103: 475–502.
Rajak, T. (1984). "Was there a Roman charter for the Jews?" *JRS* 74: 107–23.
Reed, A. Y. (2014) *Demons, angels, and writing in ancient Judaism.* Cambridge.
Reed, A. Y. (2014). "Textuality between death and memory: the prehistory and formation of the parabiblical testament." *Jewish Quarterly Review* 104: 381–412.
Reeves, J. C. (2010). "Problematizing the Bible... then and now" *Jewish Quarterly Review* 100: 139–52.
Rosental, A. (1994). "Oral Torah and Torah from Sinai—Theory and Practice" (Hebrew), in D. Rozental and M.Bar-Asher, eds., *Talmudic Studies* 2: 448–87. Jerusalem.
Rubenstein, J. L. (2010). *Stories of the Babylonian Talmud.* Baltimore.
Rüpke, J. (1996). "Controller and specialists: analyzing religious specialists." *Numen* 43: 241–61.
Rüpke, J. (2004). "Acta aut agenda: relations of script and performance," in Alessandro Barchiesi, Jörg Rüpke and Susan Stephens, eds., *Rituals in ink:* 23–43. Stuttgart.
Schäfer, P. (1978). "Das 'Dogma' von der mündlichen Torah im rabbinischen Judentum," in his *Studien zur Geschichte und Theologie des rabbinischen Judentums:* 153–97. Leiden.
Schäfer, P. (2007). *Jesus in the Talmud.* Princeton.
Scheid, J. (1990). "Rituel et écriture à Rome," in A.-M. Blondeau and K. Schipper, eds., *Essais sur le rituel II:* 1–15. Paris.
Scheid, J. (1994). "Les archives de la piété," in S. Demougin, ed., *La mémoire perdue. À la recherche des archives oubliées, publiques et privées, de la Rome antique:* 173–185. Paris.
Scheid, J. (2006). "Oral tradition and written tradition in the formation of sacred law in Rome," in C. Ando and J. Rüpke, eds., *Religion and law in classical and Christian Rome:* 1–33. Stuttgart.
Schneidewind, W. M. (2004). *How the Bible became a book. The textualization of early Israel.* Cambridge.
Schofer, J. W. (2005). *The making of a sage. A study in rabbinic ethics.* Madison.
Schremer, A. (2009). "The Christianization of the Roman empire and rabbinic literature," in L. I. Levine and D. R. Schwartz, eds., *Jewish identities in antiquity:* 349–66. Tübingen.

Schremer, A. (2012). "Thinking about belonging in early rabbinic literature: proselytes, apostates, and 'children of Israel.', or: Does it make sense to speak of early rabbinic orthodoxy?" *Journal of Jewish Studies* 43: 249–75.

Schwartz, S. (1995). "Language, power, and identity in ancient Palestine." *Past & Present* 148: 3–47.

Schwartz, S. (2001a). *Imperialism and Jewish society, 200 BCE – 640 CE.* Princeton.

Schwartz, S. (2001b). "The rabbi in Aphrodite's bath: Palestinian society and Jewish identity in the high Roman empire," in S. Goldhill, ed., *Being Greek under Rome. Cultural identity, the second sophistic and the development of empire:* 335–61. Cambridge.

Schwartz, S. (2004). "Big men or chiefs?: against an institutional view of the Palestinian patriarchate," in *Jewish religious leadership: image and reality*, ed. J. Wertheimer (New York), 1:155–73;

Schwartz, S. (2010). *Were the Jews a Mediterranean society?* Princeton.

Shemesh, A. (2009). *Halakhah in the making. The development of Jewish law from Qumran to the rabbis.* Berkeley.

Simon-Shoshan, M. (2012). *Stories of the law.* Oxford.

Simon, M. (1996). *Verus Israel. A study of the relations between Christians and Jews in the Roman empire AD 135–425.* London.

Sperber, D. (1998). *The city in Roman Palestine.* Oxford.

Stemberger, G. (2010). "Rabbinic reactions to the Christianization of Roman Palestine: a survey of recent research," in A. Laato and P. Lindqvist, eds., *Encounters of the children of Abraham from ancient to modern times:* 141–63. Leiden.

Stern, E. (2012). "Praying scripture: rethinking the role of biblical utterances in early Jewish liturgy," in C. Evans and H. D. Zacharias, eds. *"What does the scripture say?" Studies in the function of scripture in early Judaism and Christianity*, vol 2: 187–200. London.

Sussman, Y. (2005). "'*Torah she-be-'al peh': peshutah ke-mashma'ah.*" *Meḥqerei Talmud* 3.1: 209–384.

Swartz, M. (2013). "Chains of tradition from *Avot* to the *Avodah piyutim*," in N. B. Dohrmann and A. Y. Reed, eds., *Jews, Christians and the Roman empire:* 189–208. Philadelphia.

Tropper, A. D. (2004). *Wisdom, politics, and historiography. Tractate Avot in the context of the Graeco-Roman near east.* Oxford.

Tropper, A. D. (2005). "Roman contexts in Jewish texts: on *diatagma* and *prostagma* in rabbinic literature." *Jewish Quarterly Review* 95: 207–27.

van der Toorn, K. (1998). *The image and the book. Iconic cults, aniconism, and the rise of book religion in Israel and the ancient near east.* Leuven.

Veltri, G. (1990). "Zur Traditionsgeschichtlichen Entwicklung des Bewussteins von einem Kanon: die Yavneh-Frage" *Journal of Study of Judaism* 21: 210–26.

Weiss, Z. (1998). "Greco-Roman influences on the art and architecture of the Jewish city in Roman Palestine," in H. Lapin, ed., *Religious and ethnic communities in later Roman Palestine:* 219–46. Bethesda.

Whittaker, C. R. (1997). "Imperialism and culture: the Roman initiative," in D. J. Mattingly, ed., *Dialogues in Roman imperialism. Power, discourse, and discrepant experience in the Roman empire:* 143–64. JRA Supplementary Series 23.

Wimpfheimer, B. S. (2011). *Narrating the law. A poetics of talmudic legal stories.* Philadelphia.

Woolf, G. (1996). "Monumental writing and the expansion of Roman society in the early empire." *JRS* 86: 22–39.

Woolf, G. (2000). *Becoming Roman. The origins of provincial civilization in Gaul.* Cambridge.
Yadin. A. (2004). *Scripture as logos. Rabbi Ishmael and the origins of midrash.* Philadelphia.
Yinon, D. and I. Rosen-Zvi (2010). "Men's jewelry, women's jewelry: a new look at the religious status of women in rabbinic thought" (Hebrew). *Reshit* 2: 55–79.
Yuval, Y. I. (2006). *Two nations in your womb: perceptions of Jews and Christians in late antiquity and the middle ages*, trans. B. Harshav and J. Chipman. Berkeley.
Yuval, Y. I. (2011). "The orality of early Jewish law: from pedagogy to ideology," in L. Gall and D. Willoweit, eds., *Judaism, Christianity, and Islam in the course of history: exchange and conflicts*: 237–60. Munich.

Catherine Hezser

10. Between Public and Private: The Significance of the Neutral Domain (*Carmelit*) in Late Antique Rabbinic Literature

Abstract: Besides the private and public domain Palestinian rabbinic literary sources mention a third category, the so-called *carmelit*, in discussions about the carrying of objects on the Sabbath. Whereas the earlier tannaitic sources present the *carmelit* as an uncertain domain, which can neither be considered public nor private, the Talmud Yerushalmi uses the concept positively as a neutral domain in which objects can be placed from either inside or outside the house without incurring liability. In late antiquity the notion of the *carmelit* was expanded and compared with other spaces which rabbis perceived to be outside of the private/public dichotomy, such as the sea. In Roman law the sea was considered non-property, open to be used by anyone. In different contexts and for different purposes both rabbis and Roman jurists seem to have been aware of the limits of the private/public distinction. The issue of the use of spaces was as important as simple property divisions. Babylonian rabbinic texts and Sasanian legal and religious traditions seem to have differed from the Palestinian rabbinic and Roman legal concepts.

1. Introduction

Ancient rabbis distinguished between a private and a public domain and called them "the sovereignty of the individual" (רשות היחיד) and "the sovereignty of the many" (רשות הרבים).[1] The private domain comprised the individual family dwelling (בית), whether a mere room, farmstead, or villa, and may be understood as the domain over which the free male Israelite householder had absolute sovereignty. The public domain comprised the area outside of the threshold, which was used by the "many" and governed by rules beyond the individual householder's control. Besides this spatial distinction rabbis also differentiated between private and public property (e.g., a synagogue belonging to an individual

1 For a detailed discussion of the distinction between private and public in rabbinic literature in general and the Talmud Yerushalmi in particular see Hezser (1998) 423–579.

or a group) and ritual objects (e.g., the sacrifice of the individual and the community; the Torah scroll of an individual and "the town").

In all of these instances, the individual seems to be the free male Israelite householder who represented the Jewish family unit. The "many" usually remain undefined: they can consist of two or three individuals only, comprising a specific Jewish sub-group (e.g., "Babylonians" or "Alexandrians," i.e. Babylonian or Alexandrian Jewish immigrants or sojourners in Palestine), or Jewish residents of a specific city (e.g., Sepphoris or Tiberias).[2] This varied and unspecific use differs from the Roman definition of public and private based on property law distinctions and the definition of the citizen and *civitas*. Instead of imposing inappropriate Roman categories on rabbinic literature and ancient Jewish society or understanding the distinction between public and private from a modern perspective, it is necessary to ask in which contexts and for what purposes distinctions between the individual and the "many" occurred in the rabbinic sources themselves. A major context for spatial distinctions was Sabbath observance. Rabbinic discussions of the Sabbath indicate both the necessity and the flexibility of the concepts of public and private. They also require the creation of a third domain.

Rabbinic literature knows of a mysterious space called *carmelit* (כרמלית) that is distinguished from the private and public domain.[3] The literal meaning and derivation of the term *carmelit* seems to have been unclear to rabbis already in late antiquity, despite the fact that the term is mostly used in the Palestinian and Babylonian Talmuds.[4] Grammatically speaking, *carmelit* is the diminutive form of כרמל, that is, a small "plot of land" that lacked any partition and therefore was neither public nor private.[5] Rabbis appropriated the word and used it as a technical term for any area that did not easily fit the public/private classification.

In the Talmud Yerushalmi the meaning of the term is discussed in tractate Shabbat. In an explanation attributed to R. Hiyya *carmelit* is derived from an in-between state of barley (כרמל), which is "neither green nor dry but between

2 See ibid. 434–38 for examples and references.

3 In the Erfurt ms. version of Tosefta Shabbat 1:1, a so-called "free" place of non-liability (מקום פטור) is distinguished from the *carmelit*. This domain reoccurs in the Babylonian Talmud, cf. Bavli Shabbat 100b and the discussion in section 4 below.

4 In the Hebrew Bibel the term appears only twice to denote Abigail, "the Carmelite woman" (1 Samuel 27:3 and 1 Kings 3:1). No connection between this geographical term (derived from Mt. Carmel) and the rabbinic technical term can be discerned.

5 See Lieberman (1992) 3. Moscovitz (2002) 116, translates the term in a literal context with "planted field."

the two (בינוני)" (Yerushalmi Shabbat 1:1, 2d). The assumption seems to be that the barley is not ripe, either, and cannot be defined.[6] In contrast to this metaphoric definition, the following talmudic discussion provides concrete examples of spaces which may be considered *carmelit:* the "store of Bar Yustini" and the "market stands under a colonnade," that is, concrete urban spaces late antique rabbis would have been familiar with. A different definition is attributed to Hiyya the son of Rav: "All that prevents stepping into the public domain is considered *carmelit*" (ibid.), that is, areas and architectural features delimiting the private and constituting the borderline zone separating private from public space. Rabbis of Caesarea allegedly added that "even thorns, even glass" that prevent one from walking from one domain into the other can be considered *carmelit.*

In order to fully understand the rabbinic notion of *carmelit*, we need to examine the contexts in which the term appears and the functions it played within rabbinic thinking. What is clear is that the notion of *carmelit* was a rabbinic innovation and invention that served particular halakhic purposes, especially in connection with Sabbath observance. Biblical Sabbath law instructs Israelites to remain in their houses during the day of rest (Exodus 16:29: "Let everyone remain where he is: let no one leave his place on the seventh day"; v. 30: "So the people remained inactive on the seventh day"). Venturing outside would be considered "work" and was potentially dangerous, threatening the calm and peacefulness of the day. Whether and to what extent such strictures were ever observed remains uncertain. At least at the time of Philo Sabbath observant Jews seem to have left their houses to attend prayer meetings and probably also to visit relatives.[7] The rabbinic distinction between private and public and the associated notion of *carmelit* were meant to regulate Jews' movement on the Sabbath within the boundaries of biblically ordained law by enabling actions that were necessary or customary (e.g., carrying food out of the house on the Sabbath).

Since the rabbinic notion of *carmelit* emerged in Roman times it will be interesting to see whether any analogies existed in the Roman cultural context. From an anthropological point of view one may ask whether a strict distinction between public and private requires the concept of an uncertain or neutral domain in order to be practicable, just like the buffer territories adjacent to some national borders nowadays. The distinction between public and private – and accordingly also the *carmelit* – can have a spatial or a property-related connotation or both. One might imagine the *carmelit* as a space that belonged to no one or to

---

6 Jastrow (1985) 671 translates the term with "early ripened and tender barley."

7 See Doering (1999) 353 – 4, with reference to Philo, *De Vita Mosis* 2.214 and *De Specialibus Legibus* 2.251.

both an individual and the public. It could be seen as a space located between a private house or room and the street and public thoroughfare. With regard to all such definitions one needs to keep in mind, however, that the rabbinic notion of *carmelit* was first and foremost a theoretical notion constructed for the purpose of religious observance rather than a specific and well-defined space within everyday lived reality.

Interestingly, in political thought Carl Schmitt has already noted that the neutral always has the potential to become contentious so that another neutral has to be found: "Europeans always have wandered from a conflictual to a neutral domain, and always the newly won neutral domain has become immediately another arena of struggle, once again necessitating the search for a new neutral domain."[8] What seems to be criticized here is the "shallow formality" of political discourse.[9] In both political and religious thought the "neutral" is used as a device that enables action by avoiding definition, but as such it remains shallow and imprecise. The rabbinic *carmelit* was difficult to fathom, complicating distinctions between public and private by creating fluid boundaries that could endanger the very meaning and usefulness of these categories.

2. The Tannaitic Construction of the *Carmelit*

The term *carmelit* appears only very rarely in the Mishnah and Tosefta. The only reference in the Mishnah refers to a courtyard in a private house whose wall towards the public domain is broken so that there is an opening from the courtyard into the public domain. According to the opinion attributed to R. Eliezer, a person who carries something from this opening into the private domain or vice versa on the Sabbath transgresses the Sabbath, since this space is considered public domain and carrying something from one domain to the other is considered illegitimate work. According to sages, however, the person is not liable, "since it [the opening in the wall] is like a *carmelit*" (Mishnah Erubin 9:2), that is, a space that is neither public nor private. The term *carmelit* is not explained here and the assumption is that rabbis know what it means. The text suggests that a space between clearly definable public and private domains, that is, a space that cannot unambiguously be defined as either public or private, can be considered *carmelit* – but not everyone must necessarily agree with this definition, as R. Eliezer's statement indicates. As this *mishnah* already shows, the

8 Schmitt (2007) 90.

9 Sunic (1990) 84. For another interpretation of Carl Schmitt's text see Bessette (2013) 364.

concept of *carmelit* serves a more lenient understanding of Sabbath law, enabling practices that a more strict understanding of spatial divisions would find objectionable.

The entire *mishnah* speaks about internal courtyards of houses: small, large, and interlinked ones. Internal courtyards were part of many buildings, both in Roman Palestine and in the Roman world at large. They could be part of villas and one-family houses as well as apartment buildings (*insulae*) in which a number of individual family units opened into a shared courtyard.[10] The text's assumption is that the courtyard borders on the public domain, that is, a wall separated the courtyard from the street. The wall itself would probably have been part of the private building. If it was broken and there was a large opening (defined as wider than ten cubits), this space would have been open towards the public domain yet not really part of it, a situation that resulted in halakhic uncertainty. Non-residents may have used the open space to sit there and objects from the public domain may have invaded the space. Declaring this space *carmelit* solved the legal uncertainty and gave it a definition and name.

Other areas of uncertain definition are mentioned in Mishnah Erubin 10:3, where the term *carmelit* is not used: the threshold that separates a private house from the public domain and the empty space between the border of the roof and the public domain of the street. The lack of the term *carmelit* here and elsewhere in the Mishnah suggests that the editors of the Mishnah thematized doubtful areas only sparingly and refrained from clear-cut definitions between public and private. It is interesting, though, that *tannaim* already noticed certain gray areas between houses and the street, spaces that could not be defined easily as either public or private. Anyone who has visited Roman towns such as Pompei and Herculaneum has seen the many nooks and crannies between buildings. With regard to contemporary architecture Larry Ford has investigated *The Spaces Between Buildings* (2000), that is, "spaces that surround, enclose, and channel our activities."[11] Interestingly, he points out that such spaces "are often multipurpose and have different meanings for different people at different times. There is a danger that giving a name to a type of space might overly define it."[12] Nevertheless, some of these spaces "that surround and even cloak buildings" are nowadays called "semiprivate," such as "doorways, stairways, and porches."[13] Although ancient rabbis' concern with these spaces was halakh-

---

10 On domestic architecture in Roman Palestine see Galor (2010) 420–39. See also Hirschfeld (1995).

11 Ford (2000) xii.

12 Ibid. 5.

13 Ibid.

ic rather than architectural or property-law related, they were aware of gray areas in urban architecture which defied easy definitions of public and private.

In contrast to the Mishnah, the Tosefta provides a clear definition of the private and public realm: a private space needs to be within an enclosure that separates it from public streets for which various terms are used (Tosefta Shabbat 1:1–2). Especially interesting is the following sentence that mentions the *carmelit:* "But the sea and the valley and the *carmelit* and the colonnade and the threshold are neither private not public domain" (Tosefta Shabbat 1:4).[14] A person is not supposed to carry anything from these areas into the private or public domain or vice versa on the Sabbath – but if (s)he happens to do so, nevertheless (s)he remains free from liability. The *carmelit* seems to be distinguished from other, better known areas here because of its lack of specificity and undefinability except in a negative way: the nooks and crannies of urban settlement areas, which would have emerged as a consequence of decay and the collapse of architectural features, lacked specific other names that could define them. A *carmelit* was not a particular object or feature but a state of undefinability that could apply to a variety of spaces in the context of Sabbath observance, when clear-cut definitions of private and public were necessary.

From an anthropological point of view, rabbis' need to define the public and private and to invent a third category for ambiguous areas can be explained by their need to control their environment for ritual purposes. Ritual required order. As Mary Douglas has already pointed out, "ideas about separating, purifying, demarcating and punishing transgressions have as their main function to impose system on an inherently untidy experience."[15] In reality, public and private areas were not always easy to define (and rabbis do not even provide the criteria by which they distinguish between the two domains). For rabbinically defined Sabbath observance clear-cut distinctions were necessary, however, for otherwise transgression could not be determined. Therefore rabbis invented the *carmelit* as a third classification besides the private/public distinction. In this way rabbis engaged in "positively re-ordering our environment, making it conform to an idea."[16]

Another area in which private/public distinctions were halakhically relevant and in which the Tosefta introduces *carmelit* were damages to private property. The owner of cattle which entered another landlord's private domain and damaged something was liable to pay full damages (Tosefta Baba Qamma 1:6). This

---

14 For a more detailed discussion of this text and other rabbinic references to the mentioned locations see Hezser (1998) 443–51.

15 Douglas (2002) 5.

16 See ibid. 3 in connection with purity rules.

obvious statement is followed by an additional clause: if the cattle damaged something in an area classified as *carmelit*, the owner of the cattle has to pay full damages as well (ibid.), that is, it is treated like the private domain. In the case of a pit, however, which needs to be surrounded by a fence if it was dug by an individual, the area is considered public domain if its classification is uncertain (*carmelit*, cf. Tosefta Baba Qamma 6:15).[17] In these contexts where property issues are discussed, an uncertain area is classified as either private or public, that is, it is specified for the purpose of damage control. A spatial category of ambiguity, which introduced greater leniency to Sabbath law (see above), is deprived of its indeterminacy in property law, where clear decisions about the payment of damages were required. The comparison between these different contexts indicates the conceptual and ideational notion of *carmelit* which was used as a device to serve particular halakhic purposes.

The very fact that the public and private were not well defined in real life enabled rabbis to play with these categories in halakhic contexts. In connection with Roman architecture Andrew Wallace-Hadrill has already pointed out that the terms should not be understood "in terms of a black/white polarity" but as "a spectrum that ranges from the completely public to the completely private."[18] The context in which he refers to these terms is social interaction rather than legal discourse. The privately owned house had areas that served more or less public functions. Whether and to what extent a space was considered public or private not only depended on strict property-based definitions but also on other, less clearly definable issues: the social function of the space, common habits, associations, and attitudes.

Rabbis' own social status as neither solely private individuals nor public officials may also have prompted their identification of gray zones. Rabbis assumed religious leadership functions without being officially authorized in their roles.[19] Their self-imposed practice of providing legal advice was carried out in the ambiguous space of the semi-private or semi-public realm. In contrast to members of the Roman upper strata of society, who usually held official titles, rabbis would have been more likely to think beyond the private-public distinction. The fact that rabbinic *halakhah* itself was unofficial allowed them to think in categories which defied clear-cut dichotomies.

---

17 See Lieberman (1992) 3.

18 Wallace-Hadrill (1994) 17.

19 See Hezser (1997) 450–66.

3. The Palestinian Talmud's Presentation of the *Carmelit* as a Neutral Domain

The term *carmelit* is mentioned dozens of times in the Palestinian and Babylonian Talmuds, the large majority in Yerushalmi tractate Shabbat and Bavli tractates Shabbat and Eruvin. Since *carmelit* is a halakhic category, it is almost completely absent in midrashic contexts. From the Talmuds' discussions it is clear that the notion of *carmelit* has its proper place in rabbinic Sabbath law, which seems to have been adapted in Babylonia under the specific cultural conditions of Sasanian times. Altogether, the notion of *carmelit* served to make the strict biblical Sabbath laws more lenient, to allow rabbinic Jews to leave the private domain of the house and to carry items over the threshold. At the same time it seems that the discussions about the *carmelit* were mainly theoretical rather than practicable.

In the Talmud Yerushalmi the term appears in four passages of tractate Shabbat (Yerushalmi Shabbat 1:1, 2c-d; 10:2, 12c; 11:1, 13a; 11:5, 13b). Mishnah Shabbat 1:1 deals with the issue of carrying an object from the private to the public domain and vice versa on the Sabbath, an action in which two people are involved: a householder standing inside the house and a beggar who stands outside. Can they transfer food from one domain to the other without one or both of them becoming liable to a transgression? The *mishnah* divides the transaction into separate acts of each of the two people involved and examines whether any of these acts can be considered an illegitimate crossing of domains. At the same time a way of circumventing the transgression is suggested: if the hands of the householder and beggar meet and transfer an object in the middle, on the threshold between the private and public domain, that is, if neither of them carries the object from one domain into another, none of them can be considered liable of a transgression. The threshold serves as a neutral domain here that evades the public-private distinction of illegitimate transactions. It is important to note, though, that the *mishnah* neither mentions explicitly the "threshold" nor the *carmelit*. The distinction is merely between the person inside (the house) and the one standing outside. It is only the Tosefta, as mentioned above, that gives names to domains which are neither private nor public (see Tosefta Shabbat 1:4), thereby creating new categories for purposes of halakhic reasoning.

In the Talmud Yerushalmi the discussion continues. Palestinian *amoraim* seem to have been familiar with the categories of both the threshold and the *carmelit* and used them deliberately in their discussions of carrying objects and crossing domains on the Sabbath. In Yerushalmi Shabbat 1:1, 2c-d the *carmelit* appears as a domain by itself, that is, something that was arrived at by exclusion in the Mishnah (neither private nor public) has now become manifest and is given a name. One could say that naming gives reality to something that did not exist before or was perceived as a negative only: in the Yerushalmi the *carmelit* is no longer an uncertain but a neutral domain.

In a statement attributed to R. Yochanan "carrying [an object] from the private to the public domain through the *carmelit*" is declared transgressive, since the boundaries between the private and public domain are crossed and the neutral domain has no function in such an action. If, by contrast, an object were laid down in the neutral domain and then collected by someone in the other domain, the two actions would be permissible. In this statement the halakhic function of the *carmelit* becomes clear: it extends the domain to which it is attached and creates a buffer zone between private and public, enabling the transfer of objects across domains under the stipulated conditions. Whether and to what extent such a scenario was practicable and practiced or mere theoretical speculation remains uncertain.

In the following discussion the *carmelit* is identified with the threshold of a house (but not limited to it). When carrying something from a private house into the public domain through the neutral domain of the threshold, the neutral domain as such does not make this action permissible. According to Mishnah Shabbat 10:2, "He who brings out [of the house] foodstuffs and put them on the threshold, whether he [himself] returns and takes them out or whether someone else takes them out [into the public domain], he is exempt, because he did not do his work in one go." The term *carmelit* is not used in this *mishnah* but in the Yerushalmi's commentary the threshold is identified with the *carmelit:* "And is the threshold not *carmelit?*" Therefore the carrying of objects through the neutral domain has no effect – only if an object is placed within the neutral domain or taken out of it, the neutral domain serving as an extension of the domain in which the carrier of the object is standing, is the action considered permissible. Since Palestinian *amoraim* saw the *carmelit* as an extension of either the private or the public domain, one could understand the *eruv*, that is, the rabbinic idea of a local Sabbath boundary in whose parameters the carrying of objects, especially food, is allowed, as an extension of the idea of the neutral domain, despite the fact that certain differences between the concepts remain. The halakhic discussion concerning the *eruv* is very complex and cannot be dealt with here.

A further question discussed in the Yerushalmi concerns the space occupied by the *carmelit:* should one envision the *carmelit* as two-dimensional or three-dimensional, that is, as a flat space on the ground or as a space that includes the air above the ground? Obviously, the private and public domain were seen as three-dimensional: both the house and the public street and market place were living spaces rather than mere areas on a map. With the *carmelit* the situation was different, however, since it was not a space that was evident in reality. The issue of the spatial dimension of the *carmelit* became relevant in connection with throwing an object from the private into the public domain on the Sabbath, through an area that could be perceived as *carmelit*. According to the discussion in Yerushalmi Shabbat 1:1, 2c, the general rabbinic view was that such an action should be seen as a transgression, since the air above the *carmelit* was not identical with the *carmelit* itself: "It is the opinion of all that the air of [i. e. over] the *carmelit* is not [the same as the *carmelit*] itself." The passing through the air between a private and public domain could therefore not neutralize the illegitimate crossing of the Sabbath boundaries. At the same time the Talmud mentions the allegedly exceptional view of Ben Azzai who treated the air above the *carmelit* as identical to the *carmelit*, allowing the throwing of objects from the home through the door into the public domain on the Sabbath. Ben Azzai's view is presented as more lenient than the view of other rabbis. In both cases the person who throws the object is considered to have remained in the private domain him- or herself. The Talmudic discussion shows that once the notion of the *carmelit* has been introduced, thinking in terms of this category becomes increasingly complicated since its parameters have to be defined.

This is also evident in the Palestinian Talmud's discussion of the scenario presented in Mishnah Shabbat 1:1, where the transfer of an object between a beggar and a householder is discussed (see above). The Mishnah declared such an action permissible if their hands meet in the middle, above the threshold of the door. In the Yerushalmi the issue is more complex since the airspace above the different domains is taken into account. Specific measures are suggested that render the actions of the beggar and householder permissible or prohibited and the standing position of the beggar in relation to the wall of the house and the street is taken into account (Yerushalmi Shabbat 1:1, 2c). Only the airspace within ten cubits from the ground is considered part of the respective domain. In addition, a domain is supposed to be four cubits wide. The Yerushami stipulates that the transaction between the beggar and the householder is permissible only if their hands meet in the space of ten by four cubits above the threshold. Various biblical passages are alluded to in support of these measurements (ibid. 2d: height of the ark of the covenant; height of a wagon).[20]

The problems with such a definition are obvious, for how should the space higher than ten cubits from the ground be defined? Merely suggesting that it con-

---

20 The measurement of ten by four cubits already appears in Tosefta Shabbat 1:1 with regard to the private and public domains.

stitutes a “different domain” (see ibid.) would be insufficient. Therefore the following *sugya* presents the opinions of Rabbi, Ben Azzai, and R. Aqiba, who allegedly stated that the airspace above a domain should be treated as part of that domain (see ibid. Yerushalmi Shabbat 1:1, 2d). This is a much more simple solution with which the editors of the Talmud seem to have agreed (the *sugya* ends with these rulings).

Besides the threshold, Tosefta Shabbat 1:4 already mentioned the sea, valley, and colonnade as areas that do not easily fit the private/public dichotomy. They are basically treated like the *carmelit* as far as the transfer of objects on the Sabbath is concerned: if a person carried an object into such an area from either the private or public domain, he or she is exempt from liability. The discussion of these areas is continued in the Yerushalmi, where relevant Mishnah texts are cited in connection with each of them (Yerushalmi Shabbat 1:1, 2d). The question is whether the entire sea can be considered a neutral domain or only the immediate strip adjoining the land on which a person stands. If the latter is the case, what should be the maximum measurement of this part of the sea? While some rabbis wanted to apply the mishnaic four cubit measure to the sea (cf. Mishnah Shabbat 11:4: only one who throws an object up to four cubits into the sea is exempt), others seem to have viewed the entire sea as a neutral domain into which objects could be thrown on the Sabbath (see also Yerushalmi Shabbat 11:4, 13a). This more lenient position seems to have been shared by the editors.

As Fenn has pointed out, in Roman law the second-century C.E. jurist Marcianus was the first to state “that the sea and its coasts are common to all men.”[21] He concludes: “it follows that the doctrine of the common right of all men to a free use of the sea was a law of the Roman Empire at the beginning of the second century, although this law was not put into codified form until the sixth century.”[22] The free “use” included the right of fishing. Fenn argues that the notion of a “common use” is supported by the fact that “no records have been preserved of any legal doctrine of a *mare clausum*; or of a claim to dominion over the sea or part thereof on the ground that the waters are adjacent to the territory of the state or government setting up the claim, or for any other reason.”[23] No government claimed “any sort of property right in the sea itself, that is, the claim to *imperium* was not developed into a claim to *dominium*.” Furthermore, what is most important with regard to rabbis, popular opinion considered the “use” of the sea and the “appropriation” of the fish “open or common to all

21 Fenn (1925) 716, with reference to the Digest 1.8 pr. and 1.8.1.

22 Ibid.

23 Ibid. 717.

men."[24] Since "there was no *extension* of state jurisdiction seaward," the closeness to the shore was irrelevant: "The exercise of maritime jurisdiction carried with it no implication of a right by a state to appropriate the sea, or to restrict the right of access to it. A claim to jurisdiction did not and could not involve a claim to ownership."[25]

This notion is supported by other texts in the Digest, according to which "the shores of the sea were not considered subject to the ownership of the State (Digest 41, 1, 14, pr.), but simply as under its supervision or jurisdiction (Digest 43, 8, 3, pr.)."[26] Therefore the sea could not simply be associated with either the public or private sphere. The Roman state "might exercise all those rights of exclusive use that a private proprietor did"; or the state could allow public use of the sea and harbour: "This left an extremely shadowy sort of ownership in the State."[27]

According to Baillat, "by natural law these things are common to all: air, running water, the sea, and as a consequence: the shores of the sea. By its very nature, water was considered as not being subject of ownership and therefore was neither state property nor private property."[28] The sea, sea bed, and sea shore belonged to no one and were classified as *res nullius* according to "the law of nations," that is, assumed legal consensus.[29] As open access non-property (things unowned) *res nullius* was distinguished from both public (*res publicus*) and common property (*res communes*). Milun quotes Gillian Rose: "*Res nullius* (in Roman law) were either things unappropriated by anyone, such as things common, unoccupied lands, wild animals; or things which cannot be appropriated: sacred things... and sanctified things, such as the walls and gates of a city...."[30] Roman law allegedly "demonstrated an interest in the sorts of things that were outside the domain of private and public property."[31]

It seems, then, that both rabbis and Roman legal experts considered areas and objects beyond the private/public dichotomy and used particular terms to categorize them. The Roman concept of *res nullius* appears in the context of prop-

24 Ibid.
25 Ibid. 718.
26 Hunter (1803) 311. *Dig.* 41.1.14.*pr.: ... nam litora publica non ita sunt, ut ea, quae in patrimonio sunt populi, sed ut ea quae primum a natura prodita sunt et in nullius adhuc dominum pervenerunt... Dig.* 43.8.3.*pr.: Litora, in quae populus romanus imperium habet, populi romani esse arbitror.*
27 Hunter (1803) 311.
28 Baillat (2010) 26.
29 See Milun (2011) 72.
30 Quoted in Milun (2011) 72, cf. Rose (1984) 49. Ulpian (*Dig.* 1.8.9) distinguishes between sacred places "dedicated by the state (*publice*)" and the *sacrarium*, that is, a "place in which sacred objects are kept," which "may exist in a private building."
31 Milun (2011) 72.

erty law, however, whereas the rabbinic concept of a neutral domain or *carmelit* is associated with Sabbath law. Despite certain analogies the respective contexts and functions are different, just as the rabbinic notion of private and public was different from the Roman.[32] Interestingly, discussions of the notion of *res nullius* reoccurred in the legal argumentation surrounding the exploration of the New World in the sixteenth and seventeenth centuries and in philosophical thinking of the Enlightenment period.[33] The issue is still relevant for the mining and fishing industries today.[34] A related notion is that of *terra nullius* applied to certain geographical regions.[35] The Roman and later discussions of *res nullius* indicate that rabbis were not the only ones who considered public/private distinctions inadequate for covering all types of spaces and objects and practices. A third category was necessary in addition to those which were clearly public or private.

If the sea could be regarded as a neutral domain, how should one categorize a ship and a rock in the middle of the sea? Would rabbis allow the carrying of objects on a ship or rock or the throwing of objects from them into the sea or vice versa on the Sabbath? The case of a boat is already addressed in Mishnah Shabbat 11:5, but the problem is discussed in more detail only in Yerushalmi Shabbat 11:5, 13a-b. The Mishnah does not state to which domain a boat belongs but declares the throwing of objects from a boat into the sea or onto another boat permissible. The related action of carrying objects from a boat into the sea is addressed in the Tosefta (Tosefta Shabbat 10:14). Unlike the throwing of objects through the air, carrying is generally not allowed, despite the fact that the sea is regarded as neutral domain. According to one opinion, the size of the boat matters: if it is less than ten cubits high, one may carry things from it and deposit them in the sea but not into the other direction. In the Yerushalmi this regulation is justified with reference to the possible danger at sea: in order to survive, it may be necessary to relieve the load the boat is carrying. Bringing items into the boat, e.g., fish caught in the sea, would be considered work not permitted on the Sabbath, though.

Can a rock in the sea be considered neutral domain and part of or separate from the sea? According to the Tosefta, the size of the rock matters: if it is at least

---

32 See Hezser (1998) 434: "Der besonders im Zusammenhang mit der Sabbatobservanz thematisierte 'Bereich des einzelnen/der vielen' wird nie explizit besitzrechtlich definiert."

33 New World: Schmitt (2003) 175 ("*Is the Free Sea* Res Nullius *or* Res Omnium?"). See also Benton and Straumann (2010). Enlightenment philosophy: Milun (2011) 73, with reference to Kant's *Metaphysical Elements of Justice*.

34 See, e.g., Shaw (2004).

35 Edward Said criticized the alleged Zionist representation of Palestine as a *terra nullia*, see Said (2001) 161–78.

ten cubits high, it is seen as a separate domain (Tosefta Shabbat 10:12). Rabbinic statements transmitted in the Yerushalmi suggest that such a rock may be considered a partition (R. Ila). At least with regard to a smaller rock R. Hananiah is said to have ruled: "Since the sea surrounds it on all sides, it is as if the whole [area] is one *carmelit*" (Yerushalmi Shabbat 11:5, 13b), that is, the rock is seen as part of the sea. One may assume that a larger rock might be considered an island under certain circumstances. According to Roman law, unoccupied lands in the form of a rock or island in the sea would be considered *res nullius.* If someone took possession of an unoccupied island or built a protrusion into the sea, such an island or protrusion would be seen as private property.[36] Rabbis who considered a natural rock part of the neutral domain *(carmelit)* of the sea would have been in line with Roman definitions, even if they did not think from a property law perspective.

Finally, an additional issue which Palestinian rabbis considered relevant in connection with proper Sabbath observance was the space occupied by an object in the neutral domain: objects placed on the threshold of a house could be so large that parts of them reached out into the public domain. Mishnah Shabbat 10:2 refers to a basket full of produce as an example. If one took something out of the basket, one is exempt from liability, even if most of the basket reached into to street, "unless he takes out the entire basket." In the Talmud Yerushalmi (Yerushalmi Shabbat 10:2, 12c) the additional example of a shelf is mentioned, another type of container too large to fit into a small "neutral domain" completely. Is one allowed to take something out of the shelf or rearrange things? According to a statement attributed to R. Mana, such actions are permissible if the shelf is open into one domain only and therefore considered part of that domain. If a shelf is placed on the threshold, closed towards the street and open towards the house, one is allowed to take things out of it and bring them into the house on the Sabbath. For a basket such an arrangement is not imaginable, though (cf. R. Yose's reply), unless one turns it on its side (see the discussion in the next *sugya*). At the end of this discussion a general rule is stated anonymously: "There is nothing that is moved in the public domain and made [i.e., treated as] *carmelit* except for a human being alone," meaning that only a person can move around and be carried in the public domain on the Sabbath but not an object, certain exceptions that are further discussed in the Mishnah and Talmud notwithstanding (see the discussion in Mishnah Shabbat 6:1–4 and the respective Talmudic commentary).

---

36 Island: see Mousourakis (2012) 139, with reference to *Dig.* 41.1.7.3 and Justinian, *Institutes* 2.1.22. Protrusion: see Marzano (2007) 26–7, n. 65, with reference to further literature.

4. The Delimitation of the *Carmelit* in the Babylonian Talmud

The term *carmelit* appears thirty-four times in the Babylonian Talmud. With three exceptions, all of these occurrences are in tractates Shabbat and Eruvin. This means that Sabbath law remains the context in which the concept of the uncertain or neutral domain is thematized. Did Babylonian *amoraim* and/or the editors of the Bavli make any changes to the concept, perhaps in accordance with the Sasanian political, social, and cultural context in which they lived? How did they continue and augment the discussion begun by Palestinian sages? What is obvious is that they had additional *baraitot* (tannaitic traditions) available that they integrated into the discourse. For example, in Bavli Shabbat 6b the status of the valley or plain is discussed. In Tosefta Shabbat 1:4 the valley is said to be *carmelit*. In the Bavli this identification is questioned, however. A *baraita* is quoted, according to which in both the summer and winter a valley is private domain in regard to the Sabbath. No reason is given why this should be so. Perhaps the growth (summer) and sowing (winter) of agricultural produce would keep trespassers off the fields so that the areas outside of public roads could be considered different from the roads themselves. Obviously, privately owned fields would also be considered private domain according to Roman law. The discussion continued amongst Babylonian *amoraim*. According to R. Ashi, such an area can be called private domain only if it is located within an enclosure, that is, if it has a barrier that separates it from the public domain of the road. A statement by Ulla in the name of the Palestinan *amora* R. Yochanan is quoted according to which an uninhabited enclosure detached from a dwelling is still considered a private ground for purposes of carrying objects on the Sabbath (ibid.).

The logical continuation of this discussion is whether the other areas identified as *carmelit* in Palestinian tannaitic sources, namely the sea and the colonnade, might not be *carmelit*, either, but could also be identified as either private or public (cf. Bavli Shabbat 7a). Interestingly, the discussion continues with reference to R. Yochanan's opinions, a Palestinian sage who was one of the nodal points of the rabbinic network connecting Palestine and Babylonia.[37] It seems that certain Palestinian traditions concerning the *carmelit* are transmitted in the Babylonian Talmud only. According to opinions attributed to R. Yochanan and transmitted by R. Dimi, a corner area outside a house adjacent to a street

37 See Hezser (forthcoming in 2015).

as well as the area between two pillars, although sometimes populated by crowds, would be in the status of *carmelit*. In both cases the reason provided is that the public cannot make proper use of these spaces, that is, the use and function rather than ownership of the areas (cf. Roman law) is considered relevant here.

The definition of the area between the pillars of a colonnade was disputed amongst rabbis, however (see the continuation of the discussion in Bavli Shabbat 7a). Some rabbis considered this area part of the public domain and some suggested that only the elevation at the bottom (or "in front") of the pillars should be considered *carmelit*, since the public could not make proper use of this space, whereas people could usually walk between pillars. One may assume that market traders used these spaces to exhibit their goods, just like unsolicited street vendors nowadays. In this discussion the tannaitic identification of the colonnade as *carmelit* is specified and delimited: not the entire colonnade but only those parts of it that are not regularly used by the public are seen as neutral domain.

A narrowing of the notion of a neutral space that is neither public nor private is also evident in Bavli Shabbat 8b, where the threshold is discussed in relation to Mishnah Shabbat 10:2 (see above). In the anonymous discussion of the Babylonian Talmud the notion of the threshold is not considered self-evident but requires further definition: surely, the threshold of a public road should be considered public and the threshold of a private house private, that is, the threshold is seen as part of the public/private dichotomy rather than constituting a separate domain for the purpose of carrying objects on the Sabbath. Even the "thes-hold of a *carmelit*," however such a space was imagined (it seems to be an entirely theoretical concept here) is considered questionable with regard to permitting the transfer of objects from one domain to another on the Sabbath.[38] At the end of the discussion a statement of R. Dimi in the name of R. Yochanan (see above) is quoted as a solution to the problem: Only in a space (whether threshold or *carmelit*) that is less than four cubits wide may one deposit (but not transfer) objects carried from either the public or the private domain on the Sabbath.

It seems that the Babylonian editors who constructed these discussions, and perhaps also Babylonian *amoraim* before them, were stricter than Palestinian sages concerning the transfer of objects on the Sabbath. They were less willing to use the notion of a neutral domain to enable such transfers and more inclined

38 For the distinction between a private, public, and *carmelit* threshold see also Bavli Shabbat 91b and Bavli Erubin 98a.

towards strict distinctions between private and public domains. This also becomes evident when the case of someone standing in either the private or public domain and drinking (probably with his hand stretched out) in the *carmelit* is considered (Bavli Shabbat 11b). According to Abaye, such an action is not permissible as such. A statement attributed to Rabbah suggests that this prohibition might be considered a preventive measure (היא גופה גזירה).[39] Since one preventive measure should not be used to safeguard another preventive measure (standing in one domain and drinking in another by leaning the greater part of one's body into the domain where the action takes place), this conclusion becomes invalid.

Interestingly, the Bavli creates a new "free space" or "space of non-liability" (מקום פטור) in distinction from the *carmelit*, which it limits. When discussing the Mishnah's statement that someone who throws something from the sea onto dry land or into a ship or vice versa on the Sabbath is not culpable, the Bavli limits the *carmelit* to an area within four by ten cubits, measured from the sea bed, so that most of the sea would not be identified as neutral domain (Bavli Shabbat 100b). As we have seen above, the discussion of the issue in the Yerushalmi concludes with viewing the entire sea as a neutral domain (Yerushalmi Shabbat 11:4), in analogy with Roman law. In addition to limiting the area of the *carmelit* to four by ten cubits of water, the Bavli suggests a new domain of non-liability which covers the entire sea above ten cubits from the sea bed as well as the airspace above the sea.[40] This new category was necessary to avoid contradicting earlier mishnaic regulations concerning the throwing of objects at and into the sea on the Sabbath.

It is obvious, however, that Babylonian sages and editors were not as comfortable with the notion of the *carmelit* as their Palestinian colleagues and tried to limit its applicability. Unfortunately, as Maria Macuch has pointed out, the sparseness of Sasanian source material has prevented research on the private/public distinction in ancient Persian culture so far.[41] She notes, however, that "spaces played an important role in different spheres, also in Zoroastrian ritual."[42] Clearly defined ritual spaces existed for carrying out specific practices, such as oaths. Although a distinction between private and public spaces probably existed in Sasanian society, "the Sasanian concept of property ownership dif-

---

39 See also Bavli Erubin 99a, where a statement attributed to Rabbah again insists that the notion of the *carmelit* serves as a preventive measure only.

40 The issue is taken up by Maimonides: since the sea is considered *carmelit* and/or "space of non-liability" as far as Sabbath observance is concerned, sea travel is permitted on the Sabbath if the sea is at least ten handbreadths deep. See the discussion in Davidson (2011) 183.

41 Maria Macuch by email (23 June 2013).

42 Ibid.

fers from classical Roman law."[43] The Babylonian rabbinic "space of non-liability" was unrelated to property law or administrative regulations and concerned the religious sphere of Sabbath observance only. By creating this category Babylonian *amoraim* and editors could maintain certain tannaitic regulations by, at the same time, adjusting them to the environment in which they and their fellow-Jews lived.

5. Summary

Late antique Palestinian rabbis turned the tannaitic category of an uncertain domain into a neutral domain as far as carrying and throwing objects on the Sabbath were concerned. The invention of the *carmelit* as an alternative domain that defied private/public distinctions was a rabbinic innovation that served halakhic purposes. Within rabbinic discourse the discussions around the *carmelit* seem to have primarily served theoretical purposes rather than being practicable in daily life: once introduced the concept became increasingly complex and difficult to define, as the discussions in both the Palestinian and Babylonian Talmuds show. Unlike the notion of the *eruv*, which is still widely practiced by Jewish communities nowadays, the notion of the *carmelit* is largely confined to the theoretical context of Talmud study.

Perhaps the Roman legal category of *res nullius*, applied to areas and objects that were neither private nor public property and could be used by anyone, such as the sea, can provide a partial analogy. Whereas the Roman notion of *res nullius* appears in the context of property law, however, the *carmelit* is never defined in these terms. If a pragmatic reason for the definition is alluded to at all, it is the use of an area (by an individual or "the many," an undefined mass of people) rather than ownership that determined its identification.

The concept of the *carmelit* seems to have had its proper place in Palestinian rabbinic discourse in late antiquity. Babylonian *amoraim*, especially those associated with the Palestinian sage R. Yochanan, seem to have brought the idea to Babylonia, but Babylonian Talmudic discussions delimit its definition and applicability. A possible lack of analogies to the *carmelit* in the Persian cultural context and a stricter division between spaces may have caused Babylonian rabbis to confine this Palestinian concept and to revert to a greater stringency.

---

43 Ibid. with reference to Macuch (2008) 126–38.

Works Cited

Baillat, A. (2010). *International Trade in Water Rights: The Next Step.* London.

Benton, L. and B. Straumann. (2010). "Acquiring Empire by Law: From Roman Doctrine to Early Modern European Practice." *Law and History Review* 28: 1–38.

Bessette, M. (2013). "The crisis of the West, the challenge of technology, and the reaffirmation of political philosophy," in Gavriel Salvendy *et al.*, eds, *Advances in Design for Cross-Cultural Activities*, vol. 2: 359–68. Boca Raton, Florida.

Davidson, H.A. (2011). "Maimonides and Samuel Ben Ali," in Resianne Fontaine, ed., *Studies in the History of Culture and Science. A Tribute to Gad Freudenthal:* 171–88. Leiden.

Doering, L. (1999). *Schabbat. Sabbathalacha und -praxis im antiken Judentum und Urchristentum.* Tübingen.

Douglas, M. (2002). *Purity and Danger. An analysis of concept of pollution and taboo.* London and New York.

Fenn, P.T. Jr. (1925). "Justinian and the Freedom of the Sea." *The American Journal of International Law* 19: 716–27.

Ford, L.R. (2000). *The Spaces Between Buildings.* Baltimore.

Galor, K. (2010). "Domestic Architecture," in C. Hezser, ed., *The Oxford Handbook of Jewish Daily Life in Roman Palestine:* 420–39. Oxford.

Hezser, C. (1997). *The Social Structure of the Rabbinic Movement in Roman Palestine.* Tübingen.

Hezser, C. (1998). "'Privat' und 'öffentlich' im Talmud Yerushalmi und in der griechisch-römischen Antike," in P. Schäfer, ed., *The Talmud Yerushalmi and Graeco-Roman Culture*, vol. 1: 423–579. Tübingen.

Hezser, C. (forthcoming in 2015). "Crossing Enemy Lines: Network Connections Between Palestinian and Babylonian Sages in Late Antiquity," in M. Mullet and A.M. Schor, eds, *The Social Network in Byzantium and Its Neighbors.* Dumbarton Oaks Colloquium Papers. Washington, D.C.

Hirschfeld, Y. (1995). *The Palestinian Dwelling in the Roman-Byzantine Period, Jerusalem: Franciscan Printing Press*, 1995.

Hunter, W.A. (1803). *A Systematic and Historical Exposition of Roman Law in the Order of a Code*, 4th ed. London.

Jastrow, M. (1985). *Dictionary of the Targumim, the Talmud Bavli and Yerushalmi, and the Midrashic Literature.* Jerusalem.

Lieberman, S. (1992). *Tosefta Kifshutah. A Comprehensive Commentary on the Tosefta*, Part III: *Order Moed: Shabbat – Eruvin* [Hebrew], 2nd ed. Jerusalem.

Macuch, M. (2008). "An Iranian Legal Term in the Babylonian Talmud and in Sasanian Jurisprudence: *dastwar*," in Shaul Shaked and Amnon Netzer, eds, *Irano Judaica VI: Studies Relating to Jewish Contacts with Persian Culture Throughout the Ages:* 126–38. Jerusalem.

Marzano, A. (2007). *Roman Villas in Central Italy: A Social and Economic History.* Leiden.

Milun, K. (2011). *The Political Uncommons: The Cross-Cultural Logic of the Global Commons.* Farnham.

Moscovitz, L. (2002). *Talmudic Reasoning: From Casuistics to Conceptualization.* Tübingen.

Mousourakis, G. (2012). *Fundamentals of Roman Private Law.* Heidelberg.

Rose, G. (1984). *Dialectic of Nihilism, Post-Structuralism and Law.* Oxford.

Said, E. (2001). "Michael Waltzer's *Exodus and Revolution:* A Canaanite Reading," in E. Said and Ch. Hitchens, eds, *Blaming the Victims: Spurious Scholarship and the Palestinian Question,* 3rd ed.: 161–78. London and New York.
Schmitt, C. (2003). *The Nomos of the Earth in the International Law of the Jus Publicum Europaeum.* New York.
Schmitt, C. (2007). *The Concept of the Political,* expanded ed. Chicago and London.
Shaw, L.E. (2004). *Res Communis vs. Res Nullius: The Problem of Seabed Mining Under the United Nations Law of the Sea Treaty III.* Denver.
Sunic, T. (1990). *Against Democracy and Equality: The European New Right.* New York.
Wallace-Hadrill, A. (1994). *Houses and Society in Pompeii and Herculaneum.* Princeton.

Ahmed El Shamsy

11. Shame, Sin, and Virtue: Islamic Notions of Privacy

Abstract: The Islamic notion of an all-seeing God led to a reconfiguration of the pre-Islamic idea of shame and prompted the theorization of two distinct realms of human existence and action: one public, carried out before fellow humans, and the other private, known only to God. This essay traces the emergence of this distinction and its ramifications in the fields of Islamic law and asceticism. The conceptualization of privacy as the realm of the divine gaze gave rise to particular notions of sin versus crime and sincerity versus hypocrisy, and it contributed to the process of individuation that accompanied the urban spread of Islam.

1. Introduction

Classical Arabic possesses no direct or obvious equivalents for the terms "public" and "private." However, notions of privacy and the public sphere are clearly evident in several conceptual pairs and clusters used in the Quran and in Islamic religious literatures to denote distinct but complementary realms of human existence and action. For example, the discourse of Islamic law recognizes a qualitative difference between the rules of ritual law (*ʿibādāt*) and those of interpersonal law (*muʿāmalāt*), the former primarily applicable to an individual's private relationship to God and the latter governing interactions in society. The norms of personal conduct between genders, in turn, vary according to degrees of familiarity and closeness determined largely on the basis of kinship. Also in the field of law, criminal sanctions for theft recognize a difference between property guarded within a private dwelling and property displayed out in the open. More broadly, the sanctity of the home is firmly established by Quranic and prophetic norms that prescribe strict limits on external surveillance and intrusion by the authorities (Alshech 2004). And from at least the ninth century CE onward, Arabic literary culture developed a concept of private reading that was juxtaposed with the traditional practice of open, communal recitation and dictation of books. The list could go on.

This paper excavates an Islamic notion of privacy as an internal space of conscience, ethical consideration, sin, and guilt, as theorized by classical Muslim scholars. I first show how the concept of *ḥayāʾ*[1] evolved from an externally triggered emotion of shame in the pre-Islamic period to mean both shame in front of others and shame in front of the ever-watchful eye of God. This shift broadened the meaning of the term to encompass guilt as well as shame. Second, I argue that this matrix of shame and guilt led jurists to distinguish between two types of transgression against the norms of the sacred law: private sin and public crime. Third, I contrast the definition of privacy in the context of legal misconduct with a parallel but different notion of privacy in the context of virtuous behavior. In all three arenas, the public and the private are conceptualized as two distinct domains within a moral order in which the individual self unfolds by interacting with the divine, on the one hand, and with society, on the other.

2. External and internal shame

Our sources on pre-Islamic Arab societies are slim, comprising a body of poetry and early Islamic traditions that claim to describe the *status quo ante*. While these sources have to be used with caution, recent studies have shown that they can yield useful information on pre-Islamic Arabian society and its norms (Crone 2012, 424). One such report concerns the marriage between the Prophet Muḥammad (d. 632) and the wealthy widow Khadīja, which took place before the start of Muḥammad's prophetic mission. Khadīja, facing the challenge of persuading her father to agree to her marriage to a man whose position within his tribe was compromised by his orphan status, invited her father together with prominent guests from Muḥammad's tribe, the Quraysh, to a feast of food as well as wine. Once her father was drunk, she presented him with the proposal, and he agreed. When he had sobered up, he revoked his permission, but Khadīja retorted, "Are you not ashamed (*a-lā tastaḥī*, derived from the same root as *ḥayāʾ*) to lose face in front of the Quraysh, with people saying that you were drunk?" (Ibn Ḥanbal 2008, 5:46–47). Her father was cowed and accepted the marriage. This anecdote exemplifies the usage of the root *ḥ-y-y* to denote shame before someone else. In accounts of the pre-Islamic era, shame is always used to express disgrace in the eyes of other people.[2]

1 *Ḥayāʾ* is not the only term used to describe shame; the related *istiḥyāʾ* and the terms *iḥtishām*, *ḥishma*, and *taḥashshum* are synonyms.

2 See the pre-Islamic and Umayyad court poetry reproduced in *Lisān al-ʿArab*, s.v. "ḥ-sh-m" and "ḥ-y-y." The Umayyad poetry, though postdating the emergence of Islam, preserves many of the cultural forms of its pre-Islamic precedents, including an external sense of shame as relating to other people.

With the coming of Islam, however, the use of the term widened. On the one hand, Muḥammad stressed the ethical value of a sense of shame, proclaiming, "If you feel no shame, then do as you please" (al-Bukhārī 2001, no. 3,484). He is also reported to have said that "a sense of shame is part of belief" (al-Bukhārī 2001, no. 24). This statement is puzzling at first sight, because it conflates the internal phenomenon of belief with the externally triggered emotion of shame. The connection becomes clearer, however, when considering a report about Muḥammad's son-in-law and later caliph ʿUthmān (d. 655). According to the report, ʿUthmān would not undress fully to bathe even in the privacy of his house, "for it was a sense of shame that prevented him from leaving his loins uncovered" (Ibn Ḥanbal 2008, 1:554). Shame here is not an emotion affecting only the public persona of an individual; it also penetrates his personal space and his relationship with God.

The reason for this extension of shame from the public to the private lies in the theological dimension that Islam introduced into Arab ethical discourse: it was no longer only before the collective that the individual ought to fear disgrace, but also before God. Muḥammad is reported to have instructed his followers to "be adequately ashamed before God" and then explained that "shame before God means being mindful of your head and what it holds, and your belly and what it contains; it is to remember death and calamities. And whoever wishes for the hereafter leaves the luxury of this world. Those who do this are those who feel shame before God" (al-Tirmidhī 1937, no. 2,458). The aim of this reframing and internalization of shame is, to quote another saying of Muḥammad, to "worship God as if you saw Him; because even though you do not see Him, He certainly sees you" (al-Bukhārī 2001, no. 50). A preexisting mechanism of behavioral control, the concept of shame, was thus both extended and intensified through reference to an all-knowing, all-seeing God from whom nothing can be hidden—not actions performed in private, nor even fully internal phenomena such as thoughts.

This view leads to an emphasis on the intentions behind actions; as Muḥammad put it, "Actions are [judged] according to their intentions" (al-Bukhārī 2001, no. 1). It establishes an ethical continuity from the most private internal processes to the most public behavior. As Muḥammad's statement regarding shame before God shows, divine judgment in the hereafter provides both the motivation for feeling shame before God and the promise of ultimate justice in the evaluation of an individual's actions, as opposed to the sanctions of the law that apply only incompletely and are mostly limited to the public realm.

Furthermore, Muḥammad's sayings seek to set limits on individuals' sense of shame before others in order to prioritize the imperative to act righteously before God. On one occasion Muḥammad was leading a congregation in prayer when one of the participants broke wind, thereby invalidating the ritual purity that is a precondition for performing the prayer. Muḥammad exclaimed that the person in question should get up and perform the ablution in order to reestablish his ritual purity, but the culprit was clearly too embarrassed to identify himself by rising. Muḥammad said, "God is not ashamed of the truth,"[3] but still nobody stirred. Finally, someone resolved the impasse by suggesting that everyone present redo the ablution in order to allow the culprit to perform his prayers in a valid manner without exposing him (Ibn Sallām 1994, 400). In connection to another private matter, Muḥammad explicitly forbade men to have anal intercourse with their wives, adding that "God is not ashamed of the truth" (Ibn Sallām 1994, 397); that is, the need to understand the rules of the sacred law on this point prevails over the embarrassment that discussion of the topic would ordinarily provoke. The phrase recurs in a report according to which a woman asked Muḥammad whether women need to perform ritual ablution after experiencing a sexual dream. Ignoring the titters of other women present on the occasion, the questioner prefaced her query by saying, "God is not ashamed of the truth" (al-Bukhārī 2001, no. 6,091).

None of these instances calls into question a sense of shame as such. Rather, they indicate an ethical hierarchy in which emotions of shame do not establish absolute values and instead must be overcome when they clash with "the truth," which is a value that transcends the value of appearances guarded by shame. An ethical system based solely on shame would discourage individuals from revealing embarrassing private experiences, but the emphasis on an objective truth established by the deity, who can see beyond appearances, may necessitate contravening proper public behavior in order to guarantee proper private or internal conduct.

This shift in the understanding of shame brought about by the emergence of Islam appears to be part of a transformation that resembles the one described by Eric Robertson Dodds in the transition from the Homeric to the classical Greek age, namely, the emergence of a guilt culture out of a shame culture (Dodds 1951, chap. 2). In both situations, the mode of control over behavior shifted from a focus on performing for the gaze of other members of the community to the establishment of an internalized stage on which the individual had to justify himself or herself.

This division of human existence into life observed by others and life witnessed only by God created two distinct realms with two different legal and eth-

3 This peculiar phrase has its origin in Quran 33:53, which states that although Muḥammad is ashamed to rebuke his guests because they are guests, God is not ashamed.

ical logics. These realms can usefully be labeled private and public, a distinction that sheds light on the particular cultural phenomena that emerged in Islamic societies.

3. Privacy and transgression

The dichotomy between the public and private dimensions of a person's life that can be detected in the shifting connotation of the term "shame" also came to structure Islamic legal thought. Although Islamic law encompasses obligations concerning behavior that we would consider private as well as behavior that takes place in public, it nevertheless clearly differentiates between the two realms and establishes boundaries between them. A respect for the privacy of the domestic sphere is rooted in the Quran in such verses as 24:27, "O you who believe, do not enter houses other than your own until you ascertain welcome and greet their inhabitants. That is best for you; perhaps you will be reminded"; and 49:12, "O you who believe, shun much suspicion; for indeed some suspicion is a crime. And spy not, neither backbite one another. Would one of you love to eat the flesh of his dead brother?" The force of these injunctions against intrusions on individual privacy can be seen in an anecdote involving the second caliph, ʿUmar (d. 644), who reportedly approached a house in which lights were burning at night and scaled the roof to discover the inhabitants drinking wine, the consumption of which is prohibited by Islamic law. When the caliph reproached them, the owner of the house retorted:

> If I have sinned once, you have sinned three times. The Quran says, "Do not spy," and you have done so. The Quran says, "Enter houses through their doors," and you entered over the roof. And the Quran says, "Do not enter houses other than your own until you ascertain welcome and greet their inhabitants," and you have not greeted me.

The caliph was embarrassed and left without pursuing the matter (al-Ghazālī 1992, 2:427; see also Ibn Abī Zayd 1999, 14:318).

The sanctity of the home thus also shields legal transgressions taking place within it, enveloping them in the protection accorded to the private domestic sphere. The recurring metaphor through which this protection is explained and justified in legal discussions is the covering of one's nakedness (*sitr al-ʿawra*). Muslim jurists agree that human beings are obliged to conceal parts of their bodies from the public gaze: men and slaves of both genders must cover the region between their knees and their navels, free women everything except their faces, hands, and feet. Muḥammad himself is reported to have used the image of the cover in a metaphorical sense, encouraging his followers to "abstain from immorality, but whoever commits it, let him cover himself with God's cover (*sitr Allāh*) and repent. For whoever draws aside this cover, we shall apply the law of God to him" (Mālik 1985, 2:825). Muslim jurists understood this statement as admonition against self-incrimination: as long as an individual's transgression has not been detected by others, deliberately revealing it would constitute a wrongful act akin to the exposure of one's nakedness in public. (The explanation thus implicitly appeals to a sense of shame.) A private misdeed unknown to others can be expiated through repentance, that is, through cessation of the sinful activity, sincere regret, and determination not to repeat the offense. Once the action enters the public realm, however, it becomes subject to the law and thus punishable.

Clearly, this preference for keeping illegal acts secret clashes with other revealed norms that stipulate that violations of the rights of others necessitate compensation. Muslim jurists resolved the apparent contradiction by means of a crucial conceptual distinction between two types of rights: the rights of humans (*ḥuqūq al-ādamiyyīn*, *ḥuqūq al-ʿibād*) and the rights of God (*ḥuqūq Allāh*). This distinction is not found explicitly in the Quran or in the prophetic traditions, which constitute the second major source of Islamic normativity, but it is present in the earliest legal literature (e.g., al-Shāfiʿī 2001, 7:369). The rights of humans are based on the principle of just exchange between individuals; they

> include the law of transactions, the rules governing marriage, family and inheritance and parts of the penal law. The "claims of men" are considered to be the property of private legal persons who dispose of their claims at their own free will and who decide of their own accord whether they want the authorities to interfere with their business. In principle, it is only the request of a private party with a valid claim which justifies the interference of the political authority or the judiciary with the *ḥuqūq al-ʿibād*. (Johansen 1999, 200)

A violation of these rights requires a rebalancing, primarily in material or financial terms through the return of stolen property, the payment of an indemnity, or such. The rights of God, on the other hand, include in their purview ritual law, taxation, and certain aspects of penal law (such as consumption of alcohol and adultery, but not murder). Muḥammad's injunction to keep one's transgressions secret is taken to apply only to the rights of God. As soon as the rights of other individuals are affected, the need to determine and enforce a suitable remedy necessitates the involvement of public authorities.

But what purpose is served by keeping infringements of divine rights a secret? One might hypothesize that such secrecy is simply meant to serve the interests of individual transgressors by shielding them from sanctions, but several statements attributed to Muḥammad contradict this interpretation. One such statement promises an afterworldly reward for those who cover their fellow Muslims' misdeeds and threatens those who expose them, again using the metaphor of physical nakedness: "Whoever covers the nakedness of his fellow Muslim, God will cover his nakedness on the Day of Judgment, and whoever exposes the nakedness of his fellow Muslim, God will expose his nakedness, so that he will be dishonored even in his own house" (Ibn Mājah 1972, no. 2,546). The strong condemnation of subjecting the faults of others to public view suggests that such exposure would entail violation of a right to privacy held by the original transgressor. This privacy consists of an abstract, protected space that shields the individual from the gaze of the public and that can be analogized to the parts of the human body that others should not see.

Another prophetic tradition excludes from divine forgiveness those who publicize their own, previously unknown wrongdoing: "My community is forgiven, except the publicizers (*al-mujāhirīn*). Publicizing means that a man commits something at night, and the next morning, although God has covered his deed, he says: 'O So-and-so: yesterday I did such-and-such'" (Ibn Ḥajar 2005, 13:633). Here it is the transgressor himself who sins by breaching the privacy of his actions.

Therefore, the privacy of transgression, like the privacy of physical nakedness, is not a right that one can voluntarily relinquish; rather, it also entails obligation, an obligation to be ashamed of exposing what is private. But to whom is this obligation due? The category of transgressions against God displays a curious feature. If a transgression is committed in private, the transgressor, as well as anyone else aware of the act, should conceal it from public knowledge. Through sincere, private repentance, the culprit can absolve himself of the sin and receive divine forgiveness. However, once the transgression is publicized, simple divine forgiveness is no longer available, and the organs of the state have no choice but to prosecute and punish the transgressor. The majority of Muslim jurists and theologians hold that punishment applied in accordance with the law serves as expiation for the transgression (Ibn Rajab 2008, 407–408). Therefore, while the private sin can effectively be remedied by the internal act of repentance, the publicized sin is expiated through the external imposition of punishment, which involves both an element of physical or financial harm to the transgressor and the public symbolism and spectacle of punishment. Violations of the individual rights of humans can be voluntarily forgiven by those affected (including the family of a murder victim), but no such forgiveness is possible in the case of a transgression against a divine right that has become public (Peters 2005, 53). It is therefore legitimate to call the publicized violation of a divine right a public crime. This relationship between God's rights and the public was clear to premodern Muslim jurists, who identified the rights of God with the public interest (*maṣāliḥ al-ʿāmma*) (Johansen 1999, 211).

Once a potential violation of God's rights has come to the attention of a Muslim court, the court is obliged to investigate it. However, Islamic law goes to great lengths to make a conviction unlikely. As Baber Johansen aptly put it:

> In respect to control over the performance of acts of worship a special "law of evidence" allows for a person accused of neglecting his ritual prayers to acquit himself by mere verbal statement claiming the contrary. In fiscal law, only a few taxes and levies are considered to be legitimate. In criminal law, special forms of evidence are demanded, witnesses are asked not to give testimony against their fellow human beings, judges are admonished not to extract confessions from the accused. All proceedings are governed by the *šubha*-rule, according to which no penalty may be imposed should there be any doubt that not all the necessary conditions for demanding a penalty have been completely met. (Johansen 1999, 214)

The rules of legal evidence further discourage the airing of sins, particularly sexual misconduct: the false accusation of adultery, for example, carries a Quranically mandated penalty of eighty lashes (Quran 24:4). Jurists define false accusation (*qadhf*) so broadly that even if the requisite number of eyewitnesses (four) to the act of adultery is reached, a significant difference in their testimonies is sufficient to make each of the witnesses guilty of false accusation (Peters 2005, 12). As a result of such procedural rules, only those transgressions against God's rights that have been performed in full public view stand a chance of successful prosecution in court. Such deliberate obstacles clearly seek to dissuade the state from investigating private behavior, and the historical record indicates that they did indeed pose a by and large effective deterrent (Lange 2008, 44–48).

The bias against scrutiny of private misconduct is based on an ethical model that is encapsulated in an often cited statement of Muḥammad: "A transgression that is hidden harms only its perpetrator, but a publicized transgression that is not censured harms the community" (Ibn Taymiyya 1984, 2:302). In other words, private violation of the rights of God constitutes a sin, but performing it publicly or exposing it to publicity afterward constitutes a crime. The reason for the legal sanctions against publicizing one's own sinful act is that such publicity would constitute "a denigration of God, His prophet, and the righteous" (Ibn Ḥajar 2005, 13:636), because it implicitly denies the shameful nature of the act and would thus serve to normalize sinful behavior in public (Ibn Taymiyya 1984, 2:302).

The distinction between the rights of humans and the rights of God thus establishes the latter as the rubric under which public obligations are theorized: the rights of humans govern the relationship of an individual with other individuals, whereas the rights of God apply to the relationship between the individual and the Muslim public. Individuals do, of course, remain answerable to God for all of their actions, so the distinction between human rights and divine rights does not mean that the former can be considered secular while the latter are religious. Rather, calling public obligations the rights of God specifies the object of these obligations. Had they been theorized as being due to society as a collective of individuals, they would be contingent as the individuals could choose to relinquish their rights; but the function of the rights of God is to serve as an unchanging, fixed standard.

Paradoxically, however, the rights of God are routinely trumped by the rights of humans in the application of the sacred law. Since the human-divine relationship, in contrast to human interactions, is not one of reciprocity, as God has no needs to fulfill, whenever the rights of humans clash with the rights of God in legal disputes, the former take precedence (al-Shāfiʿī 2001, 7:369; Johansen 1999, 213). The priority granted to interpersonal justice reflects the overall tendency of Islamic law to limit the legal sway of the public on the individual and to concern itself first and foremost with regulating interactions between individuals.

With regard to the rights of God, the state functions as the enforcer of public norms, but its reach is constrained by a range of legal mechanisms developed by jurists to safeguard individual privacy. This privacy is not simply the right of the individual, to dispense with at will. Rather, it is an ethical construct that seeks to protect society from the effects of the individual's sinning and the individual, in return, from the societal sanctions that follow when sinning is publicized and turns into a crime. Privacy is thus constructed as a space in which the individual is alone with God and unfettered by the societal consequences of his or her actions, and thereby has the opportunity to develop a sincere and non-hypocritical relationship to God.

4. Virtue and hypocrisy

The same distinction between private and public is found in discussions concerning the performance of good deeds, such as charity and supererogatory devotional practices. The primary locus of these discussions is not law but rather the discourses of asceticism (*zuhd*) and mysticism (that is, Sufism). Perhaps surprisingly, also these realms developed a clear preference for the private sphere, with Muslim thinkers with an ascetic bent widely encouraging believers to do good in secret. The reason for this stance was the fear of hypocrisy.

Already the Quran tackles the issue of religious hypocrisy. During the Meccan period, when the Muslims were a persecuted minority, any individual Muslim's faith could be assumed to be sincere. But after the Muslims' emigration to Medina and the establishment of an autonomous Muslim community, adherence to Islam could bring about worldly benefits. The Quranic verses originating in the Medinan period deal with the phenomenon of hypocrisy as a state in which a person is outwardly a believer, but inwardly rejects Islam.[4]

In Islamic thought, this phenomenon gave rise to a deep ambivalence toward acts of public piety: even if a worshipper genuinely believed in God, the worldly benefits in terms of enhanced reputation that could accompany the public performance of acts of worship threatened the sincerity of the act as genuine worship and ran the risk of turning it into a hypocritical display of false virtue (*riyāʾ*). This potential for corruption of faith is the context for the dichotomy of secret (*sirr*) versus openness (*ʿalāniyya*), which is already found in the prophetic traditions. In one such tradition, Muḥammad distinguishes between true believers and hypocrites by noting that the former do good both openly and in secret, while the latter do good only when the good deeds are seen by others (Ibn Baṭal 2003, 1:94). The preference for privacy in virtuous behavior is tempered, however, by the fact that while transgressions against the rights of God embody a potential threat to public order and morality, the public performance of virtuous acts can have a positive social effect by setting a good example. Consequently, the emphasis on privacy is stronger in the context of legal misbehavior.

Nevertheless, the superiority of secret good deeds over public ones is attested in countless statements. Ibn Masʿūd (d. 653), a companion of Muḥammad, is reported to have claimed that "the superiority of prayer at night over prayer during the day is the superiority of secret over open charity" (Ibn Rajab 2008, 609). Another companion, Abū Umāma al-Bāhilī (d. 657), not only seems to have considered private devotion preferable to public worship but also frowned upon dramatic displays of piety in public; he once addressed a man whom he encountered in the mosque sobbing and immersed in prayer, "No, no, if only you did that in your house!" (al-Dhahabī 1985, 3:361). The same suspicion regarding the public display of virtues animates the advice given by Abū Ḥāzim Salama b. Dīnār (d. between 751 and 761): "Hide your good deeds better than your bad ones" (al-Dhahabī 1985, 6:100).

The discourse on hypocrisy and its avoidance was particularly pronounced in the "inner sciences" (*ʿulūm al-bāṭin*) of asceticism and Sufism. Whereas the rules of the law regulated public actions but consciously refrained from revealing private behavior, the inner sciences sought to reform the individual's nonsocial self, which was hidden from the public gaze and was thus considered more

4 E.g., Sūra no. 63, entitled "the hypocrites" (al-Munāfiqūn).

genuine. It was this private self that had to be reformed in order to achieve salvation. Some currents within this movement of inner reform went so far as to avoid systematically any public signs of religiosity as part of the program of private transformation. These " people of blame" (*malāmatiyya*), as they came to be known, sought a kind of religious anonymity in which they could develop their faith without the pressure of public scrutiny, and they appear to have been particularly well represented among urban artisanal and merchant groups from the late ninth century onward (Karamustafa 2007, 48–51).

Those tending to ascetic and mystical religiosity privileged the private self as the locus of salvation, while jurists as well as philosophers saw the self as inextricably formed in public life. These two approaches were not necessarily mutually exclusive, either in theory or in the practical lives of ascetic jurists or strictly law-abiding ascetics.[5] Nevertheless, the divergent emphases created polemical tensions and gave rise to distinct arenas of religious discourse and practice. But what the partisans of both approaches agreed on was a shared conception of two different realms of human life. Even though the religious norms governing these realms did not differ in content, their private and public context, respectively, endowed them with different roles and meanings.

5. Conclusion

In this essay I have sought to sketch the outlines and functions of one particular conceptual analog to the private–public dichotomy in Islamic thought. This analog is located in a semantic field related to vision, encompassing terms such as cover (*sitr*), nakedness (*ʿawra*), secret (*sirr*), open (*ʿalāniyya*), hypocritical display (*riyāʾ*), and shame (*ḥayāʾ*). The reason for the differentiation between the public and the private lies in the nature of action, which in this scheme has two ontologically distinct audiences: the divine and society. Accordingly, the life of the individual, progressing toward its eventual salvation or damnation, unfolds in the two distinct arenas of private and public, and for the sake of the persistence of an ethical order, the two ought to be kept separate to prevent both societal and individual corruption.

By establishing, maintaining, and cultivating this distinction between private and public, Islamic legal and pietistic discourses embodied both a socializ-

5 See, for example, the well-known fourteenth-century Sufi and jurist Ibn al-Mulaqqin, who in his legal commentary cannot help but remark that it is better to give charity in secret (Ibn al-Mulaqqin n.d., 132).

ing impulse expressed in the theorization of obligations to others and an individuating drive in the construction of a private, internal locus. Here, shielded from public view, the all-seeing divine gaze forced the individual to face and fashion a self that stood apart from social interactions and comprised his secret deeds, thoughts, and motivations. This finding indicates a potentially fruitful entry point for investigating the intellectual underpinnings of a broader historical movement.

The rise of Islam was not just an urban phenomenon but an urbanizing one (Berkey 2003, 119–23). The Islamic calendar began in 622 with the formation of an autonomous polity in the oasis town that came to be known as Medina (literally "the polis"). This political community transcended tribal affiliations in favor of a contractual political framework (the so-called Constitution of Medina). The subsequent spread of Islam was characterized by the expansion of old cities (such as Damascus and Alexandria), the foundation of new ones (such as Kufa, Baghdad, and old Cairo), and successive waves of sedentarization of nomadic cultures, such as the Arabs, the Turks, the Berbers, and the Mongols. While it is true that urbanization can function as a cause of greater individuation by releasing people from "social cages" (Woolf 2013, 152), the rise of Islam appears to demonstrate also a reverse causality. Islam's novel conceptualization of the individual self and its private relationship with God provided an effective counter model to existing systems of social organization based on the organic networks of family and tribe. In this scheme, the individual is the primary locus of ethico-religious obligations and "shame before God," which supplants public shame as the primary mechanism of social control. He or she is then able to interact with other, similarly constituted actors not just as members of familial collectives but as individuals charged with adhering to the divine law in both their private and their public affairs. The gradual diffusion of this conceptualization of private and public that accompanied the spread of Islamic monotheism thus gave rise to an intellectual structure within which new, complex, non-familial forms of association could emerge.

Works cited

Alshech, E. (2004). "Notions of privacy in classical Sunni Islamic thought." PhD dissertation. Princeton University.

Berkey, J. P. (2003). *The formation of Islam: religion and society in the Near East, 600–1800.* Cambridge.

al-Bukhārī, Muḥammad b. Ismāʿīl. (2001). *Ṣaḥīḥ al-Bukhārī.* Edited by Muḥammad Zuhayr al-Nāṣir. Beirut: Dār Ṭawq al-Najāh.

Crone, P. (2012). *The nativist prophets of early Islamic Iran: rural revolt and local Zoroastrianism.* New York.
al-Dhahabī, Shams al-Dīn. (1985). *Siyar aʿlām al-nubalāʾ.* Edited by Shuʿayb al-Arnāʾūṭ et al. Beirut: Muʾassasat al-Risāla.
Dodds, E. R. (1951). *The Greeks and the irrational.* Berkeley.
al-Ghazālī, Abū Ḥāmid. (1992). *Iḥyāʾ ʿulūm al-dīn.* Edited by Muḥammad al-Dālī Balṭa. Sidon: al-Maktaba al-ʿAṣriyya.
Ibn Abī Zayd. (1999). *al-Nawādir wa-l-ziyādāt.* Edited by ʿAbd al-Fattāh al-Ḥulw and Muḥammad Bū Khubza. Beirut: Dār al-Gharb al-Islāmī.
Ibn Baṭal. (2003). *Sharḥ Ṣaḥīḥ al-Bukhārī.* Edited by Abū Tamīm Yāsir b. Ibrāhīm. Riyadh: Maktabat al-Rushd.
Ibn Ḥajar al-ʿAsqalānī. (2005). *Fatḥ al-bārī.* Edited by Naẓar al-Faryābī. Riyadh: Dār Ṭība.
Ibn Ḥanbal, Aḥmad (2008). *Musnad al-imām Aḥmad ibn Ḥanbal.* Edited by Shuʿayb al-Arnāʾūṭ and ʿĀdil Murshid. Beirut: Muʾassasat al-Risāla.
Ibn Mājah. (1972). *Sunan Ibn Mājah.* Edited by Muḥammad Fuʾād ʿAbd al-Bāqī. Cairo: ʿĪsā al-Bābī al-Ḥalabī.
Ibn al-Mulaqqin. (n.d.). *Sharḥ Mukhtaṣar al-Tabrīzī.* Edited by Wāʾil Zahrān. Fayyum: Dār al-Falāḥ.
Ibn Rajab al-Ḥanbalī. (2008). *Jāmiʿ al-ʿulūm wa-l-ḥikam.* Edited by Māhir al-Faḥl. Damascus: Dār Ibn Kathīr.
Ibn Sallām, Abū ʿUbayd al-Qāsim. (1994). *al-Ṭahūr.* Edited by Mashhūr Salmān. Jeddah: Maktabat al-Ṣaḥāba.
Ibn Taymiyya. *Jāmiʿ al-rasāʾil li-Ibn Taymiyya.* Edited by Muḥammad Rashād Sālim. Jeddah: Dār al-Madanī.
Johansen, B. (1999). *Contingency in a sacred law: legal and ethical norms in the Muslim fiqh.* Leiden.
Karamustafa, A. (2007). *Sufism: the formative period.* Edinburgh.
Lange, C. (2008). *Justice, punishment and the medieval Muslim imagination.* Cambridge.
Mālik b. Anas (1985). *al-Muwaṭṭaʾ.* Edited by Muḥammad Fuʾād ʿAbd al-Bāqī. Beirut: Dār Iḥyāʾ al-Turāth al-ʿArabī.
Peters, R. (2005). *Crime and punishment in Islamic law.* Cambridge.
al-Shāfiʿī, Muḥammad b. Idrīs (2001). *al-Umm.* Edited by Rifʿat Fawzī ʿAbd al-Muṭṭalib. Mansura: Dār al-Wafāʾ.
al-Tirmidhī, Muḥammad ibn ʿĪsā. (1937). *al-Jāmiʿ al-ṣaḥīḥ wa-huwa Sunan al-Tirmidhī.* Edited by Aḥmad Muḥammad Shākir. Cairo: Muṣṭafā al-Bābī al-Ḥalabī.
Woolf, G. (2013). "Ritual and the individual in Roman religion," in J. Rüpke, ed., *The individual in the religions of the Ancient Mediterranean:* 136–160. Oxford.

Contributors

Clifford Ando, 1115 E. 58th Street, Chicago, IL 60637, USA.
clifford.ando@uchicago.edu

Elisabeth Begemann, Dept. Religious Studies, University of Erfurt, Postfach 900 221, 99105 Erfurt, Germany.
elisabeth.begemann@uni-erfurt.de

Natalie B. Dohrmann, Herbert D. Katz Center for Advanced Judaic Studies, University of Pennsylvania, 420 Walnut Street, Philadelphia, PA 19106, USA.
dohrmann@sas.upenn.edu

Esther Eidinow, Humanities Building, University Park, University of Nottingham, Nottingham NG7 2RD, United Kingdom.
esther.eidinow@nottingham.ac.uk

Ahmed El Shamsy, Department of Near Eastern Languages and Civilizations, The University of Chicago, 1155 East 58th Street, Chicago, IL 60637.
elshamsy@uchicago.edu

Judith Evans Grubbs, 221 Bowden Hall, Emory University, 561 S. Kilgo Circle, Atlanta, GA 30322–3651, USA.
jevansg@emory.edu

Edward M. Harris, c/o American School of Classical Studies, 54 Souedias Street, 106 76 Athens, Greece.
edward.harris@durham.ac.uk

Catherine Hezser, Dept. of the Study of Religions, School of Oriental and African Studies (SOAS), University of London, 10, Thornhaugh Street, London WC1H 0XG, United Kingdom.
ch12@soas.ac.uk

Adriaan Lanni, Harvard Law School, 1525 Massachusetts Avenue, Cambridge, MA 02138, USA.
adlanni@law.harvard.edu

Harry O. Maier, Vancouver School of Theology, 6000 Iona Dr., Vancouver, British Columbia, Canada V6T 1 L4.
hmaier@vst.edu

Rubina Raja, Institute for Culture and Society, Aarhus University, Nobelparken, Jens Chr. Schous vej 4, building 1461–326, 8000 Aarhus C, Denmark.
Rubina.Raja@cas.au.dk

Jörg Rüpke, Max Weber Center, University of Erfurt, PO Box 900 221, D-99105 Erfurt, Germany.
joerg.ruepke@uni-erfurt.de

William Van Andringa, 57 rue du faubourg Saint-Martin, 75010 Paris, France.
william.va@free.fr

Index

compiled by Benjamin Sippel

Bei Fragen zur Produktsicherheit wenden Sie sich bitte an:
If you have any questions regarding product safety,
please contact:

Walter de Gruyter GmbH
Genthiner Straße 13
10785 Berlin
productsafety@degruyterbrill.com